AFTER DAR~

Creative storytelling is the beating heart of Darwin's science. All of Darwin's writings drew on information gleaned from a worldwide network of scientific research and correspondence, but they hinge on moments in which Darwin asks his reader to imagine *how* specific patterns came to be over time, spinning yarns filled with protagonists and antagonists, crises, triumphs, and tragedies. His fictions also forged striking new possibilities for the interpretation of human societies and their relation to natural environments. This volume gathers an international roster of scholars to ask what Darwin's writing offers the future of literary scholarship and critical theory, as well as allied fields like history, art history, philosophy, gender studies, disability studies, the history of race, aesthetics, and ethics. It speaks to anyone interested in the impact of Darwin on the humanities, including literary scholars, undergraduate and graduate students, and general readers interested in Darwin's continuing influence.

DEVIN GRIFFITHS is an associate professor of English and Comparative Literature at the University of Southern California. His book *The Age of Analogy: Science and Literature Between the Darwins* (2016) was a finalist for the British Association for Romantic Studies (BARS) and British Society for Literature and Science (BSLS) book prizes. His work has appeared in *Critical Inquiry*, *Victorian Studies*, *ELH*, and *Book History*. He's now working on a study of ecocriticism and the energy humanities.

DEANNA KREISEL is an associate professor of English at the University of Mississippi. She is the author of *Economic Woman: Demand, Gender, and Narrative Closure in Eliot and Hardy* (2012), and has published articles in *PMLA*, *Representations*, *ELH*, *Novel*, *Victorian Studies*, *Nineteenth-Century Literature*, and elsewhere. Her current book project is on utopia and sustainability in Victorian culture.

AFTER SERIES

This series focuses on the legacy of several iconic figures, and key themes, in the origins and development of literary theory. Each book in the series attempts to isolate the influence, legacy and the impact of thinkers. Each figure addressed not only bequeathed specific concepts and doctrines to literary study, but they effectively opened up new critical landscapes for research. It is this legacy that this series tries to capture, with every book being designed specifically for use in literature departments. Throughout each book the concept of 'After' is used in 3 ways: After in the sense of trying to define what is quintessential about each figure: 'What has each figure introduced into the world of literary studies, criticism and interpretation?' After in a purely chronological sense: 'What comes after each figure?', 'What has his/her influence and legacy been?' and 'How have they changed the landscape of literary studies?' Lastly, After in a practical sense: 'How have their respective critical legacies impacted our understanding of literary texts?' Each book is a collaborative volume with an international cast of critics and their level is suited for recommended reading on courses.

Published Titles

After Foucault: Culture, Theory, and Criticism in the Twenty-First Century
Edited by LISA DOWNING
University of Birmingham

After Derrida: Literature, Theory and Criticism in the 21st Century
Edited by JEAN-MICHEL RABATÉ
University of Pennsylvania

After Lacan: Literature, Theory, and Psychoanalysis in the Twenty-First Century
Edited by ANKHI MUKHERJEE
University of Oxford

After Said: Postcolonial Literary Studies in the Twenty-First Century
Edited by BASHIR ABU-MANNEH
University of Kent

After Queer Studies: Literary Theory and Critical Interpretation
Edited by TYLER BRADWAY and E. L. MCCALLUM
SUNY Cortland and Michigan State University

After the Human: Literature, Theory and Criticism in the 21st Century
Edited by SHERRYL VINT
University of California, Riverside

After Marx: Literature, Theory and Value
Edited by COLLEEN LYE and CHRISTOPHER NEALON
University of California, Berkeley, and Johns Hopkins University

After Darwin: Literature, Theory, and Criticism in the Twenty-First Century
Edited by DEVIN GRIFFITHS and DEANNA KREISEL
University of Southern California and University of Mississippi

AFTER DARWIN

*Literature, Theory, and Criticism in
the Twenty-First Century*

EDITED BY

DEVIN GRIFFITHS

University of Southern California

DEANNA KREISEL

University of Mississippi

CAMBRIDGE
UNIVERSITY PRESS

CAMBRIDGE
UNIVERSITY PRESS

University Printing House, Cambridge CB2 8BS, United Kingdom

One Liberty Plaza, 20th Floor, New York, NY 10006, USA

477 Williamstown Road, Port Melbourne, VIC 3207, Australia

314–321, 3rd Floor, Plot 3, Splendor Forum, Jasola District Centre, New Delhi – 110025, India

103 Penang Road, #05–06/07, Visioncrest Commercial, Singapore 238467

Cambridge University Press is part of the University of Cambridge.

It furthers the University's mission by disseminating knowledge in the pursuit of education, learning, and research at the highest international levels of excellence.

www.cambridge.org
Information on this title: www.cambridge.org/9781009181174
DOI: 10.1017/9781009181167

© Cambridge University Press 2023

First published 2023

A catalogue record for this publication is available from the British Library.

A Cataloging-in-Publication data record for this book is available from the Library of Congress

ISBN 978-1-009-18117-4 Hardback
ISBN 978-1-009-18115-0 Paperback

Contents

Figures

Contributors

B. RICARDO BROWN is Professor of Social Science and Cultural Studies at Pratt Institute. His research and teaching explore the history and sociology of science, critical theory, Epicureanism, and environmental studies. His works include "Darwin, Slavery, and Science" (2010) and *Until Darwin: Science, Human Variety, and the Origins of Race* (2010).

MIRANDA BUTLER is an assistant professor of English at Snow College. She regularly speaks, writes, and podcasts about nineteenth-century science studies for a popular audience. Her archival research has earned many awards, including the best graduate student paper at the Victorian Interdisciplinary Studies Association of the Western United States.

CAROL COLATRELLA is Professor and Co-director of the Center for the Study of Women, Science, and Technology at Georgia Tech. She has published *Evolution, Sacrifice, and Narrative: Balzac, Zola, and Faulkner* (1990), *Literature and Moral Reform: Melville and the Discipline of Reading* (2002), and *Toys and Tools in Pink* (2011).

WAI CHEE DIMOCK taught at Yale for many years, and is now at the Harvard University Center for the Environment. Her books include *Empire for Liberty* (1989), *Residues of Justice* (1996), *Through Other Continents: American Literature across Deep Time* (2006), and *Weak Planet* (2020). Her new book explores the coevolution of humans and nonhumans.

IAN DUNCAN is Florence Green Bixby Professor of English at the University of California, Berkeley. He is the author of *Modern Romance and Transformations of the Novel* (1992), *Scott's Shadow: The Novel in Romantic Edinburgh* (2007), and *Human Forms: The Novel in the Age of Evolution* (2019).

PATRICK FESSENBECKER is an associate professor in the Program for Cultures, Civilizations, and Ideas at Bilkent University and a teaching faculty member at the University of Wisconsin-Madison. He is the author of *Reading Ideas in Victorian Literature: Literary Content as Artistic Experience* (2020), which includes an expanded version of his award-winning essay "In Defense of Paraphrase."

KATHLEEN FREDERICKSON is the author of *The Ploy of Instinct: Victorian Sciences of Nature and Sexuality in Liberal Governance* (2014), which was awarded Honorable Mention for the Sonya Rudikoff Prize for the best first book in Victorian studies. She has published articles on science and sexuality in journals including *differences*, *Nineteenth-Century Literature*, and *Victorian Studies*.

DEVIN GRIFFITHS is an associate professor of English and Comparative Literature. His book *The Age of Analogy* (2016) was a finalist for British Association for Romantic Studies (BARS) and British Society for Literature and Science (BSLS). His work has appeared in *Critical Inquiry*, *Victorian Studies*, *ELH*, and *Book History*. He's now working on a study of ecocriticism and the energy humanities.

ALEXIS HARLEY is the author of *Autobiologies: Charles Darwin and the Natural History of the Self* (2015), associate editor of *Life Writing*, the immediate past president of the Association for the Study of Literature, Environment and Culture, Australia and New Zealand, and a senior lecturer in English at La Trobe University.

CAROLINE HOVANEC teaches at the University of Tampa, and her research interests include animal studies, environmental humanities, and modernism. She is the author of *Animal Subjects: Literature, Zoology, and British Modernism* (2018), as well as various essays on science, literature, film, and television.

DEANNA KREISEL is an associate professor of English at the University of Mississippi. She is the author of *Economic Woman: Demand, Gender, and Narrative Closure in Eliot and Hardy* (2012), and has published articles in *PMLA*, *Representations*, *ELH*, *Novel*, *Victorian Studies*, *Nineteenth-Century Literature*, and elsewhere. Her current book project is on utopia and sustainability in Victorian culture.

TRAVIS CHI WING LAU researches and teaches eighteenth- and nineteenth-century British literature and culture, health humanities, and disability studies. Alongside his scholarship, Lau frequently writes for venues of public scholarship like *Public Books*, *Lapham's Quarterly*, and the *Los Angeles Review of Books*.

GEORGE LEVINE is Professor Emeritus at Rutgers University, and winner of Guggenheim, Rockefeller Foundation, and National Endowment for the Humanities fellowships. He was the founder and director for twenty years of the Rutgers Center for Critical Analysis. His books include *Darwin Loves You* (2008), *Darwin and the Novelists* (1988), *Darwin the Writer* (2011), *The Realistic Imagination* (1981), *Dying to Know* (2002), and *Reading Thomas Hardy* (2017); he is also the editor of *The Cambridge Companion to George Eliot* (2011).

ALLEN MACDUFFIE is an associate professor at the University of Texas at Austin. His book, *Victorian Literature, Energy, and the Ecological Imagination* (2014), won the Sonya Rudikoff Prize from the Northeast Victorian Studies Association (NVSA). He has published articles in *Representations, ELH, Victorian Studies, PMLA, Cultural Critique,* and other venues.

NIKOLAJ NOTTELMANN is the author of one monograph, *Blameworthy Belief* (2007), and the editor of an edited volume, *Belief: Constitution, Content and Structure* (2013). He has published a number of articles in premier philosophy journals, including *Mind, Philosophical Studies,* and *Synthese,* and contributed several chapters to edited volumes.

ANGELIQUE RICHARDSON is a historian of science and medicine, and Professor of English at Exeter. Her books include *Love and Eugenics in the Late Nineteenth Century* (2003), *After Darwin: Animals, Emotions, and the Mind* (2013), and *Women Who Did: Stories by Men and Women* (2005), and she writes regularly for a wide public.

HAUN SAUSSY teaches in the departments of East Asian Languages and Civilizations, Comparative Literature, and Social Thought at the University of Chicago. He is the author of *Great Walls of Discourse* (2001), *The Ethnography of Rhythm* (2016), *Translation as Citation* (2017), *Are We Comparing Yet?* (2019), and *The Making of Barbarians: China in Multilingual Asia* (2022).

JESSE OAK TAYLOR is an associate professor of English at the University of Washington in Seattle. He is the author of *The Sky of Our Manufacture: The London Fog in British Fiction from Dickens to Woolf* (2016), which won both the Association for the Study of Literature and Environment Book Award in ecocriticism and the NVSA Sonya Rudikoff Prize for a first book in Victorian Studies. He is also coeditor of *Anthropocene Reading: Literary History in Geologic Times* (2017).

CHAPTER I

Introduction
After Darwin: Ecology, Posthumanism, and Aesthetics in the Twenty-First Century

Devin Griffiths and Deanna Kreisel

Why Darwin *now?*

In the past two centuries, the world has seen radical change. With cultural and technological revolution came catastrophic alterations to the Earth itself, from the wholesale destabilization of the climate system to the devastation of environments that once awed Darwin. To live in the wreckage of the Anthropocene – as Anna Tsing and her collaborators so eloquently put it – is to live among the "ghosts" of broken environments, and amid the "monsters" created by our entanglement with other forms of life (Tsing et al., 2017).

What can Darwin tell us about the problems that haunt the world now? Even biology, the science most changed by Darwin's discoveries, has been dramatically altered since his time by the DNA revolution and the revelations of the microbial world. Speaking at Darwin College, Cambridge, on the sesquicentennial of the 1859 publication of *On the Origin of Species*, the philosopher John Dupré gave a succinct answer to this question: we should admit that Darwin was a scientist, not a soothsayer; "we should not expect him to tell us 150 years later what we should think today .... Darwin is part of history, not [the] present" (Dupré, 2009).

Yet if Darwin *was* a scientist, he has *become* much more. The essays included in this book explore the profound and continuing influence of Darwin's theories well beyond the biological sciences, from his contributions to critical understandings of human difference, including race, sex, and gender; to aesthetic theory and philosophy; and, above all, to the complex interrelations of people, their societies, and nonhuman nature. To paraphrase Adam Phillips, whether or not we read Darwin, he still reads us, and we still use a version of his language (Phillips, 1999: 13). Darwin helps us see that we are ourselves part and parcel of the world around us. He asks us to confront our deep entanglement with the living world and

I

its radical uncertainties, including its histories of violence and disposses-
sion: to accept that we are born of both ghosts and monsters.

The essays in this collection, in their dexterous engagement with the
myriad possibilities of Darwin's writings and philosophy, engage a different side of the Darwinian legacy than is provided by standard histories
of his life or by orthodox readings of the history of science – that is, the
Darwin beyond or behind what Janet Browne (2018) terms the "Darwinian
tradition." His importance today, these essays argue, does not rest upon his
status as a representative and flawed figure of Victorian science, nor even as
the co-discoverer – with Alfred Russell Wallace – of the theory of natural
selection. Many previous collections have studied Darwin both as a figure
in the history of science and as an influence on the creative imagination,
from Cambridge Companions to recent collections exploring his legacy
in psychology, genres of speculative fiction, and art history (Hodge and
Radick, 2009).[1] They show that it is possible to consider Darwin's flaws
without reducing him to a modern Pandora – releasing all subsequent
evils, including social Darwinism, eugenics, and the Holocaust, from the
box of human biology.

Building on that work, the present collection asks: what comes *after?*
How might we look beyond natural selection for the wider possibilities of
Darwin's thought, particularly as a resource for critical humanism? Darwin
himself saw that natural selection was inadequate to explain the complexity of life, especially social life. After 1859, he placed increasing emphasis on
various other mechanisms that might explain the complex relations within
and between species, including sexual selection, Lamarckian inheritance,
symbiosis, and what he termed "pangenesis." These explorations have often
been treated as accessories to his theory of evolution by natural selection,
but in fact they point to Darwin's more foundational attempt to understand – given the precariousness of life and the lack of a higher power or
master design – how life, in its full complexity, *hangs together*, as a complex
network of relations that keeps going and keeps changing. Darwin had
more than one dangerous idea. His works should be approached less as a
unified system, orbiting any single conceptual center, than as a constellation of sometimes competing, sometimes cooperating concepts – an intellectual ecology of sorts.

Darwin's account of what he termed the "struggle for existence" is
a good point of departure. Often treated as an alternative to Herbert
Spencer's "survival of the fittest," or as a more casual paraphrase of
natural selection itself, the struggle for existence in fact points toward
the essential precarity of life. In the chapter of the *Origin* that explores

its character, Darwin begins not with competition between individuals, but rather with the "exquisite adaptations of one part of the organisation to another part, and to the conditions of life, and of one distinct organic being to another being" – that is, to the *ecological* adaptations that align organisms internally and with their environment. As examples, he gives the "beautiful co-adaptations … in the woodpecker and missletoe … in the structure of the beetle which dives through the water; in the plumed seed which is wafted by the gentlest breeze" (Darwin, 1859: 60–61).[2] Darwin's wonderment in this passage marks his own effort to amplify the significance of life's prehensile condition, its struggle to hold on, and the resulting conceptual challenge "constantly to bear this … in mind" (62).

Darwin knew his readers would, like Augustin de Candolle and Thomas Hobbes, tend to interpret "struggle" as a battle between individuals, as when two dogs "struggle with each other which shall get food and live" (62). Yet all struggle, he cautions, is more fundamentally about *dependency*, not *competition*: "But a plant on the edge of the desert is said to struggle for life against the drought, though more properly it should be said to be dependent on the moisture" (62). Here, as elsewhere in his writing, Darwin struggles with language itself, attempting to wrestle, from any story's tendency to slip into narratives of competition and division, a more extensive tale of precarious need and interdependence.[3] Struggle, in this larger vision, names the fragile condition of living. Its challenge precipitates change and interconnection; living is hard, but life struggles *together*. In the face of this essential dependency, this mendicant life, living things develop "co-adaptations," learn to work together, forge interspecies alliances, care for their young, even build societies. That is, they coevolve.

If we are still struggling to understand the complexity of these interactions, the ecologies that support both human and more-than-human life, this difficulty underscores the scale of the conceptual and descriptive challenge Darwin presented nearly two centuries ago. Karl Marx privately criticized natural selection as a projection of capitalist competition onto nature, but Marx also greatly admired the "epoch-making" nature of Darwin's fundamental insight into the evolution of interdependence and the deeply material relation between natural and human history (Marx, 1990: 1:461 fn. 6).[4] As we seek to better grasp the interaction of natures and cultures, and the collapse (as Dipesh Chakrabarty [2009] observes) of the distinction between human and natural history, perhaps it is time to return to the ecological side of Darwin's thought.

1.1   Humanism and Literary Studies

We hope this collection will provide inspiration to any reader interested in the wider possibilities of Darwin's work, but it is especially intended to develop new theoretical resources for students and scholars in the humanities, especially literary studies. Darwin has a unique place in scholarship on the relation between science and literature. The publication of Gillian Beer's *Darwin's Plots* (1983) and George Levine's *Darwin and the Novelists* (1988) initiated a sea change, transforming how literary scholars interpreted scientific works and their legacies. Earlier critics and historians of ideas studied the influence of science on societies and their literatures, or less commonly, the beauties of scientific prose. The revitalized field of science and literature set out by Beer and Levine, by contrast, gave equal attention to the influence of specific literary works, genres, and modes of description upon the core work of science: producing new, factually grounded accounts of the natural world. As Beer famously put it, studies of the "traffic" between science and literature would now be "two-way" (Beer, 2000: 6).[5]

Why did Darwin provide a fulcrum for this pivot? For one, his writings have had a massive impact on virtually every aspect of the modern imagination of nature, being, and time, and pose lasting problems for how people think about morality, religion, and human society. Major reinterpretations of his theories have kept Darwin in the headlines and in the minds of literary scholars and historians: the development of eugenics in the later nineteenth century; the "modern synthesis" of genetics and evolution at the turn of the twentieth; the mid-century formulation of the "central dogma" of biology in wake of the discovery of DNA; more recent critiques of the neo-Darwinian dogma; and periodic controversies over the place of natural selection in public education, which reached fever pitch in the 1980s, 1990s, and 2000s. Darwin remains an object of troubled fascination.

Yet the imaginative nature of his work asserts a more immediate claim to humanist attention. Creative storytelling is the beating heart of Darwin's science. Given the extraordinarily long timescales he postulated for evolutionary change, the fragmentary evidence of the geological record, and the unclear connections between existing species, Darwin relied as much on speculative fiction as on direct empirical proof to support his account of how life changed over time. The agenda he set for evolutionary biology was necessarily *retrospective* and *descriptive*, in contrast to *experimental* and *predictive* sciences like physics.[6]

All of Darwin's writings drew on a mountain of information gleaned from a worldwide network of scientific research and correspondence, along with Darwin's own painstaking observations. But they hinge on moments in which Darwin steps back from this mass of information and asks his reader to imagine *how* specific patterns came to be over time, spinning yarns filled with protagonists and antagonists, crises, triumphs, and tragedies.

From the beginning of his publishing career, critics have mocked this facet of Darwin's writing as a species of "romance," that is, the fabulation of imaginative fictions on par with the fables of Scheherazade's *Arabian Nights* or the "historical romances" of Walter Scott (Wilberforce, 1860). Yet Beer and Levine, in teasing out the imaginative weave of Darwin's science and demonstrating the power of his narratives, clued scholars in to the modes of imagination and literary expression that thread through the more general practice of science.[7] Darwin's writing brims with literary devices like metaphor, analogy, and personification, as well as complex strategies of plotting and focalization, alongside powerful moments of aesthetic reverie, wonder, and disenchanting despair. It is writerly science. And in this way, Darwin's works furnish a paradigmatic case for the capacity of literary analysis and humanist study to explore the inner workings of science and its complicated relation to other modes of human experience. They undermine the generic and conceptual contrast between fact and fiction, and expose how fictions help equip science with useful facts, which flourish in the creative interplay of observation and imagination. Darwin helps us recognize fiction not as the antithesis of stable fact, but as a process of making and of discovery.

His fictions also forged striking new possibilities for the interpretation of human societies, their relation to natural environments, and the forces shaping their practices. Darwin's deeply historical and materialist reading of the natural world and the place of humanity within it overturned Enlightenment schemas of human reason, history, and the orderliness of nature. For this reason, he was essentially the first modern to answer classic problems regarding human nature and perception in terms of relatively irrational, contingent processes. In the years since, many have taken up some of his interpretations and reworked them until they have developed into well-traveled avenues of thought. We return to Darwin today with an eye toward roads not taken – trails of thought blazed but not pursued. In what follows, we trace three tracks in Darwin's thinking that merit further exploration: process philosophy, the critique of human distinction, and aesthetics.

1.2   Darwin as Philosopher

Despite Darwin's unease with the title "philosopher" (he went to great effort to present himself as a sober empiricist), his manuscripts demonstrate a deeply speculative and wide-ranging imagination.[8] His printed works continue to prove a rich resource for what Louis Althusser once termed the "spontaneous philosophy of the scientists" (Althusser, 1990: 114–115). Darwin's core ecological insight – that life is deeply interdependent and contingent – marks an ontology rooted in relation and constant change. This vision has had considerable (if unrecognized) impact in the field of speculative thought known as "process philosophy," a way of reading the complexity of both natural systems and human behavior that has become increasingly important in gauging the manifold complexity of the Anthropocene. In her *Minimal Ethics for the Anthropocene* (2014), Joanna Zylinska explains how process philosophy offers a moral and philosophical perspective on the way "humans are making a difference to the arrangements of what we are calling 'the world'" (Zylinska, 2014: 20–21). And in their "Manifesto for a Processual Philosophy of Biology" Dupré and Nicholson (2018: 21) describe how process philosophy reads the interdependencies of the living world, in which "organisms persist by virtue of the intricate webs of relations they maintain with one another" in much the same way that "ecological communities or consortia, such as biofilms, holobionts, and superorganisms, are not collections of relatively autonomous things but deeply entangled meshes of interdependent processes."[9]

Histories of process philosophy generally overlook Darwin's contribution to this thinking, tracing it to classical philosophers like Heraclitus, German thinkers like Leibniz and Hegel, and more recent speculative theorists like Gilles Deleuze and Alain Badiou (Zylinska, 2014: 37). Yet modern process philosophy is essentially a response to Darwin's work and the challenge of the eventful, contingent, yet patterned nature he revealed. The key commitments of this tradition – a focus on process over stable things or "substances"; the continuity of mind and cognition with material operations; the idea that human meaning is historical and contingent – are central components of Darwin's vision.[10] If Darwin's influence on process philosophy is generally overlooked, it may be because other important contributors to modern process philosophy, especially Friedrich Nietzsche, Henri Bergson, and Alfred North Whitehead, were explicitly hostile to specific implications of Darwin's theories – especially the mindlessness of natural selection. Complaining that Darwin "forgot the mind," Nietzsche responded by formulating a dynamic philosophy that made space for human self-creation as an ennobling, progressive force (Nietzsche, 1990: 87).[11] Bergson's *élan vital* similarly replaced the "mechanistic" theory of natural selection with an immanently creative evolutionary force on par with our own consciousness (Miquel, 2007). And Whitehead, for his part, was dismayed by the theological implications of Darwin's unthinking nature, and worked to formulate a process theism that could reconcile process theory with metaphysics – a path taken by later writers like Gregory Bateson and Charles Hartshorne (Lucas, 1985).

Darwin's place in this genealogy matters because it can help us get past the organicist impasse in process thinking. Organicism remains one of the dominant modes of imagining the way collectives work together; for this reason, as Nicholson and Dupré note, it is a major component of modern process theory. Yet organicism assumes that part and whole are tightly locked in an instrumental relation through which, as Kant (2001: 247) originally put it, "everything is an end and reciprocally a means as well." Organicism engrafts teleology – a preconcerted purpose – into the tissues of the body and into the logic of a system's parts. In this way organicism, as Denise Gigante points out, is not so much the *antithesis* as the synthetic *culmination* of mechanistic thinking: it interprets natural systems as the internalization of the instrumental structure of the machine, in a closed loop of ends and means (Gigante, 2009). This leaves it ill-equipped to describe the essential messiness of nature, the way its relations exceed instrumental utility. Nature, in the organicist view, is reduced to grist for instrumental reason – simply a means to our ends – with disastrous repercussions for the environment: "a wholly enlightened earth radiant with triumphant calamity" (Horkheimer and Adorno, 2007: 1).[12]

Like Donna Haraway, Anna Tsing, and Stacy Alaimo, we see the need for a more open reading of ecologies and bodies, a way of reading living creatures and their environments as not simply means for other's ends or in terms of their instrumental value, whether to humans or other creatures (Alaimo, 2016; Haraway, 2016; Tsing, 2017). The time is ripe for such thinking. The "Anthropocene is marked by severe discontinuities" not only in the climate system, as Haraway explains, but in the way "assemblages of organic species and of abiotic actors make history, the evolutionary kind and the other kinds too" (Haraway, 2015: 159, 160). As Jesse Oak Taylor and Allen MacDuffie discuss in Chapters 2 and 5, respectively, Darwinian thinking remains crucial for understanding the scale of humanity's impact on the environment and the destructive nature of human species being. And as Caroline Hovanec writes in Chapter 3, Darwin's work is important for activists and environmentalists fostering a better understanding of the animal kingdom and forging more just and ecological patterns of life. In order to read these histories and knowledges "in a moment when models of political collectivity seem to be buckling and failing daily," what we really need, Ella Mershon proposes, are collective theories of *inorganicism* (Mershon, 2020: 280).

It is time to return, with fresh eyes, to Darwin's earlier vision of nature and society as a "seamless spectrum of degrees of intertwining" and see what it might offer to this inorganic thought (Nicholson and Dupré, 2018: 21). If, as we have argued elsewhere, Darwin's ecological vision was forcibly wrenched into an organicist paradigm by later ecologists, it's worth reconsidering how his study of the fragile dependencies of nature might dismantle strictly instrumental analyses (Griffiths and Kreisel, 2020). In 1872, Darwin added a passage to the *Origin of Species* that summarized the expansive sweep his ecological vision took over time:

> [W]ith organic beings we should bear in mind that the form of each depends on an infinitude of complex relations ... and this depends on the surrounding physical conditions, and in a still higher degree on the surrounding organisms with which each being has come into competition, – and lastly, on inheritance (in itself a fluctuating element) from innumerable progenitors, all of which have had their forms determined through equally complex relations. (Darwin, 1872b: 101)

The relational and dynamic reading of organisms set out here looks like a relatively orthodox summary of process biology. The key question is whether "organisms" are understood in strictly organic terms, and whether their "complex relations" and dependencies are strictly governed by the logic of means and ends.

We propose that this passage, often cited for its deeply ecological flavor, should be read as a kind of speculative proposition – a statement of theory that underlines Darwin's philosophical commitment to the *inorganic* dimensions of living forms. Organisms, in this view, are not tightly integrated parts and wholes, because their network of dependencies in fact extends well beyond their bodies, to an "infinitude of complex relations" to other beings and to the physical world. Their environment teems with accidents and errant encounters. Life is a process of radical interaction and fluctuation, a process of continual, uncertain change. It is a world in which things fail as often as they work, a world filled with the useless as well as the useful.

This fertile failure is evident if we consider how the "fluctuating element" of inheritance draws upon Darwin's ongoing speculations about the deep contingency of reproduction and growth. The theory of "pangenesis" is sometimes treated as an embarrassing cul-de-sac in Darwin's thinking, but we think it should be taken much more seriously as a window into Darwin's reading of all living processes. As M. J. S. Hodge has shown, it marked the culmination of decades of private speculations on the nature of growth, reproduction, and organic differentiation – speculations that predate the theory of natural selection (Kohn et al., 2014). Published as a hypothesis for the mechanism of inheritance in his 1868 study *Variation under Domestication*, pangenesis posits that all of the individual parts of an organism emit "gemmules," small particles that together communicate heritable information to descendants. This theory decomposed the organism into a messy assembly, "a host of [smaller] self-propagating organisms" (Darwin, 1868: 2:404).

Rather than interpreting his gemmules as organic components of the body itself (and thus relocating organicism to a lower level of organization), Darwin emphasized the radical *uncertainties* and continual *failures* of this process, comparing living bodies to "a bed of mould [i.e. plot of soil] full of seeds, most of which soon germinate, some lie for a period dormant, whilst others perish" (Darwin, 1868: 2:404). The seedy plot offers a radically inorganic way to read living bodies, including our own. And it suggests that all living assemblies, from organs to organisms to ecologies, have not one purpose or end, but many, with many relations exceeding purpose entirely. In this view, all creatures are feral, unruly assemblages, no more organized (and just as dependent, uncertain, and rangy) as the ecologies within which we live. Our interest does not depend on the accuracy of this theory of inheritance (although we note not only the fact that Hugo de Vries drew upon pangenesis in formulating modern gene theory, but also the recent revival of epigenetic theory). Rather, it is precisely *because* pangenesis was such a speculative leap that it opens a window into Darwin's wildly inorganic imagination of the living world.

1.3   Darwin's Difference

The anti-organic dimension of Darwin's reading of process is, to crib a phrase from Bateson, the difference which makes all the difference in his philosophy (Bateson, 1992: 445). To our knowledge, it has not been noted that pangenesis's vision of the complex autonomy and independence of the elements making up the human body is incompatible with essentialist theories of sex, gender, or race: its implication is that all of the distinctions that individual societies associate with categories of the human are relatively autonomous, contingent, and inessential. In recent years – and despite the many classist, racist, and sexist judgments incorporated into works like *The Descent of Man* – a range of philosophers and humanists have found, within Darwin's writings, critical elements for more equitable, anti-racist, gender-positive frameworks of analysis.

There is a long tradition, as S. Pearl Brilmyer notes, of "Darwinian feminisms" that derived, from Darwin's writings, strategies that "brought human traditions and norms under the critical gaze of science," including critiques – explored in Chapter 9 by Carol Colatrella – of Darwin's own sexism (Brilmyer, 2017: 32). Feminist philosopher Elizabeth Grosz has done more than any other thinker to highlight how Darwin's reading of "difference, pure biological difference, as the very matter of life itself" (Grosz, 2004: 46) offers the conceptual grounds for a "nonessentialist understanding ... of sexual dimorphism" — and polymorphism (Grosz, 2004: 67).[13] Darwin's analysis of sexual selection, in its focus on unruly aesthetics of desire, has been particularly important as a framework for recognizing the radical potentiality of sexual life. For this reason, trans studies scholar Eva Hayward sees in sexual selection a potent formulation of the self-altering "forces" impelling "trans-sex dynamics ... the expressive over-spilling of sensoriums, a passionate rapport that advances a creature's further transformation" (Hayward, 2010: 235–236). As Kathleen Frederickson argues in Chapter 8, Darwin's theory of domestication can also furnish an important resource for queer theory, both as it bridges sexual and natural selection and as it demonstrates the importance of aesthetic criteria within the economy of nature.

There has been an even more extensive discussion of the anti-racist commitments of Darwin's science. Darwin's interpretation of race was more complex than is often acknowledged. On the one hand, he subscribed to a belief in the cultural superiority of the "civilized [i.e. white] races" and was disturbed, as Cannon Schmitt observes, that his commitment to a common history of the human species necessitated kinship to populations like the "barbarous" Indigenous people of Tierra del Fuego (Schmitt, 2013). Yet Darwin was horrified by his encounters with African slavery in the Americas, and remained a staunch and active abolitionist. Adrian Desmond and James Moore identify this commitment as the "*moral* passion firing his evolutionary work," including his lifelong effort to prove that humanity was a single species descended from a common human ancestor (Desmond and Moore, 2009: xviii). His ultimately successful efforts to refute the racist theory of polygenesis (the thesis, advanced by Louis Agassiz, Ernst Haeckel, and others, that different human races were either independently created or separately evolved) extended throughout his career. As Gregory Radick has shown, the argument for monogenesis was a central focus not only of the argument in *The Descent of Man*, but of the architecture of *The Origin of Species* and the evidence gathered for *The Expressions of Emotion* (Radick, 2018).[14]

An equally important objective in the *Descent* is to show that the differences between human populations are largely superficial, physiologically unimportant, and inconsistent (Darwin, 1871: 1:214). In arguing that these differences were the generally idiosyncratic results of sexual selection, rather than fit adaptations to specific climates and environments (as racial theorists had long argued), and in documenting the wide variations of aesthetic judgment in distinct societies, Darwin went a long way toward demonstrating that racialized aesthetics and race itself were rooted in cultural norms. Darwin's continued efforts to develop, refine, and defend the theory of sexual selection, as Evelleen Richards notes, was in part motivated by this attempt to explain (and partly explain away) racial distinction (Richards, 2017). For this reason, Kwame Anthony Appiah reads Darwin's analysis as a turning point in the slow dismantling of biological theories of "racial essence" (Appiah, 1994). As Irene Tucker observes, in Darwin's analysis "the arbitrary racial sign and its critique come into being with one and the same gesture" (Tucker, 2013: 199).

Sylvia Wynter's work provides one of the most extensive efforts to wrestle with the conflicting readings of race offered in Darwin's writings. If she sometimes simplifies Darwin's perspective (for instance, asserting in several places that Darwin insisted that natural selection was "the only directive agency of evolution"), Wynter also came to see her own lifelong project as a "meta-Darwinian" theory of how human societies evolve beyond the selective pressures of natural selection, and ultimately, beyond prejudicial readings of what that history implies about racial being (Wynter, 2015: 198 fn. 18 and 22). More recently, Arun Saldanha has turned to Darwin's ecological thought to sketch a critical geography of race as the intersection between phenotype – produced by the interaction of "genetic endowments, environmental conditions, exercise, hormones, diet, disease, ageing" – and the languages that "*charge*" phenotype, and so "circumscribe what it is capable of doing" (Saldanha, 2006: 18). However, as B. Ricardo Brown argues in Chapter 7, Saldanha's argument is symptomatic of the way human sciences have continued to deploy race as an organizing concept, despite Darwin's interventions, and even as those interventions have furnished an important resource for ongoing antiracist work. In a similar fashion, and as explored by Travis Chi Wing Lau in Chapter 6 and Wai Chee Dimock in Chapter 10, Darwin's evolutionary redescription of human diversity has provided grounds for contrasting analyses of the status of disability, from cognitive ablism to neurodiversity. In Chapter 14, Angelique Richardson similarly explores how Darwin's emphasis on interdependence can counter authoritarian disregard for the vulnerable and disadvantaged. And in Chapter 11, Ian Duncan reads Darwin's divided legacy with his own account of empire and moral evolution, demonstrating how "social instinct," which Darwin characterizes as the human capacity to imagine past, present, and future states as well as others' points of view, impels human becoming as an uncertain struggle between imperial genocide and the global extension of sympathy across the boundaries of kinship and nation.

1.4   Darwin's Aesthetics

In *The Descent of Man*, an expanded account of sexual selection transforms the perception of beauty into a key mechanism of human evolution and a central axis of social organization – including, as Alexis Harley explains in Chapter 13, the development of human language. In this way, Darwin awarded vast significance to aesthetics as a "distribution of the sensible" essential not only to art, but also to custom and political life. In this way, he provided, as Jacques Rancière (2014: 32) puts it, "the germ of a new humanity, of a new form of individual and collective life." As Ian Duncan has explained, Darwin was not the first to organize human evolution around sensibility (Duncan, 2020). Decades earlier, Friedrich Schiller had proposed the "free play" of art as the evolutionary leap that lifted humanity above animal nature. But Darwin radically altered that account in momentous ways, arguing *both* that aesthetics is part of the texture of ecological relations beyond the human (from the link between flowers and their pollinators, to the evident attraction between animal sexes) *and* that human aesthetic judgment does not respect a universal standard set by an idealized man (as Kant had argued).

Darwin's aesthetic revels in wildly various and idiosyncratic tastes; this "love of excitement or novelty" is what continues to afford his aesthetic account its revolutionary potential (Darwin, 1871: 1:65). Moreover, in the fascinated attention Darwin gave to the range of the aesthetic sensorium, from the lilting qualities of birdsong – as explored by Miranda Butler in her discussion of Darwin and sound studies in Chapter 4 – to the "pleasure" we take in a "sweet perfume," from the various flavors of floral scents to the "music" of the spoken word, he gave beauty its fullest sensory amplitude (Darwin, 1872a: 198). Darwin challenged the priority that contemporaries gave to vision and specular experience. His complex aesthetic influence extended well beyond his own time; as Haun Saussy discusses in Chapter 15, neo-Lamarckians in turn-of-the-century France protested the reduction of inheritance to features of the gene by drawing vital analogies between aesthetics and the sciences of biology, chemistry, and psychology. At a moment when many scholars are questioning the mixed legacies of the Enlightenment, it is worth recognizing how Darwin's writings tolled the demise of normative reason, recasting both cognition and aesthetics as both profoundly irrational and imminently meaningful. As Patrick Fessenbecker and Nikolaj Nottelmann argue in Chapter 12, Darwin's theories had a significant impact on moral philosophy, permanently untethering the existence of moral feeling from divine design. Darwin, in forging the sort of "illiberal humanism" Kandice Chuh has recently called for, still has much to say to humanists concerned with the role of taste, perception, and pleasure in mundane and political life (Chuh, 2019).

Darwin's unruly aesthetic gives the lie to ostensibly "Darwinian" interpretations of literature, art, and beauty that insist that certain behaviors or modes of thought were programmed by an earlier evolutionary advance in human development, and are thus fixed for the present. The field of evolutionary psychology, for example, has come under intense scrutiny for its "narrow" tendency to assume a modular, hard-coded model of mind, and its simplification and even neglect of the methodological challenge of distinguishing learned and innate human behaviors (Grossi et al., 2014). In an aligned critique of Darwinist aesthetics and theories of art's evolution, Matthew Rampley notes the failure of evolved and universal aesthetic predispositions to explain the radical differences in art practices between cultures and across historical time, highlighting the "vulgar and shallow interdisciplinarity" of such approaches (Rampley, 2017: 105). And Jonathan Kramnick, in a review of literary Darwinists who assert that the pleasures and components of literature (like language itself) are adaptive traits, skewers accounts that fail to demonstrate the "adaptive function" of literature as such, and thus fall back on more general claims about literature's capacity to cultivate imagination or sympathy (Kramnick, 2011: 331).

Yet few have pointed out how evolutionary-psychology approaches, in judging social behavior and aesthetics in terms of evolutionary or cultural "fitness," ignore Darwin's insistence that aesthetics, which originates in *sexual* not *natural* selection, is not governed by fitness or function. Sexual selection, as Grosz explains, "unhinges the rationality of fitness that governs natural selection ... selecting according to terms other than those related to fitness – beauty, appeal or attractiveness" (Grosz, 2011: 132).

Darwin, as much as anyone, was committed to the notion that art and pleasure can exist for their own sake, that aesthetics operates as a "mode of enhancement," not survival. As humanists, working on and with Darwin, the easiest way to avoid "vulgar and shallow" interdisciplinarity is to actually *work with Darwin*: read his works, in their complexity, within historical perspective, and with the aid of an extensive body of scholarship written to help us interpret his aims.[15]

1.5 Conclusion

We live after Darwin, yet in a world that Darwin recognized: a simultaneously natural and cultural world of deep entanglement and uncertainty, defined by complex networks of care as well as violence, a world constantly changing, and threatening to fall apart. Darwin gave the first truly modern account of an Earth stripped of design and intent. In doing so, he delivered responsibility for this planet into our hands. The climate crisis is the ultimate test of that charge. It is also a race to complete his work. Darwin's struggle was to explain how we can both be part of nature *and* have developed capacities that radically remake that nature. Our challenge looking forward is to square the manifold pleasures we take in this world with the struggle for it (and so for us) to survive.

Notes

1 For an account of non-Darwinian evolutionary thinking, see Lightman and Zon (2017). For more on Darwin, aesthetics, and psychology, see Larson and Flach (2013), Richardson (2013), and Voigts-Virchow et al. (2014). For more focused studies of the reception of Darwin in different national and regional contexts, see Engels (2014), Saul and James (2011), and Gianquitto and Fisher (2014).

2 Further references given by page.

3 In a classic essay that raises the stakes of this challenge, Amitav Ghosh observes the failure of contemporary novels to narrate the complexity of the climate crisis (Ghosh, 1992).

4 That same note belies Marx's critique of analogies drawn between capitalism and nature, insisting on the deep continuity between organic evolution and the interlocking development of machinic labor. In one of his many introductions to *Capital*, Marx approvingly quotes a reviewer who comments that "Marx treats the social movement as a process of natural history ... analogous to the history of evolution" (Marx, 1990: 1:100).

5 For a more detailed genealogy of Darwin and the field of science and literature, see Griffiths (2018).

6 For discussion of the narrative structure of evolutionary explanation in the philosophy of science, see Grimaldi and Engel (2007), Gallie (1964), Beatty (2016), and Gould (2002).

7 For now-classic discussions of the literary dimensions of Darwin's writing, see Hyman (1962), Beer (2000), and Levine (1988; 2011).

8 Most of his printed works, as well as his manuscripts, are published at "Darwin Online": darwin-online.org.uk. And a majority of his known correspondence can be found at the "Darwin Correspondence Project": www.darwinproject.ac.uk.

9 As Grosz (2004: 10) puts this, "Nietzsche is perhaps more Darwinian than he would like to admit.... He ontologizes and moralizes Darwin; he makes his own version of Darwinism the beginning of a philosophy of becoming."

10 As Seibt (2018) observes, "the early phase of process philosophy was mainly motivated by an effort to come to terms with the far reaching philosophical implications of the Darwinian theory of evolution" – more precisely, the wider implications of a Darwinian *philosophy* .

11 See discussion in Birx (1991).

12 For an analysis of the problem of instrumental value in environmental ethics, see Sarkar (2010).

13 Grosz's initial analysis of the gender binary, as many have noted, tended to underline and essentialize the male–female dichotomy, and overlooked Darwin's more basic insistence on radical uncertainty and his deep engagement with modes of differentiation beyond the binary – for example, his fascination with plants that have more than two sexes, or with hermaphroditic sea life (a point Grosz herself acknowledges in later work) (Grosz, 2011).

14 Along similar lines, Sarah Winter has explored how the "biosemiotic" analysis proposed in the *Expressions* "prefigures a postracial science" by arguing for the universal character of human communication (Winter, 2009: 131).

15 Jonathan Smith's *Charles Darwin and Victorian Visual Culture* is a foundational consideration of Darwin's own artistic sensibilities, while two excellent collections have done much to set Darwinian aesthetics in a wider historical and disciplinary context: Diana Donald and Jane Munro's *Endless Forms* and Barbara Larson and Sabine Flach's *Darwin and Theories of Aesthetics and Cultural History* (Smith, 2006; Donald and Munro, 2009; Larson and Flach, 2013).

PART I

Environments after Darwin

CHAPTER 2

Darwin after Nature
Evolution in an Age of Extinction

Jesse Oak Taylor

If there is an official account of nature in the modern world, it has Darwin's name on it. Walk into a natural history museum anywhere in the world, and you will find Darwin: his image, his name, his form etched in stone, his luminous words adorning portholes into the biosphere (Figure 2.1). Darwin is the patron saint of ecology, not merely as the science that seeks to understand "how everything is connected to everything else," but also as an ethical position following from that insight: the recognition that "we" are not unique or separate from the natural world, but rather one species among many, evolved and evolving within a dynamic planet (Commoner, 1971: 35). As Elizabeth Hennessey points out, the thousands of tourists who visit the Galapagos each year aren't simply visiting a biodiversity hotspot, they are making a pilgrimage to a mythic landscape: the origin of the *Origin*, and hence of the convergence between nature as *evolved* (and evolving) and nature as *vulnerable* that is foundational to modern ecology (Hennessy, 2019). Indeed, in arguing for the establishment of a national laboratory on the Galapagos, Julian Huxley described the islands as "a living memorial of Darwin," and a "museum of evolution in action" (quoted in Hennessy, 2019: 118).

Despite their celebration of biodiversity and natural beauty, these exhibitions tell a more ominous story as well. Natural history museums are mausoleums. They present an idea of nature constituted in and through death: the visitor is surrounded by corpses, the taxidermized specimens convey the diversity of the living world as a memory, something that had to be snuffed out for the display to come into being.[1] This has always been true of the individual animals on display, but that was justified by a sacrificial logic, in which the death of the individual stood in for the species and thus enabled a greater understanding of (and value for) the whole. We are now forced to ask whether the death on display is actually that of nature itself, by which I mean not only an idea but a particular configuration of the biosphere. At present, wild animals constitute only 3 percent of

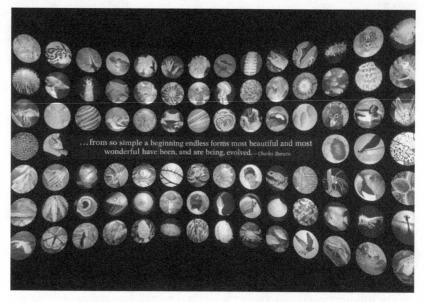

...from so simple a beginning endless forms most beautiful and most wonderful have been, and are being, evolved. —*Charles Darwin*

Figure 2.1   Darwin Exhibit at the Field Museum of Natural History, Chicago.
Author's photograph.

living mammals, with the remainder made up of humans (36 percent) and our pets and livestock (60 percent) (Bar-On, et al., 2018);[2] another recent study estimated that the weight of human manufactures exceeds all living biomass (Elhacham, et al., 2020). These figures offer a reminder that the "end of nature," in Bill McKibben's memorable phrase, is not only a question of whether we conceptualize nature and society as separate; it is also a horrific rending of the web of life, remaking the substance of the planet itself (McKibben, 1989).[3]

This chapter asks what it means to read Darwin in the middle of what appears to be the seventh mass extinction in Earth's history, and the first caused by the actions of a single species, our own.[4] When Darwin set sail on the *Beagle,* he journeyed into a world in which the human footprint was much smaller (though growing larger and faster than at any previous point in history), in which intact ecosystems still covered much of the planet, and, with CO_2 hovering around a comfortable 284 parts per million, the climate had yet to be altered by the combustion of fossilized life. Nature still outweighed humanity in more ways than one. Understanding this shift means grasping not only the degree to which our intellectual milieu is indebted to Darwin's work, but also the fact that his world was profoundly different from our own precisely because of the greater scope and power of what Carolyn Merchant calls "autonomous nature" within it (Merchant, 2016). The historical distance separating us from Darwin marks not only a profound shift in the *idea* of nature, but in the ontological state of nature itself, which is to say the configuration of existing (and/or vanishing) species and ecosystems completely apart from our ideas of them.⁵ We need to reckon with both sides of that equation, and the relationship between them, if we are to understand Darwin's relevance for our own efforts to forestall mass extinction in the present.

•••

Charles Darwin and Alfred Russel Wallace conceived the theory of natural selection in the midst of an unprecedented movement of species and specimens around the globe. Their work is historically convergent with both the shift to fossil fuels and the extractive infrastructures of European empire. The science of geology (including the stratigraphic method now being used to date the Anthropocene) proceeded in conjunction with mining. The invention of the steam engine enabled deeper shafts and accelerated the demand for subterranean resources, most notably coal (Torrens, 2016; Rudwick, 2008). While Earth's deep history was uncovered in the quest to extract mineral resources from its physical depths, the living world was mapped through the geographic expansion of empire and the search for new resource frontiers. As Alan Bewell explains, natural history's "revolutionary character lay in the project of *producing natures that could travel.*" Species were "named and classified so that they could be exchanged and transferred within the broader project of biologically refashioning the globe" (Bewell, 2017: 26).

The study of natural history was bound up with empire from the start. Whether in cabinets of curiosity, botanical gardens, and glasshouses whose interest derived largely from the exoticism of their inhabitants, or through Linnaean taxonomy, the effort to collect, catalog, and understand the living world proceeded in consort with European conquest and the discovery that nature harbored a far greater diversity of life than was imaginable from a strictly European perspective. As Tobias Menely has argued, even a work like Gilbert White's *Natural History of Selbourne*, with its resolute attention to the local ecology, derives its form from travel writing, and thus treats an English province as equivalent to a distant climate (Menely, 2004). A global imaginary proved essential to bringing nature (even local, English nature) into view. As a way of seeing, natural history was an inherently global (indeed, planetary) project.

That planetary frame would prove vital to both Darwin's and Wallace's understandings of evolution, since the theory of natural selection was conceived in large measure as an attempt to account for the distribution of species, as evidenced by Wallace's insight that "Every species has come into existence coincident in both time and space with a pre-existing closely allied species" (Wallace, 1855: 186). This was a key step in the development of Wallace's evolutionary thinking (articulated in an article that influenced Darwin even before the famous Ternate paper in which he revealed his own theory of natural selection), because it situated evolution in time and space. The "coincidence" of allied species not only showed them responding to similar conditions, but also provided the context in which speciation occurred in the wild. Whereas one might expect that a creator would have designed similar species to populate comparable habitats the world over, Wallace showed that this was not in fact the case: similar habitats could be home to very different kinds of species, an insight he formulated most famously in "Wallace's Line" separating the fauna of Australia and Southeast Asia. This understanding of the geographical distribution of species, in other words, was central to Wallace's ability to understand them as *historical* – forms produced by the friction of time and space.

A planetary vision was also crucial to perceiving nature as a single, interconnected system, a perspective owed above all to Alexander von Humboldt, whom both Darwin and Wallace read as inspiration for their own travels (Wulf, 2015). However, this planetary vision was also bound up with the globalizing infrastructure of imperial power. The *Beagle* was on a cartographic mission: mapping the world for the British Navy. Even Wallace, who operated outside such official channels, was a frequent guest at plantations and timber operations in both the Amazon and Malay Archipelago, and reported that the fringes of such disrupted locales were some of his best collection sites. A Darwinian view of nature aligns with the emergence of the Anthropocene because they emerged out of the same geohistorical conditions. In a Darwinian world, all species (or, to use the term both Darwin and Wallace preferred, *forms*) can be explained by locating them in time and space, situating them at particular junctures within planetary processes. The same is true for ideas. When we situate Darwin and Wallace within the Earth system, it becomes evident that their insights were made possible in part because of the particular convergence between human and planetary history in which they lived, as imperial capitalism reconfigured the biosphere to its own ends.

The theory of natural selection was a product of the Anthropocene frontier. It became visible on the Anthropocene's leading edge, in those novel spaces brought into being by what Jason Moore calls the "world-ecology" of capitalism as a global (indeed, planetary) system for organizing nature (J. Moore, 2016a). The global trade in specimens and the use of botanical gardens to cultivate profitable plants far from their native climates can be understood in this context, which places it in the midst of the commodification of nature that lies at the root of the extinction crisis.[6] And it is vital to understand this not simply as an *idea* of nature, but as a shift in the state of nature itself, one composed of the movement of species (both intentionally and otherwise), the clearing of large swathes of forest, the mining of subterranean resources, and, of course, the combustion of fossil fuels.

Crucially, these changes were not wrought by the intrusion of humanity into an untouched nature, but rather by the violent conquest of existing human cultures. As Anna Tsing provocatively argues, by replacing "complex webs of dependency and interdependence" with antagonism, the plantation regime "changed the very nature of species being" and remade "the practice of being human" (Tsing, 2012: 144, 149) In a similar vein, Bewell suggests that "we need to speak of colonialism in terms of the biological resettlement of the globe. Natures were not only being renamed but also being remade, transformed, or translated into something else" (Bewell, 2017: 16). Hence, when Bewell credits Darwin with inventing a "modern conception of nature" predicated on mobility and flux, it is important to recognize that this is not simply a modern *idea* of nature, but rather emerges out of the remaking of actual living ecosystems (27). "Modern" nature is both concept and empirical reality. Empire refashioned both the biosphere and the "practice of being human" within it. Finally, this transformation of nature was not invisible in the nineteenth century: Darwin and Wallace commented on it directly. While neither went as far as George Perkins Marsh's *Man and Nature, or, the Earth as Modified by Human Action* (1865), now often mentioned as an important precursor to the Anthropocene concept, their work nonetheless displays frequent, if ambivalent, hints that "man is everywhere a disturbing agent" within the natural world they study (Marsh, 2003 [1865]: 36).

The reshaping of the biosphere through human intervention of multiple kinds, and at multiple scales, was the *enabling condition* of Darwin's thinking. This is most obvious in his reliance on "artificial selection," in which he saw the human capacity to modify living forms through breeding as the paradigm for how evolution functions in nature. As Darwin writes, "We have seen that man by selection can certainly produce great results, and can adapt organic beings to his own uses .... But Natural Selection ... is as immeasurably superior to man's feeble efforts, as the works of Nature are to those of Art" (108). Despite his insistence on the difference in *scale* between artificial and natural selection, they bear a reciprocal relationship in the development of his thinking. As Devin Griffiths explains, "Darwin had to argue against contemporary wisdom regarding *both* natural *and* domestic species: insisting that domestic selection could produce new species *and* that natural selection does so in nature" (Griffiths, 2016: 34–35). For Darwin, natural selection essentially boils down to domestication writ large, while domestication becomes a force of nature.[7] While this feature of his work is well known, its implications for the idea of nature that Darwin brings into view is less often remarked. Not only does the "plasticity" (Darwin's term) of living forms render nature *mutable*, but the wholesale transformation of the world through large-scale domestication of both plants and animals provides his key evidence base.

Conquest and domestication provide key threads suturing Darwin's account of the origin of species to the emergence of the Anthropocene. Darwin's insight about the correlation between artificial and natural selection corresponds to a shift that Tsing sees in agriculture itself: "Domestication is ordinarily understood as human control over other species. That such relations might also change humans is generally ignored" (Tsing, 2012: 144). Darwin's arguments about domestication are similarly reciprocal: the analogy between artificial and natural selection defines nature in terms of domestication writ large. (For further discussion of domestication in Darwin, see Chapter 8.) Furthermore, this relationship is not limited to his discussion of domestication or artificial selection narrowly defined; it also recurs in the numerous examples he draws from disrupted ecosystems in the wild. For example, Darwin invokes the prevalence with which "our domestic animals of many kinds" now "run wild in several parts of the world" as evidence for the rapid rate of reproduction under favorable circumstances (*Origin* 1859, 64). While not explicitly framed as an example of artificial selection, this turn to introduced, feral, or invasive species is nonetheless one of many in which human interference serves to illustrate a natural principle, in part by accelerating or exacerbating it. It thus underscores the degree to which Darwin's theory is predicated on breaching the "wall between human and natural history," to borrow Dipesh Chakrabarty's influential formulation of the Anthropocene.[8]

The fact that Darwin draws his understanding of nature from the human modification of nature means that he ends up defining nature in and through its modification and mutability. In so doing, he locates his theory within the wholesale transformation of the biosphere. This becomes particularly evident in the way that his discussion of evolution and extinction is saturated with the language of conquest: "foreigners" and "natives" struggle for "firm possession of the land," with the invaders frequently emerging victorious (*Origin* 1859, 83). Empire provides the dominant metaphor, or set of metaphors, through which he describes the "struggle for existence" (*Origin* 1859). Moreover, that relationship is not purely metaphorical. It is *because* biological and cultural conquest provided the context for Darwin's observations that it became a central model for his understanding of how nature works. The ramifications of this insight become particularly acute in relation to extinction.

•••

Natural selection is as much a theory of extinction as it is of evolution. The means of "selection" is death: the absent force which carves away traits embodied in innumerable nonreproductive lives. Darwin was explicit about this, arguing that in "natural selection the extinction of old forms and the production of new and improved forms are intimately connected together" (*Origin* 1859, 317). That is why Darwin faces extinction with relative equanimity: "We need not marvel at extinction; if we must marvel, let it be at our presumption in imagining for a moment that we understand the many complex contingencies, on which the existence of each species depends" (*Origin* 1859, 322).

And yet, this equanimity about extinction is the exact opposite conclusion of the one drawn by environmentalists today. Darwin's commitment to gradualism and his overriding opposition to human exceptionalism led him (and even more so, others who followed in his footsteps) to misconstrue the unique intervention marked by the large-scale transformation of the biosphere that was unfolding before their eyes (Sepkoski, 2020: 9, 66–69, 80–81). Remarkably, he did so despite using evidence of anthropogenic extinction in the present to interpret the fossil record, as when he argued that "rarity precedes extinction": "we know that this has been the progress of events with those animals which have been exterminated, either locally or wholly, through man's agency" (*Origin* 320). Whereas widespread evidence of anthropogenic extinction now appears as a radical rupture in Earth's history, Darwin interpreted it in precisely the opposite terms, as a lens through which to understand the fossil record as an account of *change,* rather than stable forms fixed in stone.

This is part of a broader pattern that Allen MacDuffie has identified, in which Darwin's nineteenth-century readers interpreted his insights in a manner diametrically opposed to the way they appear to environmental readers in the present: "although we might expect that Darwin's discussion of the complex interconnectedness of all life would raise serious concerns about industrial growth and the rippling consequences of things like invasive mining practices, large-scale forest clearing, and increasing fossil-fuel consumption, in fact it became in many quarters an important argument for that very regime" (MacDuffie, 2018: 549). Hence, it was precisely by *downplaying* the distinctiveness of the human and emphasizing the separation of technology from natural processes that Darwin and his followers overlooked or dismissed the uniqueness of anthropogenic extinction and the human capacity to wreak havoc on the biosphere. This is perhaps most evident in the positions taken by T. H. Huxley, "Darwin's bulldog," who argued against fishing regulations on the logic that any tendency to overfishing produced by steam-trawlers would be corrected by the same natural checks that prevent predators from hunting their prey to extinction, rather than recognizing the uniquely destructive capacity of technological innovation, especially when linked to the insatiable appetite of capital (Hirsh, 2020).

The key difference is scale and speed. Extinction *is* a constant feature of the biosphere, and hence nothing to "marvel" at. What makes the present situation a crisis is the fact that extinctions are estimated to be occurring at around 1,000 times the "background rate" of extinction under normal conditions (that is, outside exceptional events such as those that have precipitated mass extinctions in the past, ranging from asteroid strikes to rapid climate change), with the possibility of reaching 10,000 times the background rate as climate change and ocean acidification accelerate (De Vos et al., 2015).

Moreover, the extinction of species is only part of the story. As Ursula Heise notes (and Darwin himself recognized), *populations* are as important a category as species, whether for the provision of "ecosystem services" for humans or for the health of the biosphere. For example, she notes that "if bees were to disappear everywhere except in Italy, the species itself would not be extinct, but the consequences for agriculture would be catastrophic" – to say nothing of the wild species that depend on bees for pollination (Heise, 2016: 25). This is why statistics such as the cumulative weight of human/domestic versus wild biomass are at least as important as catalogs of endangered species and extinction alone. It is also why the ongoing protection of intact ecosystems, expansion of wilderness, and the connection of conservation areas into corridors that allow the movement of animal (and plant) populations are vital, as envisioned in E. O. Wilson's ambitious "half-Earth" hypothesis (Wilson, 2016). Hence, as Heise notes, many conservation biologists argue that "the conservation of species needs to be complemented by a close analysis of their geographical and ecological distribution" (Heise, 2016: 25).

An isolated patchwork of protected areas organized around individual species is ultimately little different from the conservation work done in zoos and seed banks, or even in the preservation of specimens in natural history museums: it maintains the species as *form* but not the population of living, *acting* creatures within the world. With this in mind, Gordon Sayre warns against the tendency to conceptualize biodiversity as a "library" of life, noting that "we must appreciate the differences between organisms and archives, or we may find ourselves in an impoverished biosphere clutching only our data" (Sayre, 2017: 297). In this sense, it is alarmingly appropriate to meet Darwin in a hall filled with the curated bodies of the dead.

•••

These questions become even more acute in the work of Wallace, the "codiscoverer" of evolution, who broke with his more famous interlocutor in arguing that natural selection alone could not explain the evolution of the human mind.[9] Whereas Darwin was adamant about rejecting human exceptionalism, Wallace retained it even as he offered an evolutionary account of the human-as-species. For Darwin, the question of the human boiled down to how humans were like other animals; for Wallace, the question was how evolution could have given rise to a being so different from the rest of nature. Both questions are relevant to the Anthropocene. Wallace was also far more concerned than Darwin was about extinctions, which he saw as an inevitable result of European colonization. Shortly after returning to England, he published an essay arguing for the establishment of reserves for native flora and fauna, as well as "complete collections" to be housed in natural history museums in "every country colonized by Europeans," warning that if this was not done "future ages will certainly look back upon us as a people so immersed in the pursuit of wealth as to be blind to higher considerations" (Wallace, 1863: 234).

A central passage in his *Malay Archipelago* (1869) describes a feeling of "melancholy" upon seeing birds of paradise in the wild for the first time and reflecting that "such exquisite creatures should live out their lives and exhibit their charms only in these wild inhospitable regions, doomed for ages yet to come to hopeless barbarism," and yet laments that "should civilized man ever reach these distant lands … we may be sure that he will so disturb the nicely-balanced relations of organic and inorganic nature as to cause the disappearance, and finally the extinction, of these very beings whose wonderful structure and beauty he alone is fitted to appreciate and enjoy" (Wallace, 1962 [1890]: 340).[10] Wallace thus frames extinction as an inevitable counterpoint to empire.[11] After all, that seeming eventuality – "*should* civilized man ever reach these distant lands" (italics mine) – actually registers as inevitable because Wallace himself is there.

The notion that "civilized man" alone is "fitted" to appreciate the birds' beauty is, of course, completely false.[12] Indeed, Wallace found the birds through the assistance of local hunters and was thus the direct beneficiary of their knowledge. However, Wallace wasn't just wrong about his companions' appreciation of the birds of paradise, he was also *right* about the impact of "civilized" man. By the end of the nineteenth century, the demand for bird of paradise feathers in the fashion industry led to wholesale slaughter, with some 30,000–80,000 skins per year shipped to Europe between 1905 and the 1920s, when the commercial hunting of birds of paradise was banned (De Vos, 2017: 100). Though Wallace was an ardent critic of the feather trade (and active in campaigns to stop it), he supported his research by selling most of his specimens to museums and private collections, accumulating an astonishing 125,600 specimens and documenting more than 5,000 species previously unknown to western science. If the scientific contribution is staggering, so is the death toll. Hence, the line between collecting for science and killing for profit was nowhere near as clean as Wallace might have liked.

Nonetheless, Wallace takes the birds' beauty and remoteness as an occasion to meditate on the autonomy of nature, reflecting that "all living things were *not* made for man," and that "the cycle of their existence has gone on independently of his, and is disturbed or broken by every advance in man's intellectual development" (340). He further grants the birds themselves a *meaningful* existence, imbued with "happiness and enjoyments … loves and hates," and reflects that their "struggles for existence" have reference to "their own well-being and perpetuation alone" (340). The telling phrase "struggle for existence" connects this meditation to the theory of natural selection itself, which Wallace surely viewed as an "advance in man's intellectual development," and one that is thus directly implicated in extinction.

This is a death scene, after all: that vibrant living bird is doomed to be transformed into one of the thousands of specimens that Wallace shipped home, and upon which his evolutionary theory was based. My point is not to equate scientific collecting with the exploitation of nature for profit, but rather to show how these dynamics cannot be fully extricated from one another, and that that entanglement is precisely what makes Wallace and Darwin useful in our own efforts to forestall extinction in the present.

Wallace's concern with extinction spans more than 40 years and intensifies over the course of his career. In his magnum opus *On the Geographical Distribution of Animals* (1876), he argues that "we are now in an altogether exceptional period of the earth's history. We live in a zoologically impoverished world from which all the hugest, and fiercest, and strangest forms have recently disappeared" (Wallace, 1876: 150). Wallace argued that the mass extinction was most likely due to (naturally occurring) climate change because it seemed unimaginable that early humans could have acted on such a large scale. However, by the late work *The World of Life* (1910), he was persuaded that the "dying out of so many large Mammalia, not in one place only but over half the land surface of the globe", beginning in the late Pleistocene, was due at least in part to "man's agency" (Wallace, 1916: 264). Wallace's mounting concern was linked to increasing recognition of anthropogenic extinction in the late-nineteenth and early twentieth centuries, evident in high-profile cases such as the decimation of the passenger pigeon (which would go fully extinct in 1914) (Barrow, Jr., 2009: 2, 7, 93–104). Nonetheless, he does not treat this capacity for extermination as a unique property of the modern world system, but rather reads it back onto the fossil record and hence into his understanding of the human as such.

Wallace's concern about extinction dovetails with his sharpening critiques of empire and commitment to socialism during the same period. It also aligns with his break from Darwin over natural selection as an adequate explanation for the human mind and his conversion to spiritualism. This last development did real damage to his scientific reputation and contributed to his work being largely forgotten for much of the twentieth century. However, in recent years, there has been a resurgence of interest in Wallace as a foundational figure in island biogeography, conservation biology, and extinction studies (Lomolino, 2019). What I want to highlight here is that Wallace's concern about anthropogenic extinction *proceeds from* the notion of human exceptionalism rather than being opposed to it. In this regard, his position is similar to that of Marsh, who argued that the difference between human action and that of other animals or natural forces is "of an essential character, because, though it is often followed by unforeseen and undesired results, yet it is nevertheless guided by a self-conscious and intelligent will" (Marsh, 2003 [1865]: 41). In other words, Wallace's growing alarm at anthropogenic extinction derived not only from the accelerated pace of species loss, but also from the implications of understanding it as deriving from the self-conscious actions of a self-conscious species.

My point is not to endorse Wallace's view of human evolution over
Darwin's, or to minimize Darwin's profound insights into the "tangled
bank" of ecological interconnection. Darwin's decentering of the human
remains the bedrock of ecology, but it is incomplete. Darwin's search for
origins, and his effort to understand how "man still bears in his bodily
frame the indelible stamp of his lowly origin" (*Descent* 1871a, 405) needs
to be juxtaposed to Wallace's conviction that the human mind, and especially the cumulative effect of human culture, marks something unique, a
threshold in evolution, just as the disruption of the Earth system wrought
by modern society marks a threshold within the Earth's history. Grappling
with the unique tragedy of anthropogenic extinction means recognizing
that "all living things were *not* made for man" even if we can no longer say
that they have "no relation" (Wallace 1962, 340) to human societies.

It is frankly misleading to suggest that humans are merely a species
like any other when humans and our domesticates compose 97 percent of
Earth's animals. The sheer scale on which human society has transformed
the Earth derives not simply from human biology, but from the aggre-
gate force of human history, especially the particular historical formations
of empire and capitalism as well as the magnification of human agency
through technology, including language, art, and story.[13] And that is a difference that makes a difference.

•••

It is debatable whether a latter-day Darwin or Wallace could formulate
the theory of natural selection from field observation today: nature is too
fragmented, the biosphere too fully reshuffled for the evolutionary connections between species and habitat to be observed in the wild.[14] There
is something undeniably tragic about this recognition of a "tangled bank"
torn asunder. But that isn't the whole story. Tiger populations are on the
rise in India (Ratcliffe, 2019); the snow leopard was recently taken off the
"red list" (Snow Leopard Trust, 2017); biodiversity is flourishing even in
the toxified landscape around Chernobyl (UNEP, 2020); rewilding ini-
tiatives have transformed our understanding of how ecosystems function
(Monbiot, 2014). In short, conservation works when you do it right. The
protection of intact ecosystems remains essential to conservation success; so too is recognizing that nature never stands still. Species move and
change, remaking habitats as they go. Despite the destruction wrought by
some "invasive" species, others make homes in new habitats without harm
(Heise, 2016: 29). Adaptation in a time of climate change will depend on
making space for ecological climate refugees alongside human ones. The

core of Wilson's "half-Earth" proposal, and others like it, is the recognition that expanding and connecting protected areas magnifies their regenerative potential, providing species the chance to migrate and adapt and acknowledging the autonomy of nature to make its own future.

At the end of *The Origin of Species*, Darwin writes that "There is grandeur in this view of life, with its several powers, having been originally breathed into a few forms or into one; and that, whilst this planet has gone cycling on according to the fixed law of gravity, from so simple a beginning endless forms most beautiful and most wonderful have been, and are being, evolved." (1859: 490). In a world ravaged by extinction, we must recognize that this grandeur is not a self-congratulatory celebration of scientific insight, but a sense of wonder at the sheer abundance of nature in all its variety. When Darwin described the "state of nature," he was not referring to an abstract idea, but to a vibrant world, teeming with life, in which nature's autonomy, while already fragile, remained on full display. The grandeur of his "view of life" derives not from his theory, but from the infinitely complex web of life upon which Darwin's gaze was fixed with wonder and attention, marveling at "those endless forms most beautiful and most wonderful" that "have been, and are being, evolved." And still are.

Notes

1 On the centrality of memory, vulnerability, and loss to both Darwin and Wallace's thinking see Schmitt, 2009.
2 For an overview, see Carrington, 2018.
3 For a critique of McKibben's "end of nature" thesis in relation extinction and endangered species, see Heise, 2016: 8–10.
4 New research suggests that there may have been six mass extinction events in Earth's history, which would mean that the extinction event precipitated by humans is actually the *seventh*, rather than the sixth, as popularized in a number of publications, including Elizabeth Kolbert's Pulitzer Prize-winning *The Sixth Extinction: An Unnatural History* (2014) (Kolbert, 2014). See also, Rampino and Shen (2019).
5 A number of scholars have recently argued for why the environmental humanities needs to retain a conception of "nature" as separate from human society, even (or indeed especially) in the Anthropocene. See, for instance, Malm (2018); and Crist (2019).
6 See Menely (2017). See also Dawson (2016).
7 Notably, this strong emphasis on artificial selection is one of the points on which Darwin and Wallace differed.
8 Chakrabarty describes the Anthropocene's central conceptual challenge for the humanities as reckoning with the fact that "the wall between human and natural history has been breached" (2009): 221.

9 For a comparison of Darwin and Wallace's views on evolution, see Costa (2020).

10 Further references given by page.

11 In framing extinction as an inevitable consequence of empire, Wallace fits within the Victorian discourse on the inevitable extinction of "primitive" races described by Brantlinger (2003). However, Brantlinger glosses over the extinction of other species, neglecting the way that the extinction of "primitive" or "savage" humans often served as a metaphor for extinctions in nature, and vice versa.

12 On the longstanding relations between Papuan people and birds of paradise, De Vos, 2017: 95–96.

13 Sylvia Wynter and Katherine McKittrick describe the human as "a biomutationally evolved, hybrid *species – storytellers who now storytellingly invent themselves as being purely biological.*" Wynter and McKittrick, 2015: 9–89, 11. Arguing in a similar vein to different conclusions, Simon L. Lewis and Mark Maslin ascribe the emergence of the Anthropocene proceeding across scalar thresholds (mercantile capitalism, industrial capitalism, etc.) reaching back to the human capacity for "cumulative culture." Lewis and Maslin, 2018.

14 Anna-Sophie Springer and Etienne Turpin have posed this question in their research on Wallace: "When we asked evolutionary biologists whether or not they believe it would still be possible to develop the theory of evolution, or biogeographical distribution, based on a collection of specimens from the Malay Archipelago today, most answered in the negative." Springer and Turpin, 2017: 36.

CHAPTER 3

Darwin and Animal Studies

Caroline Hovanec

It has become commonplace to say that Darwin's evolutionary theory radically overturned human exceptionalism, revealing our species as one among many. He taught us that we evolved through the same natural processes that made wolves wolves, oaks oaks, and mushrooms mushrooms. For most philosophers, Darwin's leveling of humans and other species was significant because it refigured the human as animal, thus revealing within us the continued presence of the biological, the embodied, the earthly – all of that which Western religion and philosophy had long tried to exclude from humanity. As Derrida says, "the disavowal" of the animal's gaze is not "just one disavowal among others. It institutes what is proper to man, the relation to itself of a humanity that is above all anxious about, and jealous of, what is proper to it" (2008: 14). Darwin's theory of evolution by natural selection violated this notion of propriety, avowing our animal nature and kinship with animals, and thus shocking theologians and humanists alike.

There was, however, a corollary to this relative demotion of the human: Darwin's work can also be seen as elevating the status of other animals. To persuade his readers that humans had evolved from ape ancestors, Darwin had to show that every human trait – not just physical organs such as lungs and eyes, but also the capacities for emotion, reason, and morality – had evolved from similar traits shared with other animals (2002 [1871]: 1.34–35). Thus, *Descent of Man*, a book ostensibly about human evolution, in fact reads like a catalog of animal stories, its pages full of superstitious dogs, vengeful monkeys, and avian aesthetes. The *Descent*'s animals demonstrate the diverse feelings, intelligences, and abilities within the animal kingdom.

These twin insights – the animality of the human, the subjectivity of the animal – have been foundational for animal studies, an interdisciplinary field of study that examines the social, cultural, and aesthetic significance of animals. Darwin's work has been especially generative for literary animal studies (my own subfield). In their now-classic monographs,

Margot Norris (1985), Akira Mizuta Lippit (2000), and Carrie Rohman (2009) have shown the importance of the *Origin of Species* and the *Descent* for refiguring animality. More recent animal studies works by Angelique Richardson (2013), Ivan Kreilkamp (2018), and Chris Danta (2018) have explored Darwin's lesser-known writings, including (respectively) *Expression of the Emotions, Variation of Plants and Animals Under Domestication*, and *The Formation of Vegetable Mould Through the Action of Worms*. An axiom of animal studies is that the man/animal dualism, which has sustained centuries of European philosophy, is wrongheaded and must be replaced with a different understanding of life. What Giorgio Agamben calls the "anthropological machine" – the imaginary devices for locating and excising the "animal" in order to produce the human – has enabled not only cruelty to animals, but also the denial of human status to many groups of *Homo sapiens*, including those who are Black, Jewish, or disabled. As Agamben says, the task is therefore to stop the anthropological machine (2004: 37–38).

Like many interdisciplinary fields, animal studies is riven with tensions among different factions. My aim in this chapter is less to resolve these debates than to consider how Darwin's work might offer a useful compass for navigating them. To sketch some of these concerns in very general terms: an often gendered divide exists between the (masculine) "theory" and (feminine) "praxis" poles of animal studies, with poststructuralists and vegan or animal welfare proponents having little to say to each other (Fraiman, 2012). Another problem for the field is how to balance the critique that science creates an instrumentalizing, reductionist view of animals with the recognition that biologists also offer a crucial source of knowledge about animals, which can be used to help animals flourish (Haraway, 2008: 69–73). A third source of tension is the intersection between animal studies and critical race studies. While there is little doubt that "animalization has been central not incidental to the project of racialization" (Kim, 2015: 18), many animal rights organizations have nevertheless treated racism as a thing of the past and a source of convenient analogies – for example the comparison of animal agriculture to slavery (Boisseron, 2018). Finally, animal studies has often remained strangely divorced from the environmental humanities, reflecting (among other things) a difference of scale: is the unit of ethical consideration the individual animal or is it the population, species, or ecosystem?

Darwin's work and its legacy can help us better understand these debates and how they have shaped the past, and are likely to shape the future, of animal studies. This chapter will focus on four avenues of inquiry, traversing two centuries of responses to Darwin's work and its bearing on animals: (1) Activists since the 1800s have used evolution as evidence for the existence of animal minds and feelings (and therefore animals' ethical standing). (2) Ethology, a science of animal behavior that emerged during the twentieth century, piqued public interest in the workings of animal minds and social life. (3) In the past twenty years, Donna Haraway and her followers have used Darwin's notion of coevolution to understand the relationships, from parasitism to pet-keeping, that make different species "companion species." (4) Finally, a new area of animal studies focuses on the sixth (or, as Jesse Oak Taylor notes, perhaps it is the seventh?) mass extinction.[1] Here, we see the range as well as the limits of Darwin's influence, for Darwin understood extinction as slow, rare, and natural, while the current extinction crisis is anything but. If the catastrophist Georges Cuvier (1822) is in some ways more relevant to our concerns today than the gradualist Darwin, the latter's work nevertheless has something crucial to offer the new extinction studies: a better understanding of what it is that is being lost.

3.1　Animal Advocacy Movements

Though many animal activists in the nineteenth century drew on Darwin's evolutionary theory, animal welfare sentiments predate Darwin. There are at least two schools of eighteenth-century Western thought that saw animals as sensitive subjects deserving protection. One is the empiricist tradition that ran from John Locke through David Hume, Jeremy Bentham, and John Stuart Mill, which assumed that animals could think and feel and thus warranted ethical concern (Rollin, 2007: 253–255). The other is the Christian tradition, which built its arguments for animal welfare on theological grounds that would prove antithetical to Darwinism. In eighteenth-century Britain, many clergymen advocated kindness to animals as an essential Christian duty (Spencer, 2013). Both the theologians and the empiricists believed that sympathizing with animals, and acting accordingly, constituted a moral obligation.

　　Pre-Darwinian beliefs in animal feeling and the need for animal sympathy found a practical counterpart in the establishment of early animal welfare organizations. Most notable among these was the Society for the Prevention of Cruelty to Animals, founded in 1824. The Society for Prevention of Cruelty to Animals (SPCA) (to which Darwin himself subscribed) worked within a framework of bourgeois respectability, tying its campaigns to Christian morals, national pride, and a "bettering" of the supposedly barbarous lower classes (Burkhardt, 1999: 778; Ritvo, 1987: 125–144). It was likely the fact that this version of the humane movement was politically defanged and highly classed that led Queen Victoria, in 1840, to bestow the prefix "Royal" to the SPCA's name, a title it still bears today.

Articulating Darwin's role in the history of animal ethics requires a great deal of nuance. As Jane Spencer (2013) argues, it is not the case that people prior to Darwin were unaware of animal subjectivity or uninterested in animal welfare. Nor is it the case that all of Darwin's followers committed themselves to the ethical consideration of animals that would seem to be a logical consequence of his work. Nevertheless, as Spencer puts it, "What Darwinism did encourage was ... the development of a scientific and secular discourse, rooted in biological and behavioural studies, for articulating concepts of human-animal relationship" (2013: 26). Animal lovers could use his work to derive an ethical imperative to care for animals from a belief in their biological capacity to feel and think.

There is a strong Darwinian tradition of caring for animals based on phylogenetic kinship and shared subjective capacities. Darwin himself seems to have practiced a general, untheorized kindness toward animals, especially the menagerie of dogs, cats, birds, and even worms that lived in his household. He was evidently so soft-hearted that the Victorian anti-vivisectionist Frances Power Cobbe described him as "a man who would not let a fly bite a pony's neck" (Feller, 2009: 268). To cause animals pain was intolerable to him; as he famously wrote of vivisection, "It is a subject which makes me sick with horror" (Darwin, 1871b).

As Bernard E. Rollin observes, in the late nineteenth century, "Darwin's work inspired a spurt of concern about the moral status of animals," including the work of E. P. Evans and Henry Salt, who brought evolutionary theory to bear on the question of how to act morally toward animals (2007: 257). Cobbe, too, understood Darwin's work as related to animal protection; though (as I'll describe below) they did not see eye-to-eye on the use of animals in physiological research, the two nevertheless bonded over a shared love of dogs (Feller, 2009: 265). The Victorian vegetarian movement also latched onto the *Origin*, "[taking] up the language of common origins to bolster the meat-free cause" (Richardson, 2019: 118).

On the other hand, Darwin and his acolytes also angered animal advocates because they defended the right of scientists to experiment on animals. Darwin's legacy was obviously pro-science; he pursued naturalistic explanations for biological phenomena well into the territory that had been marked off as the province of theology alone. His "bulldog," Thomas

H. Huxley, spent a lifetime promoting scientific research and education, even the sorts of which the public disapproved, (mostly) with Darwin's blessing (Desmond, 1994: 457–462). This conflict came to a head in the 1870s when the Cruelty to Animals Act, which regulated vivisection, was proposed and eventually passed. The debate over the bill pitted Cobbe and other animal activists against physiologists, including Huxley. Darwin played a mediating role, supporting modest regulations while also defending his scientific colleagues against charges of cruelty (Feller, 2009).

There is a paradox in biomedical research on animal subjects: we now know, thanks to Darwin and other biologists, that it is *because* of evolutionary kinship that animal research has any use for human medicine at all. If we were unrelated, or biologically unsimilar, then animal models could not tell us anything about human physiology. And yet, as Rollin reports, biomedicine has continued to pretend, well beyond the nineteenth century, that this similarity does not extend to the experience of pain (2007: 270–271). Although the passage of the Cruelty to Animals Act represented a partial victory (or at least a draw) for the animal activists, it by no means ended the debates over animal experimentation, which have continued to rage with more or less fervor ever since.

The animal advocacy movement, too, has not abated, and we might locate some of the antivivisectionists' spiritual heirs in the vegan and animal liberation activists of the twentieth century. However, along with the deep commitment of the Victorian antivivisectionists, the movement has also inherited the prejudices, class and otherwise, of the RSPCA. And here we can see a much more troubling legacy of Darwinism: the social-Darwinist notion that kindness to (nonhuman) animals is a sign of a "more evolved" civilization, and therefore that upper- and middle-class whites must protect nonhuman animals from "brutish" others – represented by the working classes in early Victorian England and Black, Indigenous, and Asian people in the United States (Kim, 2015).

While Darwin did not subscribe to a polygenist view of human races (in which Africans, Asians, and Indigenous people were seen as literally belonging to other, "lower" species), he did contribute to the discursive framework that placed nonhuman animals and people of color in competition with each other for ethical consideration:

> For my own part I would as soon be descended from that heroic little monkey, who braved his dreaded enemy in order to save the life of his keeper; or from that old baboon, who, descending from the mountains, carried away in triumph his young comrade from a crowd of astonished dogs – as from a savage who delights to torture his enemies, offers up bloody sacrifices,

practices infanticide without remorse, treats his wives like slaves, knows no decency, and is haunted by the grossest superstitions. (Darwin, 2002 [1871], 2.404–405)

As Bénédicte Boisseron (2018) and Claire Jean Kim (2015) argue, much of the contemporary animal rights movement has perpetuated an animals-versus-"savages" framework. Looking at several case studies, including the Michael Vick dogfighting scandal, Kim finds a continuity between this racist framework's nineteenth-century formulation – savages *are* animals – and its twenty-first-century version – Black people and Asians are savage *to* animals (2015: 6–7). With this powerful critique in mind, a challenge for the animal welfare movement going forward is how to retain the power of an evolutionary view of animal sentience while shedding the social-Darwinist prejudices that have made animal activism largely the purview of a white middle class and disconnected it from other struggles for justice.

3.2 Ethology

While the animal welfare debates focused mainly on domestic animals – working horses, laboratory dogs – Darwin was at heart a naturalist and his work contributed to new approaches to studying wild animals as well. Another, more ecologically oriented legacy of Darwin's work is ethology, a science that was championed by Konrad Lorenz and Niko Tinbergen in the mid-twentieth century and revised in the late twentieth century by figures such as Jane Goodall, Barbara Smuts, and Marc Bekoff. Ethology is the study of animal behavior; Lorenz and Tinbergen differentiated their studies from animal psychology by insisting on the importance of studying animals "in the wild." Like the naturalists who preceded them, and unlike psychologists who studied mice and rats in laboratory experiments, the ethologists believed that animals' behavior could only be properly studied in their natural habitats. This was for evolutionary reasons: behaviors, they thought, evolved just as physical traits did, and they could only truly be understood within the context of the environment that selected for that behavior (Burkhardt, 2005).

Lorenz and Tinbergen's fascination with wild animal behaviors is something that many animal studies scholars share, but in one respect they are a strange pair of influencers for our work. As Eileen Crist (1999) has detailed, Lorenz and Tinbergen were resolutely attached to mechanistic descriptions of animal behaviors, and they would not countenance any hint of subjectivism in their scientific writing about animals. Like the behaviorists in psychology, Lorenz and Tinbergen wanted to make their research scientific, which they thought required the exclusion of any whiff of the unprovable – no speculation about what animals actually feel, think, and experience (Burkhardt, 2005: 187, 435; Crist, 1999: 79).

In the 1960s, however, a new generation of ethologists-in-training turned to subjective and personal registers to describe animal behaviors. There were many reasons for this shift, but one was that excluding analysis of animal subjectivity came to seem unscientific, when some forms of awareness and volition were evidently favored by natural selection. As the founder of cognitive ethology Donald R. Griffin wrote, "it seems likely that conscious thinking and emotional feeling about current, past, and anticipated events is the best way to cope with some of the more critical challenges faced by animals in their natural lives" (2001: 3).

Most notable among the new subjectivist school of ethology were, in the 1970s and '80s, the primatologists Jane Goodall and Barbara Smuts, and the ethologist Marian Stamp Dawkins and, in the 1990s, the ethologist/activist Marc Bekoff, the primatologist Frans de Waal, as well as Griffin himself (Bekoff, 2002; Dawkins, 1980; de Waal, 1997; Goodall, 1986; Smuts, 1985). These figures represent diverse research programs and varying relationships with the animal welfare movement (Bekoff and Goodall have been outspoken in favor of it, while Griffin and de Waal have made more circumspect public statements) (Bekoff, 2002; Griffin, 2001; Mance, 2019; Phillips, 2020). But they have three crucial things in common: they believe in studying animals' subjective states, they often write for the public, and they encourage kindness toward animals as a basic corollary of their research. In this regard, they represent a turn back to Darwin's practices.

In literary studies, many scholars have analyzed ethology as an influence, context, and theory for a wide range of animal representations (Baetens and Trudel, 2014; Caracciolo, 2020; Hovanec, 2018; Kendall-Morwick, 2021; Murray, 2020; Smith, 2001). A key takeaway from much of this work is that, while there is certainly an ethical dimension to ethology, its cultural significance lies more in the intellectual realm of fascination with the uncanny workings of animal minds. Certainly, it is hard for anyone to spend much time thinking about animals' behavior without drawing some conclusions about the importance of treating them well – which, for most ethologists, requires preserving the environmental conditions that allow them to flourish. Yet the main appeal of ethology, I would argue, has more to do with pursuing curiosity. Those who wonder what echolocation feels like to a bat, how birds know how to migrate, or why dogs bow on their front legs when they are playing are drawn to this field, which offers the satisfaction of learning more about these alien others with whom we share the planet.[2] And it is its ethos of genial curiosity as much as its evolutionary framework for understanding animal behavior that links ethology back to Darwin.

3.3   Companion Species

For Donna Haraway, genial curiosity is both a scientific virtue and an ethical obligation to the animals with whom we work and live. Ethologists, she suggests, have succeeded in this regard where philosophers have not, for some ethologists "have met the gaze of living, diverse animals" and truly *responded* to them (Haraway, 2008: 21). Haraway's *Companion Species Manifesto* (2003), *When Species Meet* (2008), and *Staying with the Trouble* (2016), represent a twenty-first-century theoretical turn to the study of human relationships with other creatures. Haraway defines "companion species" as "a bigger and more heterogeneous category than companion animal," one that points to complex, evolving, and co-constitutive forms of relationality among different species (2003: 17). In other words, "companion species" refers to species that have shaped each other throughout their evolutionary history; for humans, our companion species would include not just dogs and horses but also "rice, bees, tulips, and intestinal flora, all of whom make life for humans what it is" (15).

Despite its emphasis on many different forms of relationality, *The Companion Species Manifesto* is a marker of a renewed theoretical interest in pets specifically. This turn is significant because many earlier philosophers and writers had privileged wild animals over domestic ones, imagining the former as primitive, romantic, and unsullied by human contact, and the latter as degraded and unworthy of serious inquiry (the province of little old ladies with purse dogs or too many cats) (Haraway, 2003: 27–30). But, informed by postcolonial and feminist theories, Haraway and her fellow critics bring a skepticism of notions like "wild" and "primitive," and a respect for care and relationality, to animal studies. A great deal of recent scholarship speaks to a shared conviction about the importance of animal companionship for theory and lived experience (Dayan, 2015; McHugh, 2011; Weil, 2012).

Among some of the most important explorations of species companionship in literary studies today are those which explore the overlooked, vexed, or subversive relations between marginalized people and animals. Boisseron (2018), Joshua Bennett (2020), and others discuss the history of "white dogs" in the Americas, used for centuries by slave-owners and police to terrorize Black people. But these critics are also interested in relations of mutual flourishing. Boisseron, for example, praises commensal relations in Caribbean culture, which allows dogs and other animals into domestic spaces without the obligations of pethood (2018: 90–95). Bennett similarly finds in African-American literature a vision of "kinship between humans and dogs" that exists outside the framework of "domination or sovereign power" implicit in the usual notion of pet ownership (2020: 142). Though not all of this work addresses Haraway (or Darwin) specifically, it is important for two reasons. It allows us to notice how the forms of loving companionship with animals that both Haraway and Darwin enjoyed are in part enabled by whiteness and class privilege; and it demonstrates the depth and complexity of other forms of human–animal relationships.

Although Haraway, who trained as a biologist, describes herself (only partly tongue-in-cheek) as a "dutiful daughter of Darwin," not all of the work on companion species self-consciously positions itself within a Darwinian tradition (2003: 15). Darwin's work and life, though, are richly intertwined with companion species. First, it must be remembered that the phenomenon of domestication was integral to Darwin's thought (as Kathleen Frederickson [2022] discusses in Chapter 8).[3] In the *Origin*, artificial selection, or the selective breeding of species to be useful to humans, is the prototype for the concept of natural selection (Darwin, 2002 [1859]). Darwin's later book, *The Variation of Animals and Plants Under Domestication* (2002 [1868]), testifies to his enduring interest in a wide variety of domesticated animals, from dogs and cats to livestock and fancy pigeons.

Second, Darwin's own life was spent in the company of animals, in which he found both companionship and intellectual inspiration. His lifelong love of dogs is well-known and is described in Emma Townshend's *Darwin's Dogs* (2009). His son Francis wrote that Darwin "was delightfully tender to Polly," his favorite dog, "and never showed any impatience at the attentions she required" (Townshend, 2009: 11). Cats and horses also lived with the Darwins at Down House, and Darwin obtained beehives in the 1850s while working on the *Origin* (The Evolution of Honeycomb). During those years, Darwin also built a pigeon house so that he could study pigeon breeds; as Townshend reports, the birds "toed an uneasy line between being experimental specimens and pets" (2009: 73). Toward the end of his life, Darwin even kept earthworms in his home, experimenting with them to find out which foods they preferred, how they used different materials in their burrows, and what their sensory capabilities were; he published the results in his final book, *The Formation of Vegetable Mould Through the Actions of Worms* (Darwin, 2002 [1881]; Hovanec, 2019).

Most importantly, the notion of companion species widens our understanding of coevolution. The *Origin* describes the mutual "coadaptations" of flowering plants and pollinating insects as an example of natural selection; and Darwin's later study on orchids (1862) builds on this insight by exploring how the flowers and their pollinators coevolved into extremely specialized forms. Animal studies scholars today use the concept of coevolution to revise human-exceptionalist narratives of domestication. "Evolution," as Karalyn Kendall-Morwick argues, "is always *co*-evolution," and "coevolution works both ways" (2021: 7, 8). The shared history of people and dogs goes back thousands of years, and this relationship changed the humans as well as the wolves (Haraway, 2003: 30–31). There are similar stories to be told about other companion species. The theory of coevolution has redirected emphasis away from the primal image of man, standing apart, naming and taming the animals, and toward an image of the human as ecologically embedded: open, from the very start, to the hand, paw, feeler, or flagellum of the other.

3.4 Species of Concern

To outsiders they may appear closely related, but animal welfare and environmentalism have traditionally operated as two separate, even conflicting, domains. Animal advocates have mostly been concerned with the lives of individual animals (especially domestic and food animals), while environmentalists have focused on wild creatures at the level of population or species, calling for the preservation of biodiversity. But today, we find ourselves receiving near-daily dire news confirming that ecological collapse is an animal welfare issue, and animal welfare is an ecological issue. As Sunaura Taylor points out, "Humans and 'livestock' – a word that clearly demonstrates life reduced to economics – now make up more than 96 percent of mammalian biomass on the planet. We've replaced wildlife and wild spaces with farmed animals whom we treat, not as living beings, but as parts to consume" (Taylor and Orning, 2020: 675). Taylor calls for an animal studies that attends to the interrelatedness of animality, ecology, disability, race, and labor in an age of what she calls "dead meat capitalism" (677). This call is all the more urgent in the context of COVID-19, which, as Xiao Wang (2020) observes, is a case study in how industrialized animal agriculture facilitates the spread of zoonotic pathogens.

The upshot is that, because of human activities (specifically those of capitalist countries in the Global North), we are living through a mass extinction event. Species are dying out at 1,000 to 10,000 times the normal rate (de Vos, et al., 2015). As Jesse Oak Taylor points out in Chapter 2, Darwin's theory was "a product of the Anthropocene frontier," enabled by the same forces of empire and capitalism that have made today's "nature" so impoverished that Darwin would hardly recognize it if he could see it. If it ever made sense to separate animal issues from ecological ones, under these conditions it no longer does.

For Darwin, extinction was a necessary part of the history of life. His generation had learned from Cuvier that extinction existed; prior to the nineteenth century, the disappearance of species was unthinkable because it was incompatible with natural theology's understanding of creation as ordered by God. But Darwin ridiculed Cuvier's catastrophism – the belief that extinctions were caused by great geological disasters – writing, "so profound is our ignorance, and so high our presumption, that we marvel when we hear of the extinction of an organic being; and as we do not see the cause, we invent cataclysms to desolate the world" (Darwin, 1859: 73). In the *Origin*, extinction is not apocalyptic; it is critical to natural selection, and is, like evolution itself, a slow process (318). As Gillian Beer puts it, "Time dilutes terror" (2009a: 324).

The historian David Sepkoski (2020) narrates a history of geology in which the gradualist paradigm, advanced by Charles Lyell (2002 [1830]) and adopted by Darwin, had to be replaced in the 1980s as scientists strove to account for both the current crisis of biodiversity loss and the K-T extinction of 65 million years ago, which killed off the dinosaurs. The Alvarez hypothesis, first proposed in 1980, showed that the disappearance of the dinosaurs was likely the sudden result of an asteroid impact in the Yucatán Peninsula. Sepkoski portrays a zeitgeist in the 1970s and '80s obsessed with the specter of catastrophe, in which emerging scientific knowledge about mass extinction events in the deep past coincided with a dawning recognition of the many possibilities for an anthropogenic environmental apocalypse in the present (2020: 2–4, 8–13). That end-of-the-world feeling is today as pervasive as ever.

It might seem that in the present mass extinction, the usefulness of Darwin's work reaches its limits. His gentle Victorian moderation now looks outmoded; the cataclysms of Cuvier and the Alvarezes have more imaginative power today, as we watch ice sheets crumble, fires rage, and animals die out. Even here, though, where Darwin got it at least partly wrong, I would argue that his work still offers something valuable to our ethical imagination. He recognized the sublime slowness and sheer chance that made the evolution of every species alive today the most unlikely, most wondrous of outcomes.

The sixth extinction requires a marshaling of all our critical (not to mention material) resources. We need animal studies to insist on the value of animal life, ecology to perceive the connections that life relies upon, environmental humanities to defamiliarize the clichés that too often defang environmental politics, theory to have a hope of understanding the irrational and libidinal forces driving a capitalist economy to hurtle toward and through mass death, and activism to keep us honest in all our theorizing. We need the catastrophists to disrupt the deeply ingrained but deeply wrong idea that things can go on this way pretty much indefinitely. But we need Darwin too, whose evolutionary theory first showed us the secular miracle of each species emerging slowly through a mindless, impossibly delicate process that could never be repeated in the history of life. "Species once lost do not reappear" (Darwin, 1859: 313).

The sixth extinction is, I think, the future of animal studies, but it is also likely to be the end of animal studies one way or another. Perhaps because a university system capable of sustaining intellectual study in any large-scale, networked way seems rather improbable in a world of four or five degrees of warming, or perhaps, in a more utopian vein, because in this marshaling of resources I have described above, "animal studies" will no longer be an eccentric niche within the academy. If we take the sixth extinction seriously, animal questions may rather become so fully integrated into intellectual study and praxis that they dissolve, "like water in water," and no longer need a name.[4]

Notes

1 See Chapter 2 by Jesse Oak Taylor.
2 These questions are inspired by the famous Thomas Nagel (1974) essay, "What Is It Like to Be a Bat?", but Nagel argues the title question is fundamentally unanswerable, while cognitive ethologists aim to answer such questions as closely as possible through scientific study.
3 See Chapter 8 by Kathleen Frederickson.
4 The phrase is borrowed from Bataille, who wrote, "Every animal is *in the world like water in water*" (1989: 19).

CHAPTER 4

Darwin's Birdsong
Sound Studies and Darwinian Aesthetics

Miranda Butler

As a Victorian reader and writer, Darwin not only read nature – he listened to it. In the nineteenth century, reading was "not limited to the genealogy of how we now read, in silence and using the eyes alone" (Cavallo and Chartier, 1999: 4). As Devin Griffiths explains, for the Darwin family (like so many other households), reading was "a shared family event" that often took place out loud (2016: Loc. 5458). From his earliest notes to his final publications, an urgent need to recreate sonic experiences for himself and his readers threads throughout Charles Darwin's observations. As this chapter will argue, sound studies – more particularly, acoustemology – offers the potential to reshape crucial interpretations within the history of literature and science, including readings of Darwin's work.[1]

John M. Picker adapts the term "soundscape" (originally coined by composer R. Murray Schafer) to "turn the Victorian gaze on its ear" by "investigat[ing] the two major roles that hearing played in Victorian culture: as a response to a physical stimulus and as a metaphor for the communication of meaning" (2003: 7). However, subsequent critics have suggested that as a theoretical term, the "soundscape" relies too heavily on a parallel to the visual "landscape," and furthermore, "is lined with ideological and ecological messages about which sounds 'matter' and which do not; it is suffused with instructions about how people ought to listen" (Kelman, 2010: 214). Yet in an article tellingly titled, "Sound – So what?," Mark M. Smith reviews the emergence of sound studies and suggests that, rather than pitting the eye against the ear, "sensory history generally, and the history of sound specifically, ... tend to claim that attention to the sensate and auditory past allows us a deeper appreciation of the texture, meaning, and human experience of that past" (2015: 133). In other words, sound studies does not work against existing historical inquiries, but in conjunction with them. Interrogating the past's auditory environment, Smith argues, can reveal how sounds helped shape power relations, a wide variety of lived identities, and personal experiences (2015: 132). However, in the same paragraph, Smith also asserts that sound studies "rarely makes extravagant or especially daring claims about the field's interpretive power" (133). Why not? An acoustic epistemology, Steven Feld argues, "insists that one does not simply 'acquire' knowledge but, rather that one knows through an ongoing cumulative and interactive process of participation and reflection" (2015: 12–13).

As Darwin interrogates the auditory again and again, he ultimately concludes, in Elizabeth Grosz's words, that "The sonorous and visual arts are possible only because the body finds intensities of sound, color, and form pleasing and alluring. It may be, Darwin suggests, that this most elementary form of discernment or taste is the evolutionary origin not only of all art, but of language use and intelligence more generally" (Grosz, 2011: 136). Grosz develops this argument in order to propose a larger-scale "concept of life that does not privilege the human as the aim or end of evolution" (2). However, her analysis begs sound studies scholars to attend to the role that language plays in articulating Darwin's aesthetics within nature.

In this chapter, I will highlight passages of Darwin's writings that explore phonetics and phonology in the natural world, illuminating how sound lies at the heart of his observation, and how sound studies provides new approaches to Darwin's work in literature, science, and beyond. Phonetics, J. C. Catford explains, is the study of "the basic components that go into the production of any speech sound" (2001: 11) and although this definition traditionally refers to human languages, Darwin analyzes speech production indiscriminately in both humans and animals. Phonology, which operates in conjunction with phonetics, is the study of sound patterns within and between languages, and Darwin likewise compares animal languages to human ones without a second thought.

I begin with Darwin's *Voyage of the Beagle*, comparing his handwritten notes from the last period of his journey alongside the published travelogue. These early ideas and observations are especially productive to scholars of Darwin's work, since Darwin immersed himself in his research and experienced the sounds on his voyage so viscerally. Darwin's handwritten notes from 1832–1836 constitute "an early assemblage of his personal experiences, written with the red-hot memory ... round the skeleton list of specimens" (Barlow, 1963: 204), and many of these passages served as drafts for the prose of the published *Voyage*, showing what Darwin was thinking, and how he attempted to explain it sequentially, before he returned to the constraints of printing, publication, and generic expectations.

Transcription technologies proliferated in the early nineteenth century, including shorthand writing, like Gurney's and Pitman's; phonetic transcription, for example, Dickens' depictions of dialects; and graphic systems for recording birdsong, often adapted from musical notation (Bevis, 2019). Darwin, however, was not trained in any of these methods. Yet it is precisely because Darwin was unable to use any preestablished method of sound recording that we can see the texture of his own thinking about the nature of sound and its transcription. In British and American linguistics, the turn toward the physiological study of speech and sound production was also taking place throughout the late eighteenth and early nineteenth centuries. Attention to sound similarly helped Darwin organize a shift toward "aesthetic evolution," which Ian Duncan reads – through Richard O. Prum – as a "compelling alternative to the idealist tradition" that "delivers us from the idealist mystification of art" (Duncan, 2020: 54, 56).

In Section 4.1, I outline Darwin's contributions to sound studies, using his early work to demonstrate that his writing process relies upon experiencing the sonic texture and physiological dimension of nature, as well as recreating that auditory experience within his own mind's eye (or ear) and in the imaginations of his readers. Next, I analyze Darwin's attempts to represent birdsong to foreground the importance of transcribing animal sounds for Darwin's work comparing animal species. Finally, in Section 4.3, I look beyond Darwin's depiction of birdsong, analyzing his numerous approaches to labeling sound at the intersection of different physiological, behavioral, and cultural registers, in order to identify sound and vocal communication as a critical foundation for his theories and writings.

4.1   Auditory Ekphrasis and Animal Phonetics

Scholars such as Desmond King-Hele remind us that Charles Darwin's grandfather, Erasmus Darwin, studied speech sounds as early as the 1750s and wrote about speech production in correspondence with Benjamin Franklin in 1772. In a letter to the American polymath, Erasmus proposes a theory for the difference between various vowels, suggesting that, "I think there are but four Vowels, their successive Compounds, and their synchronous Compounds. For as they are made by apertures of different parts of the mouth, they may have synchronous, as well as successive Combinations" (King-Hele, 1981: 63). To test this theory, Erasmus was said to have constructed a mechanical mouth, capable of pronouncing some sounds so precisely that listeners thought it was indeed a person speaking. The invention is said to have been in operation by 1770 (Wilcox,

1975: 212). At the end of his letter, Erasmus enquires about the rumors that someone else had built a similar "speaking machine," and asks urgently if there was any truth to such reports (King-Hele, 1981: 63).

Scholars including King-Hele, Griffiths, Martin Priestman, and others, have traced in detail the direct influence that Erasmus Darwin's writings had on Charles's theories: Charles inherited his grandfather's notes, and also invoked *Zoonomia* by name in 1837, when he first began to gather his thoughts on the mutability of species (Griffiths, 2016: Loc. 143). Charles's interest in sound experiments was also somewhat eccentric – as part of his studies of plant growth and movement in the late 1870s, he had his son play the bassoon for certain "sensitive" plants.[2] A general fascination with the physicality of sound, which anticipates major transitions in nineteenth-century linguistics, pervades Charles Darwin's writings. Both Darwins understood human speech, like all animal sounds, as physiological – and consequently, a feature that would necessarily evolve alongside species.

Charles Darwin is well-known for his "meticulous attention to the accumulation of vast and detailed examples" (Grosz, 2011: 117), which Richard Doyle has described as simultaneously his "rhetorical burden and gift" (2011: 141). Through descriptive language and idioms, Doyle explains, Darwin relies on visual ekphrasis to translate his arguments for his readers. Darwin also frequently asks his reader to imagine embodied sonic experiences. More often than not, it proves immensely challenging to inspire his reader to "hear" the right sound, and so Darwin must continually tend to and revise these instances of auditory ekphrasis in order to suit a variety of authorial purposes.

Many biographers of Darwin have highlighted how he toiled when revising and perfecting his writing in preparation for publication, but in his handwritten notebooks, Darwin toils in another sense. His notes from the *Voyage* adopt, adjust, and abandon a number of experimental approaches to sound transcription in order to capture Darwin's auditory experiences as best as he can. These quick, immediate observations reveal what Darwin's granddaughter Nora Barlow describes as his "spontaneous first impressions," as he attempts to record sounds, as well as his "difficulty of expression" (1945: 3) when standard English orthography proves insufficient.

In the *Voyage of the Beagle*, Darwin adjusts his experimental descriptions to suit the genre conventions of travel narrative, while his polemics, *On the Origin of Species*, *The Descent of Man*, and *The Expression of Emotion in Man and Animals*, pick and choose descriptions carefully in an attempt to lay out the most persuasive evidence in favor of Darwin's theories. Thus, there are discrepancies between the ways that Darwin transcribes the sounds of the natural world over time and in different contexts. An examination of some of his earliest written attempts to capture the qualia of his experience reveals the extent to which sound and its production preoccupied Darwin and informed his entire oeuvre. For example, the printed second edition of the *Voyage* describes a bird called the Carrancha, in a passage which exemplifies Darwin's multilayered analysis of birdsong in his notebooks and works. "At times, the Carrancha is noisy," Darwin writes, "but it is not generally so. Its cry is loud, very harsh and peculiar, and may be likened to the sound of the Spanish guttural *g*, followed by a rough double *rr*" (Darwin, 1845: 69). Taking a phonological approach inherited from comparative philology, he begins by listening to the Carrancha's call and comparing it to human speech. This comparison is especially notable since, as Ian Duncan has written, "Darwin's theory dethrones the human species from nature and from history. We share aesthetic enjoyment – and everything else – with other creatures" (2020: 68–69). In other words, to Darwin, human speech is similar to, rather than different from, the "languages" of birds. The only hint of a taxonomy or hierarchy is Darwin's conclusion that the Spanish language, rather than English, includes sounds better suited to capture this particular bird's song.

At this point in the passage, Darwin's ornithological notes, written from 1832 to 1836, include a speculation that the *Voyage* does not: "Perhaps the Gauchos from this cause have called it Carrancha" (1832–1836: Image 58). Both versions then observe that "when uttering this cry it elevates its head higher and higher, till at last, with its beak wide open, the crown almost touches the lower part of the back" (Darwin, 1845: 73). When taking the time to fully capture his auditory experience, an exploration of animal phonetics becomes necessary. As Grosz has written, language for Darwin "is not the uniquely human accomplishment that post-Enlightenment thought has assumed," but rather "resid[es] within the voice and in other organs capable of resonating sound, to articulate, to express, to vibrate, and thus in some way to affect bodies" (2011: 20). In order to record the call of this bird for his own future intellectual consideration, Darwin must also consider the bird's physical means of producing sound.

After this passage, the published *Voyage* diverges into other observations about the Carrancha's diet and habits. The manuscript, on the other hand, continues to describe the embodied production of the Carrancha's sound:

This fact, which has been doubted is quite true; I have seen them several times with their heads. backwards. in a completely inverted position. – The Carrancha builds a large coarse nest indifferently; in any low cliff. [*sic*] or in a bush or lofty tree. – (a)[3] I am in great doubt about the plumage of the two sexes & ages of this bird. (1832–1836: Image 58)

"Birdsong and plumage," writes Doyle, "are the veritable audio and visual media with which Darwin gathers and renders his scientific description of the world" (2011: 142). In *Charles Darwin and Victorian Visual Culture,* Jonathan Smith studies the visual media incorporated into Darwin's writings, pursuing the question: "How could natural selection, a concept almost by definition impossible to illustrate directly, be illustrated, especially when the existing visual conventions of the natural sciences were associated in varying degrees with conceptions of species fixity?" (2006: 1). In turning to Darwin's auditory ekphrasis in addition to his visual media, idioms, and analogies, academic scholarship can more deeply interpret the layers of information that contributed to his theorization of an evolutionary framework.

4.2   Birdsong and the Gradations of Language

Like many European naturalists, Darwin was passionate about ornithology and the melodious songs of birds, but his work demonstrates that he was equally interested in birdsongs that were not beautiful. In order to survive, organisms do not need to produce sounds that are melodious – only ones that are informative and, as Doyle has written, "create one of Darwin's most deployed rhetorical strategies: gradation" (2011: 149). For example, in the published *Voyage of the Beagle,* Darwin includes a passage about the Shiny Cowbird (*Molothrus niger*), which "sometimes attempt[s] to sing, or rather to hiss; the noise being very peculiar, resembling that of bubbles of air passing rapidly from a small orifice under water, so as to produce an acute sound" (Darwin, 1845: 70).

In his earlier, more immediate attempt to describe this sound in his handwritten manuscript, Darwin's passage looks like this: "I heard many of them attempting to sing or hiss for I do not know what to call it. – The noise was very peculiar resembling bubbles of air from a small orifice passing through water, but rapidly, so as to produce an acute sound. I at first thought it came from Frogs" (1832–1836: Image 17). The comparison to frogs is missing from his published work, but several things are apparent upon fuller examination of this passage: even without the rhetorical phrase "picture to yourself,"[4] Darwin is asking his reader to do precisely that (in their mind's ear); furthermore, the "picture" he and his reader attempt to imagine necessarily requires them to think about the physiological underpinnings of sounds. When he tries to describe the most similar sound he can imagine, the only way to do that is by articulating the *way* that that sound is produced: bubbles of air from a *small* orifice, in particular, moving in a specific fashion. Size and movement – concepts rooted in their physicality – are also incorporated into his detailed description.

When attempting to use comparisons and figurative language to aid in capturing this animal's sound, Darwin is more than willing to ignore established boundaries that differentiate animal species, just as he breaks down boundaries between human and animal languages, rhetorically suggesting that the differences between all animals, including humans and the "lower" species, are certainly of degree and not of kind (Grosz, 2011: 24). Although a bird and a frog share few, if any, similarities in their visual appearance, sonically, they can be virtually indistinguishable. The ability of species to produce meaningful sounds results in languages of all kinds; however, these sounds "do not culminate in human languages but include them as one means among many for the linguistic elaboration of life" (Grosz, 2011: 14).

The Shiny Cowbird is not the only example of a description in Darwin's notes which blurs the boundaries between animal species. Throughout his observations, he compares a variety of bird calls to a variety of dog sounds, including a "*little* dog giving tongue when in full chace [*sic*]" (1832–1836: Image 12), an example in which the word "little" is underlined to emphasize the difference in the sound – presumably pitch – made by a small dog compared to a big one. The sonic description additionally requires the reader to "hear" the effect that the shape of the dog's mouth (giving tongue) and movement of its body (full chase) has on that sound.

These sonic comparisons enable Darwin to comprehend differences in sound as gradations of similarities, rather than stark boundaries of separation. As he assesses species that resemble each other, he compares several ovenbird species within the genus Furnarius. He describes the smaller species thus in his handwritten notes: "At certain times it frequently utters a peculiar shrill, but gentle, quickly reiterated cry (so quickly reiterated as to make one ^running sound.) In this respect [it] resembles the Oven bird, but as widely differs in its quietness, from that active bird" (1832–1836: Image 33). The process of revision here – first adding a parenthetical explanation, and later adding the adjective "running" – demonstrates the difficulty of capturing all the necessary dimensions of sound and its production. Even though the two species within the same genus have a call that is similar in most respects, the volume ("quietness") still provides even further information that can be used to study the animal.

In the printed *Voyage*, the description of this species simply reads that the smaller Furnarius "resembles the oven-bird in a peculiar shrill reiterated cry" (Darwin, 1845: 103). This simplified version is perhaps better suited to the conventions of a travel narrative, in which readers expect to encounter a Humboldtian vision of a harmonious nature. At this early point in his career, Darwin's strategy of publication is to stabilize the uncertainties of natural description; in polemics like *The Origin*, Darwin amplifies the uncertainty because this very instability *is* his central argument. His early notebooks, in this way, indicate that long before Darwin made his theories of animal language and natural selection explicit in the *Origin of Species, The Descent of Man*, and *The Expressions of Emotions in Man and Animals*, he relied upon sound and the information it provided to draw relationships between species.

4.3   Aesthetics and Approaches to Darwin

Darwin's sonic descriptions of many animals – not just birds – show the importance of phonology and acoustemology as a general rubric for the study of the natural world. In this final section, I bring sound to the forefront of recent interventions in the study of Darwinian aesthetics, connecting these discussions to the continuity of sounds between humans and other animals that Darwin cited to establish his theory of natural selection. It was not only bird calls that urged Darwin to think about sound, its production, and its transcription. In the published *Voyage*, Darwin describes a small, mole-like creature that lives in burrows. "This animal," he writes:

> is universally known by a very peculiar noise which it makes when beneath the ground. A person, the first time he hears it, is much surprised; for it is not easy to tell whence it comes, nor is it possible to guess what kind of creature utters it. The noise consists in a short, but not rough, nasal grunt, which is monotonously repeated about four times in quick succession: the name Tucutuco is given in imitation of the sound. Where this animal is abundant, it may be heard at all times of the day, and sometimes directly beneath one's feet. (1845: 69)

Darwin's handwritten notes correspond very closely to the passage he ultimately publishes. However, when he is reflecting on his own thoughts, his writing demonstrates that the animal's sound – for which it is named – is immensely difficult to transcribe. When regular English orthography fails, the Cambridge-educated Darwin turns to one of the only possible alternatives he has – the long and short marks often used in Classics – in an attempt to better transcribe the name, which has already been "translated" from the sound of the animal itself, into Spanish, and now into English. Even the additional markings that Darwin adds prove unsatisfactory to his own recollection of the name: Darwin originally wrote "Toco-toco" in pen, and then changed those o's to u's using a fine, light pencil.

These difficulties and creative descriptions led Darwin to fascinating questions and comparisons of the tuco-tuco on the next page of his manuscript (Figure 4.1). When first listening to animal sounds, Darwin's complete attempt is as follows:

> At the Rio Negro (Lat 41°) some animal frequenting [^similar situations] makes [^also] the same kind of burrow, but its grunt or noise, although of the same class, is decidedly different from that of Maldonado. It is repeated only twice instead of three or four times, & it is more distinct, loud, & sonorous; it may be compared to the [^very] *distant* sound of the blows of an axe when a *small* tree is cut down; so close is this resemblance, that I have sometimes remained in doubt for a few minutes. –
>
> At Bahia Blanca (Lat 39°) another (or the same) animal makes a [^similar] noise, but repeated at single intervals, either at equal times or in an accelerating order. I was assured these animals are found of many different colours [^and therefore I presume are of as many species.] At B. Blanca, having caught a mouse (1284), many of the country people maintained that it was the To[^u]co, To[^u]co, & the author of the noise. – What is the truth? (1832–1836: Image 12)

In an attempt to explain the different sounds, Darwin launches into another elaborate and physiological metaphor. When he compares the noise of the similar animal to a distant sound of an ax, he feels the need to go back again and add, with a caret, that this is the "very" distant sound of the ax. Similarly, when he says that it sounds like the cutting down of a small tree, he underlines the "small," again attempting to imagine a very particular cause and effect that will generate the desired sound. Darwin recognizes that descriptions of sound are socially mediated, in that his metaphor relies on cultural touchstones like the ax. Similarly, he recognizes that sonic experience is simultaneously material, since even the same sound is perceived differently based on the observer's physical distance from the production of that sound. Much like orthography itself aims to do, Darwin's description tries to match a shared reference to a novel experience.

In the end of the passage, Darwin calls the tuco-tuco the "author" of its sound. Of course, "author" can mean "creator" or "source," especially in the nineteenth century, but in his handwritten notes, Darwin often

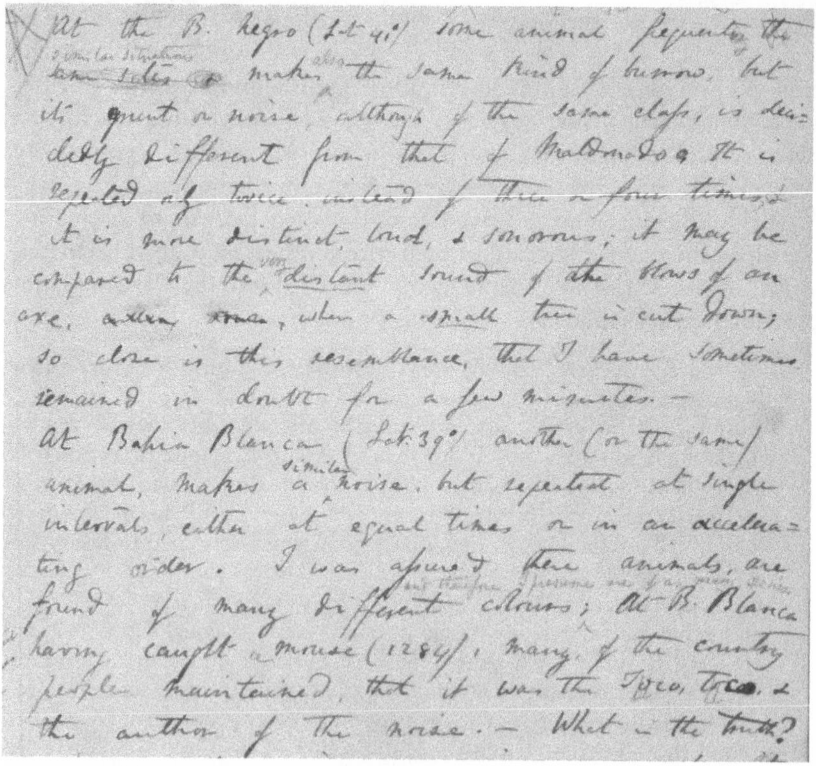

Figure 4.1   Image from Charles Darwin's "Catalogue of *Beagle* Specimens" (1832a) CUL-DAR29.1. Reproduced by kind permission of the Syndics of Cambridge University Library.

uses the phrase "author of the sound" to refer to several animals – though he does not use the term "author" in any other context related to his specimens (that I have found). This question of authorship and articulation once again destabilizes any assumptions that human language is an exceptional development among animal species. Darwin draws upon the metaphor of authorship and the idiosyncrasies of both verbal and written communication when he invokes Lyell in *The Origin*: "Following out Lyell's metaphor, I look at the natural geological record as a history of the world imperfectly kept, and written in a changing dialect; of this history we possess the last volume alone, relating only to two or three countries" (Darwin, 2003: 310). This invocation relies upon the very shortcomings of language that it describes in order to persuade the reader of Darwin's argument. Furthermore, auditory ekphrasis and animal sounds remained central to Darwin's work throughout his career. When he embarks on a longer-scale attempt to explain human communication (including writing, and explicitly rhetoric) in *The Expression of Emotion in Man and Animals*, he identifies the vocal organs in "many kinds of animals, man included," as "efficient in the highest degree as a means of expression" (Darwin, 1872: 1307).

Sound haunted Darwin. As a meticulous scientific observer who depended on effectively communicating his embodied experiences accurately in order to prove his claims, he relied on animal phonology and auditory ekphrasis to describe sound in myriad creative ways. By listening to birdsong, he struggled to differentiate animal species when comparing their sounds, and the attempt to find the right language to record sounds sharpened his experiences and his attempt to gauge sonic texture. In this way, sound studies is the connective tissue that binds together many recent interventions in scholarship about Darwin.[5] Analyzing Darwin's numerous investigations and depictions of sounds at different physiological, behavioral, and cultural registers builds a deeper critical foundation for understanding the reasoning behind his theories as well as his authorial and argumentative choices. Far from merely amplifying existing approaches to literature, sound studies empowers scholars to transform Darwinian aesthetics from an object of study situated in the Victorian field into a methodology for fresh interpretations of any works that reject idealized conceptions of nature in favor of an "imperfectly kept" record of sonic texture.

Notes

1 Steven Feld, who coined the term, defines this combination of "acoustics" and "epistemology," as a methodology designed to "theorize sound as a way of knowing," which recognizes sound "as something simultaneously social and material, an experiential nexus of sonic sensation." In doing so, Feld explains, acoustemology "inquires into what is knowable, and how it becomes known, through sound." By its very definition, acoustemology challenges scholars to reinterpret history, literature, and ways of knowing. (Feld 2015: 12, 14).

2 Darwin wrote, in an 1878 letter to John Tyndall: "The day before yesterday & today I observed (but perhaps the observation will prove erroneous) that certain sensitive plants were excited into movement, by a prolonged note on the bassoon & apparently more by a high than a low note." See Darwin (1878).

3 The (a), noted in the quotation above, is an inserted manuscript note, added between two sentences that seem unrelated to the discussion of the Carrancha. The note points the reader to a brief description of the Carrancha's diet and habits, which was ultimately published.

4 This is pointed out by Doyle (2011: 138). The phrase is used in the *Voyage* (Darwin, 2006: 420, 426); and *Descent of Man* (Darwin, 2006: 1,100).

5 For example, Griffiths (2015) coins the term comparative historicism to address the relation between Erasmus and Charles Darwin, delving into comparative philology and the way both naturalists studied language. Similarly, Duncan's (2020) discussion of "aesthetic evolution" cites developments in the study of language which offered productive counterparts to idealized visions of nature in the nineteenth century.

CHAPTER 5

Darwin and the Anthropocene

Allen MacDuffie

The "Anthropocene" concept is useful, in part, because of its capacious-ness, in the way it encompasses an almost endless variety of interlocking environmental crises. Those crises include climate change, of course, as well as the mass extinction event commonly known as the "sixth extinc-tion" that, in viciously circular fashion, causes and is caused by the pro-found and tragic diminishment of planetary biodiversity. It also includes the increasing acidification of the world's oceans and the threat it poses not just to marine ecosystems everywhere, but to the very oxygen con-tent of the atmosphere, and thus the ability for life on the planet to keep breathing. We might add the toxic "forever" chemicals leaching into the soil and groundwater, and the radioactive waste creeping from its badly constructed and inadequately imagined concrete tombs in Greenland, the Marshall Islands, and many places in between (Colgan et al., 2016; Gerrard, 2015).

The list goes on, with the common denominator of these unfolding crises being of course the *Anthropos* of Anthropocene: human beings, *homo sapiens*, us. Or to be more precise: a certain privileged, resource-intensive subset of "us" in (primarily) the so-called developed world, the Global North. Thus, as many have argued, the very term "Anthropocene" does not merely describe a crisis; it is a concept that is itself *in* crisis, or should be, insofar as by employing the universal category of "the human" it spreads blame in ways that obscure the actual histories of how "we" got "ourselves" into this mess in the first place. If the term is usefully inclusive, it is all the more important to keep track of all the things such inclusivity excludes.

This, on some level, is a question of what Timothy Clark calls "scale effects" (2015: 71–90) and Zachary Horton calls "scale framing" (2019: 5–26) – the way in which a chosen spatial and temporal perspective always conceals something in the very act of making something else visible. Connecting American consumer behavior to climate change, for example, might usefully reveal the aggregated impact of "ordinary" activities, but

57

such a scale effect might also obscure the larger players – the oil industry, the military-industrial complex, the automobile manufacturers – whose impact is far greater, and whose anti-environmental efforts are organized and well-funded. It is no accident that the term "carbon footprint" was popularized in a public relations campaign by British Petroleum in the early aughts – what better way to deflect attention from corporate culpability than by making *everyone else* responsible (Kaufman, 2020)? And yet, if the trope of a "carbon footprint" concedes too much ground to an individualizing neoliberal logic, it can also make usefully visible the grotesque difference between the average American's contribution to global emissions and that of someone in Haiti or Bangladesh. The point is that whichever scale you use to think about the environment always has both epistemological and political implications – the latter less obviously, if no less inevitably, so.

Figuring out the proper scalar perspective to understand the history of the Earth and the place of humans upon it was of central importance to nineteenth-century geology, biology, physics, and any number of other disciplines in the hard and soft sciences. In a relatively short historical span, the limited horizon of a few thousand years mandated by scripture was replaced by the vastness of geological "deep time" and the long, slow crawl of complex life forms out of the primordial stew. Meanwhile, awareness of what would come to be called "the Anthropocene" was also dawning upon nineteenth-century observers. It was not yet named such, of course, but it was, as we shall see, inferred, projected, theorized, guessed at, and *felt* all the same. Anthropogenic climatological or geological change appears in speculative or even visionary guise in literary texts by Charles Dickens, Richard Jefferies, Robert Browning, and John Ruskin (among others), and in more straightforward theoretical form in scientific works by Henry Cadell, Antoni Stoppani, and George Perkins Marsh.[1] But though the scale of evolutionary history and the scale of the Anthropocene might both be properly termed "geological," they are also distinct in terms of how and where the human fits in the frame: in one, we have a thoroughly dehumanized cosmos where the whole species rates as barely a blip; in the other, a planet apparently undergoing a relentless process of humanization. These scales were in a state of tension, if not conflict, in the nineteenth century, even if they both participated in the same widespread reconsideration of the place, size, and significance of humanity in a newly expanded and metamorphic natural order.

Darwin's place in the still-unfolding story of the Anthropocene is complex and uncertain, depending, in some sense, on which "Darwin" we are talking about and, in a way, which scale we are using to talk about him. For the ecologists Simon Lewis and Mark Maslin, for example, Darwin, along with Copernicus, is one of the towering figures in the centuries-long humbling of humanity at the hands of Western science; but in their account, "acknowledging the Anthropocene reverses this trend ... after almost 500 years of ever-increasing cosmic insignificance, people are back at the centre of the universe" (2018: 16). For Lewis and Maslin, reclaiming this mantle of centrality is not about restoring some kind of Promethean self-regard, but about recognizing the urgency of the crisis and what "we" will need to do – technologically, managerially, legally, culturally – to rise to meet it.

And yet it is fair to wonder how large a step it is from imagining ourselves "back" at the center of things to imagining ourselves as more than we really are. Lewis and Maslin may provide a careful, measured assessment of the situation, but our species seldom passes up opportunities for self-aggrandizement. "We are as gods," the eco-philosopher Stewart Brand famously wrote, "and *have* to get good at it" (2009: 20). The line may have been meant as a clarion call, but it also has a familiar act-one ring to it: the sound of Hubris rousing Nemesis. For many critics, this return of a sense of human primacy is a serious, even fatal, flaw in the Anthropocene concept: a doubling-down on the very logic that produced the crisis in the first place. Donna Haraway calls it "an almost laughable rerun" of the old story of the rise and fall of super-powered "self-making man" (2016: 47–48). For Haraway, Darwin's thorough reimagining of *homo sapiens* as one animal species among many, radically contingent on and thoroughly enmeshed in the nonhuman world (microscopically, macroscopically, and at every level in between), seems like a crucial step in the project of undoing entrenched anthropocentric categories and concepts that make "nature" seem somehow other, and thus available for exploitation and domination. Seen in this way, Darwin appears as *both* a continuous part of the long story of Western science, and a point of departure, a new kind of epistemological orientation or narrative pattern branching off from – we might say "evolving" out of – the old.

But, to apply yet another scale, this point of departure was not one that many of Darwin's fellow naturalists, or indeed the man himself, seemed to follow very far at the time. That is, although Darwin did indeed mount perhaps the most thorough and radical challenge to human exceptionalism in Western cultural history, and although he is often credited as being the "father" of ecology, his ideas were, at the time, quite readily and notoriously pressed into legitimating service for empire and capital. For many Victorians, the cosmic miniaturization of the human, along with the powerful new insights of Darwinian evolutionary thought, seemed to open a blank space for humans (Europeans) to exert a new creative dominion over nonhuman environments and natural processes, including natural selection. Take, for example, this review of *The Descent of Man* from the liberal *Westminster Review*:

> [N]ot only does Man take from Nature the power of modifying his own bodily frame, limiting its action to his cerebral organization, we find that besides he has encroached on the hitherto undivided ways of Natural Selection over the rest of the organic world; and that both in the vegetable and the animal kingdoms he tends to supplant this power. For the majority of the plants that cover the surface of the earth wherever man's power is supreme, and the majority of the animals that feed upon them, now owe their existence to Human not to Natural selection. (Anonymous, 1870)

Such tributes to the newfound scope of human agency register something of the epoch-defining transformation that is underway, but with a decidedly rosy shade cast over it. This is the Anthropocene imagined not as climate chaos and spiraling mass-extinction events, but as the rise of a benevolent new form of dynastic power. With god ousted and Nature "supplanted," a new ruler of the Earth's twin "kingdoms" steps to the throne.

Darwin of course is not responsible for the arguments of his reviewers, but, as we'll see, he did surprisingly little to promote the "environmental" (in today's sense) implications of his ideas. The point is that his ground-breaking theories could work to shrink the human to nothing or expand it to almost everything – sometimes, paradoxically and dizzyingly, at the same time – and the interplay of these various, overlapping, tension-filled, but not mutually exclusive scalar dimensions carries profound implications for environmental thought and politics in the period and beyond. As I hope to show in what follows, the "proper" scale through which to best understand and respond to the crises of the Anthropocene is by no means obvious, and finding it remains a pressing and unresolved question all these many years after Darwin.

Darwin's insistence on the immensity of the geological time scale was important methodologically, rhetorically, and even ethically. The dramatically expanded temporal horizons pushed back powerfully against a dominant scientific tradition informed by natural theology and belief in Providential design, which, for many, scaled the cosmos to cinch up rather comfortably on the human frame. As Margot Norris writes: "The affective motive behind the argument from Design was to make the world (and its Creator) familiar and tame by founding it upon those analogies to the self, reason, and human will, that assure the existence of control over Nature's power" (Norris, 1985: 28–29). It also forged a middle ground between scientific inquiry and Christian theology, allowing the former to proceed in a way that at least *appeared* less threatening to the latter. Even if most works of natural theology readily conceded that the Earth had been around a lot longer than the meager span described in the Bible, humanity remained the center and purpose and point of the system – still, for most, the proverbial measure of all things. In his journals, Darwin can often be found fulminating against the vanity of such assumptions: "Man, in his arrogance thinks himself a great work, worthy of the interposition of the deity, more humble & I believe true to consider him created from animals" (1838: 196–197); "Why is thought, being a secretion of the brain, more wonderful than gravity a property of matter? It is our arrogance, it [is] our admiration of ourselves" (166).

The vast time scale was also methodologically necessary to counter objections arising from somewhat closer quarters: fellow naturalists, even fellow evolutionists, who doubted that an undirected, chance-driven system could have possibly produced all this. But Darwin argues that natural selection only *seems* implausible as a mechanism because of how the human mind falters when confronted with the kinds of temporalities in question:

> [I]t may be objected, that time will not have sufficed for so great an amount of organic change, all changes having been effected very slowly through natural selection. It is hardly possible for me even to recall to the reader, who may not be a practical geologist, the facts leading the mind feebly to comprehend the lapse of time … a man must for years examine for himself great piles of superimposed strata, and watch the sea at work grinding down old rocks and making fresh sediment, before he can hope to comprehend anything of the lapse of time, the monuments of which we see around us. (1859: 282)

The human mind is not just imperfectly fitted to grasp the natural world; it is not actually capable of it: Darwin can "hardly" make the reader understand even the basic data. His insistence on the unfathomable time scale thus does double duty: it grants natural selection enough raw time to work at its gradual pace, and it demands of the reader an epistemic humility, an acceptance of the limits of their own mind that is, on some level, also the point.

This all makes complete sense, yet we might also ask what might be at stake epistemologically, politically, and environmentally when the vastness of this particular scale is insisted upon. When "nature" swells to such proportions, do we lose sight of human impact upon it, because, at such a scale, there simply *is* no human impact? As Darwin puts it in *The Origin of Species*: "How fleeting are the wishes and efforts of man! How short his time, and consequently how poor will be his results, compared with those accumulated by Nature during whole geological periods!" (1859: 84). The biblical cadences of this passage are unmistakable, and, in a way, part of a wider strategy Darwin sometimes uses in the book of offering his bitter medicine with some rhetorical candy coating. Here, he draws upon a familiar move in Christian theology and homiletics, where the abasement of the human serves to raise god even higher in glory. And yet, if "Nature" now slips into god's spot on the cosmic see-saw, one wonders what qualities might accompany that position – remoteness, permanence, perfection – that would set "Nature" apart from actually existing environments. Seen in slightly tighter focus, the wishes and efforts of "man" at this moment in industrial, imperial, and environmental history do not actually seem so poor and feeble, and perhaps should not be dismissed so quickly. We know now that in the period Darwin was writing *The Origin of Species*, a certain subset of *homo sapiens* was beginning to wield a massively outsized power, and was fashioning itself into an incorporate giant whose imprint could be tracked across everything from the composition of the atmosphere to the shape of coastlines and continents.[2] By 1859, the Anthropocene was underway.

And it is not, I hasten to add, simply the privilege of hindsight to point this out. The nineteenth-century Italian geologist Antonio Stoppani and the American naturalist George Perkins Marsh were, as many have pointed out, important early theorists of the Anthropocene, and the Scottish geologist Henry Cadell invokes a decidedly modern-sounding term when he remarks in an 1892 essay that "the face of the country and the geological map alike bear testimony to man's power as a geological agent here" (Cadell, 1892–1893: 280; Steffen et al., 2011: 844). But even further back than that, Darwin's grandfather Erasmus articulated, in Siobhan Carroll's words, "radical dreams of climate modification" in his poem *The Botanic Garden* (1791) (Carroll, 2013: 12). Such dreams participated in more widespread late-eighteenth century notions about "the role that science and empire might play in the global re-ordering of nature" (Bewell, 2017: 76). Noah Heringman traces Anthropocene discourse back to the French naturalist Georges-Louis Leclerc, Comte de Buffon, who, in *Epochs of Nature* (1778, quoted in Heringman, 2015), posited the latest "Epoch" of the Earth as one partly defined by fossil-fuel use and the time when "the power of man assisted the operations of nature" (Heringman, 2015: 58).

This is not to say that these writers imagined anthropogenic global change the way we do; for one thing, the idea of "humanity" having a vast and even planetary impact seemed, for many, an exciting and even utopian prospect. In his long poem *The Excursion*, William Wordsworth imagines the spread of the British Empire over the globe as an important first step in domesticating the planet:

> Change wide, and deep, and silently performed,
> This Land shall witness; and, as days roll on,
> Earth's universal Frame shall feel the effect
> Even 'till the smallest habitable Rock,
> Beaten by lonely billows, hear the songs
> Of humanized Society. (1814: 404)

This passage has a decidedly ominous ring now, given what we know not only about the climate crisis, but also about the rapacious history of settler colonialism. But as troubling or myopic as such imaginings seem, they also clearly indicate a dawning awareness of the immense power that humans, collectively imagined, were beginning to wield.

Indeed, the human impact on actually existing environments – as opposed to on capital-N Nature – is registered elsewhere in Darwin's work, if often in an understated or tacit way. In the third chapter of *The Origin of Species*, for example, he writes about the "complex and unexpected" connections between and among "organic beings" in a given habitat, using as an example the relationships of trees, insect life, and cattle in a region of Staffordshire:

> [T]here was a large and extremely barren heath, which had never been touched by the hand of man; but several hundred acres of exactly the same nature had been enclosed twenty-five years previously and planted with Scotch fir. The change in the native vegetation of the planted part of the heath was most remarkable, more than is generally seen in passing from one quite different soil to another: not only the proportional numbers of the heath-plants were wholly changed, but twelve species of plants (not counting grasses and carices) flourished in the plantations, which could not be found on the heath. The effect on the insects must have been still greater, for six insectivorous birds were very common in the plantations, which were not to be seen on the heath. (1859: 71)

Such a modest, decidedly localized set of observations might seem a far cry from the Anthropocene, but in the account of all the unintended effects radiating outward from a single human intervention in an ecosystem, it defines the ecological logic through which things like anthropogenic habitat destruction and even mass-extinction events could begin to be articulated in the period and beyond.

Marsh, for example, drew extensively on *The Origin of Species* for his landmark study *Man and Nature*, including an incisive reading of the place of the human in the above Scotch fir passage (1885: 288). Described by Jan Zalasiewicz et al. as "the first major work to focus on anthropogenic global change," *Man and Nature* tracks the unintended and often destabilizing consequences of human practices like overfishing, wetlands draining, and deforestation (2011: 835). Meanwhile, in *The Malay Archipelago* (1872), Darwin's rival and "codiscoverer" of natural selection, Alfred Russel Wallace, voices his alarm at the way the heedless spread of empire and industry spelled certain extinction for many nonhuman animal and plant species:

> Should civilized man ever reach these distant lands, and bring moral, intellectual, and physical light into the recesses of these virgin forests, we may be sure that he will so disturb the nicely-balanced relations of organic and inorganic nature as to cause the disappearance, and finally the extinction, of these very beings whose wonderful structure and beauty he alone is fitted to appreciate and enjoy. This consideration must surely tell us that all living things were not made for man. (1872: 44)

(For further discussion of this passage, and of Wallace's work in general, see Chapter 2 by Jesse Oak Taylor.) All this is to say that an understanding of the scale on which anthropogenic environmental impacts were occurring was available to Darwin, and, for some of his contemporaries, seemed to proceed inevitably from his theorization of complex, multilevel forms of ecological relationality. But, as Nancy Stepan argues, "Darwin drew no larger conclusions from this knowledge of interdependency, remaining unconcerned about conservation issues" (Stepan, 2001:78). While it is perhaps an overstatement to say that Darwin was "unconcerned" with conservation, Stepan usefully indicates how his discussion of conservation is not as robust as one might expect given his foundational contributions to ecology, as well as his first-hand accounts of the way actually existing environments were being profoundly reshaped, intentionally and accidentally, by human activity. Historian of science David Sepkoski argues that Darwin's approach to extinction and biodiversity – two concepts central to contemporary ecological thought – was premised upon a belief in nature as dynamically equilibrated and thus fundamentally stable, with extinct species always getting replenished by whatever fitter, happier, more productive variation would emerge to fill the niche:

> [T]he issue isn't whether Darwin recognized or thought natural variety was important – he certainly did – but whether he thought diversity itself could be diminished by extinction, and nature's stability could thus be threatened, which he did not .... [S]truggle and even extinction were positive forces, in

the long view – thus soothing the anxieties of Victorians about their own impact on the world. The world may be subject to constant change, but faith in the ultimate constancy of nature was not shaken. (Sepkoski, 2020: 66)

Darwin's understanding of the English "impact" on the world was informed by – as it informed – the dominant ideological construction of native lands and peoples as the British empire spread across the globe. The imperial and ecological were thus intimately and, in many ways, antagonistically related in the period. As Patrick Brantlinger argues, Darwinian science often fed into nineteenth-century "extinction discourse" in ways that both naturalized and moralized the disappearance of native populations in the process of Western colonization (Brantlinger, 2003: 1–3). It is no accident that Wallace, who lived in unusually close and sympathetic contact with native peoples during his travels in Malaysia and elsewhere, also developed a much more trenchant critique of empire and a more robust environmental imaginary. By the time he writes his era-surveying book *The Wonderful Century*, Wallace's criticism of modern extractivist practices (what he calls "the plunder of the earth") is unsparing:

> The struggle for wealth, and its deplorable results … have been accomplished by a reckless destruction of the stored-up products of nature, which is even more deplorable because more irretrievable. Not only have forest-growths of many hundreds of years been cleared away, often with disastrous consequences, but the whole of the mineral treasures of the earth's surface, the slow products of long-past eons of time and geological change, have been and are still being exhausted, to an extent never before approached, and probably not equaled in amount during the whole preceding period of human history. (Wallace, 1898: 369)

This is geological time scaled not to reduce humanity to a cosmic speck, but to register the strange temporalities of fossil fuel expenditure, in which eons of compressed life get released all at once, in a great bonfire of time. The intimations of the Anthropocene here and elsewhere make plain that responsibility for this belongs not to "humanity" writ large, but to the small subset of mostly white Europeans rapaciously and ruthlessly pursuing profits at all costs.

But troubling though Darwin's relative silence about the kinds of environmental damage that so alarmed Wallace, Marsh, and others may be, it is important not to overlook his decisive contributions to environmental thought, including his truly revolutionary undoing of so many of the foundational assumptions of human exceptionalism. Indeed, this is, for many, *the* crucial first step in addressing the various crises we face. Bruno Latour argues that the "full originality" of Darwin's thought has "still not been absorbed by public consciousness," because of how modern-day biologists persistently, if often tacitly, align their accounts of the evolutionary process with familiar human meanings and narrative tropes (2009: 470). The "blind watchmaker" metaphor, for example, popularized by the biologist Richard Dawkins, retains a mechanistic sense of the universe being engineered from above and thus also carries a whiff of a developmental patterning. After all, a watchmaker, blind or not, works toward a specific goal, even if that work gets carried out haphazardly. But Darwin, Latour writes, was after something much more challenging and radical; for him, "there is no overall narrative, no controlling divinity. Each individual organism is alone with its own risk, goes nowhere, comes from nowhere: it is creativity all the way down" (Latour, 2009: 470). If this is actually one of the implications of Darwin's work – what amounts to a total reimagining of all human meanings and narrative patterns, far more disorienting than just losing one's religion – it is no wonder that it was not at the time, and still has not been, fully "absorbed." Indeed, it is no wonder that, in response to such a challenge, something like the opposite would happen: that larger, human-centered narratives – of advancing civilization, of cultural development – would come to seem *more*, not less, important.

It is worth noting that just about all of the nineteenth-century writers who seem today much more attuned than Darwin to the onset of the Anthropocene also remained stubbornly, sometimes mystifyingly, anthropocentric in their orientation. That is, concern about the profound ecological significance of aggregated human agency almost always came accompanied by a more general metaphysical belief in human significance as such. Marsh, for example, was a believing Christian, and held fast to the notion of the kind of unbridgeable ontological distinction between humans and nonhuman animals that Darwin was working to dismantle (Lowenthal, 2009: 426). And Wallace, much to Darwin's dismay, notoriously carved out a crucial exception for humankind in the evolutionary process, arguing that something as complex as the human mind could not have arisen via natural selection alone (Wallace, 1869: 392–394). Meanwhile, though writers like John Ruskin and Gerard Manley Hopkins – both direct inheritors of the Wordsworthian legacy – vividly, and we might even say presciently, depict the destructive climatological and planetary effects of industry, they remain decidedly, even vehemently, opposed to Darwin's materialist leanings and his radical decentering of the human.[3] So while there is something refreshingly direct about the normative environmental judgments leveled by these writers, there is also something troubling, and perhaps even self-defeating, about the stubbornly human-centered worldview that informs and even enables them. If we wonder about what environmental impacts might be occluded when the human diminishes almost to the point of disappearance, we might also ask whether a focus on the magnification of human agency does not create its own blind spots, and whether there is not something problematically self-regarding about the discourse of the Anthropocene.

This has been an important line of contemporary critique, even by those who find the Anthropocene a valuable heuristic, or "conceptual halfway house," as Jason Moore (2016b: 3) puts it. Political theorist Jeremy Baskin, for example, argues that the Anthropocene concept is "a paradigm presented as an epoch," one that potentially contains "radical and emancipatory insights," but that also does its own problematic work of ideological legitimation (2015: 11). We have already touched on one of the crucial problems he raises: how the question of who is included in the "Anthropos" part of the "Anthropocene" is assumed or left implicit, often in Western-centric and even racist ways. Baskin also critiques the way the concept "reinserts 'man' into nature only to re-elevate 'him' within and above it," a paradoxical demotion-as-promotion that involves privileging instrumental reason and various technocratic "fixes" to address the crisis (2015: 11). In a similar vein, Heringman sees the concept as tacitly reinforcing teleological, anthropocentric Enlightenment tropes by presenting human civilization "as the culmination or completion of geological and anthropological time" (2015: 57). Even more scathingly, Donna Haraway finds embedded in the concept a narrowly developmentalist, patriarchal narrative patterning, and argues, instead, for new, more complexly interlinked, multi-dimensional, open, and unpredictable forms of cultural meaning-making: "we can inherit," Haraway says, Darwin's "bravery and capacity to tell big enough stories without determinism, teleology, and plan" (2016: 50). As Devin Griffiths puts it: "Darwin's philosophy continues to resonate because it shifts from reading form as inherent plan or intricate design, to reading form for the contingent history of open systems, and from seeing form as a property of individual organisms, to recognizing it as non-determinative relation between multiple things in process, including human societies" (2021: 72).

Thus, the question of human exceptionalism remains a crucial unresolved theoretical and practical issue in contemporary discussions of the Anthropocene. There are those who, like Haraway, argue that it is only through a radical epistemological and moral "revolt" against anthropocentric categories, political structures, and ideologies that we can hope to address the crisis at its source; any appeal to technological interventionism or managerial rationality will only sink us deeper into the same destructive logic that produced the problem in the first place. On the other hand, there are those who would argue that some mix of "top-down" interventions – technological, legislative, political – cannot *not* be part of the solution, given the severity of the crisis and the limited left time to prevent us – in the novelist Kim Stanley Robinson's words – "from dropping into a mass extinction event" (Canavan, 2019).

John Dryzek and Jonathan Pickering, for example, argue for "ecological reflexivity" in which the "pathological path dependencies" of Holocene institutions and modes of thought can be comprehensively rethought rather than simply discarded (2019: 34). For Jedidiah Purdy, the Anthropocene is a "call to take responsibility," a somewhat old-fashioned you-break-it-you-buy-it ethos that makes the case for legal and legislative solutions (2015: 17). Western jurisprudence, based as it is upon the discourse of human rights, is inherently anthropocentric; thus, the push in some quarters to grant "personhood" (and therefore the protections afforded to legal subjects) to nonhuman animals and even, in some cases, to natural formations like rivers and trees, is an attempt to transform the meaning and operative categories of humanism while retaining its foundational ideals. For these writers, the point is that this is not a time for less humanism, but for more – a humanism at once chastened, purposeful, self-critical, and bold; one that, they imagine, will at last live up to the principles that it has, over its long history, almost always betrayed. Such positions are, in their way, also "Darwinian," insofar as they recognize that the future history of the planet is open, undirected, and undetermined; that the category of "the human" is fluid and therefore available for creative reimagining; and that, deeply flawed and self-undermining as it has been, human intelligence remains the only power capable of reflecting upon its own disastrous history as an environmental actor, and thus the only power capable of correcting the bleak path on which it has put itself.

In this way, the Anthropocene concept forces into crisis questions about the place, significance, power, and status of *homo sapiens* in a natural order that is at once intensely vulnerable to human impact and entirely indifferent to it. We are destroying the planet, and "the planet" is not something we can destroy; after all, Earth will go on spinning in space, will almost certainly remain host to countless life forms – some now living, most yet to appear – that will evolve to survive in a catastrophically warmed world. Of course, from their point of view, it will not be a catastrophe at all. Extinction, as Darwin made clear, is simply part of the process, and, in that sense, nothing could be more natural than the Anthropocene, or more ordinary than the demise of a species with adaptations that pushed against the limits of its environment. In short, "nature" does and does not register our impact; it can and cannot feel us. Of course, we *are* nature, and it *is* us; the very idea that we are somehow meaningfully set apart from everything around us is a fiction that we habitually, quixotically, seemingly inevitably, mistake for the real thing. Language, that complexly evolved instrument with all its powers of reflexivity, abstraction, reification, and distance, expresses and enacts the very problem it also enables us ("us") to comprehend. Such are the paradoxes Darwin gave expression to, the disorienting questions he asked or made askable. Unsettling and unresolvable as they may be, they seem now to demand answers more urgently than ever.

Notes

1 For the literary connections, see Taylor (2016); Williams (2017); MacDuffie (2014). For early scientific theorizations of the Anthropocene, see Steffen et al., 2011.

2 Darwin knew the work of all three writers well. "I took much delight in Wordsworth's and Coleridge's poetry; and can boast that I read the 'Excursion' twice through," he writes in his *Autobiography* (Darwin and Darwin, 1892: 31).

3 See, for example, Ruskin's lecture *The Storm Cloud of the Nineteenth Century* (1884), and Hopkins's poems "Binsey Poplars" and "God's Grandeur" (1948: 15, 24).

PART II

Differences after Darwin

CHAPTER 6

Disability after Darwin

Travis Chi Wing Lau

6.1 Introduction

Scholars in Disability Studies have traced how Darwinian evolution came to underpin eugenic thinking in the late nineteenth and twentieth centuries with devastating consequences for disabled people.[1] As Lennard J. Davis remarks in his introduction to *The Disability Studies Reader*, Darwin's thinking about evolutionary advantage made possible the idea of a perfectible body that can be progressively improved while simultaneously condemning "disabled people along the wayside as evolutionary defectives to be surpassed by natural selection" (2013: 3). Industrial factory labor coupled with proliferating forms of urban risk tied to problems like sanitation and food safety led to a rise in the number of disabled people and types of disabilities, from feeblemindedness to madness to lameness. The solution would be the mass institutionalization and sterilization of disabled people in workhouses or asylums, and even the eugenic elimination of "defectives" to preserve a "good" genetic future for the nation, as exemplified by the infamous Nazi *Aktion-T4* campaign, which forcibly euthanized almost 300,000 disabled people. Yet, this ur-narrative in Disability Studies itself merits reevaluation as it uncritically reproduces a teleological assumption that Darwin's evolutionary writings could only lead to eugenic cooptation toward ableist ends. Can there be an anti-ableist reading of Darwin that refuses the reduction of his thinking to eugenics? In what follows, I turn to Elizabeth Grosz's feminist reworking of Darwinian evolutionary theory to reconsider the role of disability in Darwin's writings and his life.

Feminist scholars invested in denaturalizing essentialist categories that reduce identities to bodies have since revisited Darwin's theory of evolution to recover its radical framing of biological "matter as a fundamentally indeterminate and temporally conditioned phenomenon" (Brilmyer, 2017: 20). For Grosz's materialist feminist reading of

73

Darwin's theory of evolution, indeterminacy is intrinsic to the ongoing unfolding of life in "a fundamentally open-ended system which pushes toward a future with no real direction, no promise of any particular result, no guarantee of progress or improvement, but with every indication of inherent proliferation and transformation" (Grosz, 2005: 26). In this light, life is defined not by causality and linear development, but rather by dysteleological multiplicity. If natural selection hinges upon an organism's fitness, Grosz crucially insists that Darwinian "fitness" does not refer to "superiority in a given milieu or environment but the adaptability of the organism, in its given state to changing environments" (2005: 26). By emphasizing how natural selection compels life toward change without certainty of improvement or perfection of ability, Grosz provides a powerful refutation of the eugenic "survival of the fittest" narrative that champions only the forms of life that manage to survive nature's culling of biological "dead ends." In the Groszian model, to declare any organism's form or feature as indicative of its evolutionary "dead end" is not only mistaken but futile as the purposes of a particular adaptation may not yet be clear or obvious to the researcher attempting to make sense of it.[2]

Disabled people have long been figured as such "dead ends" without futures – evolutionary failures doomed to extinction because they are presumed to be incapable of surviving on their own. Such stigma surrounding disabled people is one of the consequences of ableist thinking. According to Tobin Siebers, ableism is a pernicious ideology that privileges ablebodiedness or ablemindedness as normative and desirable to the extent that it "defines the baseline by which humanness is determined, setting the measure of body and mind that gives or denies human status to individual persons" (2008: 8). "Feeblemindedness" and "dumbness" marked out disabled people as deviant, pathological, and therefore subhuman, rendering them subject to violent interventions either to cure or ameliorate their divergence from normative ability, or to prevent them from reproducing such evolutionary failures in future generations. Yet, Grosz's interpretation of evolution underscores how the naturalization of ablebodiedness is precisely ideological in its false assumption that disability must be genetic error or human lack rather than a vital part of biodiversity. With Grosz's interpretive framework in mind, I turn back to Darwin's evolutionary writings to locate in them what Rosemarie Garland-Thomson has called "counter-eugenic logics," which insist on the inherent worth of disabled life to be "conserved" in the face of developing neo-eugenic practices like genetic testing and gene editing, technologies that seek to purge and prevent disability as a undesirable state of being (2012: 341).

6.2 Beyond the Ableism of Darwin's Evolutionary Theory

After 1859, "Darwinian" came to refer to any number of developmental narratives that tried to account for the profound social and cultural changes precipitated by the rise of the British empire and rapid industrialization. Even though "evolution" as a term does not appear in Darwin's writing, and as a concept, is not applied to human beings until *The Descent of Man, and Selection in Relation to Sex* in 1871, Darwin's vision of life as a competitive struggle inspired a wave of thinkers eager to apply its principles to the management of the nation. Biologist and sociologist Herbert Spencer, already interested in evolutionary theory long before Darwin's publications, turned to Darwin's theories as a schema for achieving human perfection. His utilitarian application of evolution to social life in works such as *The Man versus The State* (1884) decried charitable support for the "bad poor" as unnatural (1884: 87). Spencer believed these "weaker" forms of life merely impeded evolutionary progress by wasting limited resources and weakening the general stock of humankind by their reproduction. Social Darwinism, a name for what were a series of sometimes-conflicting sociopolitical applications of Darwin's evolutionary theories, naturalized human competition as necessary for social progress and justified violent practices of colonial expansion and laissez-faire capitalism that saw "lesser" races and nations as expendable. To maintain this trajectory toward improvement also meant discouraging the reproduction of undesirable traits while encouraging the reproduction of those with competitive fitness who seemed more capable of surviving. This was what Charles Darwin's half-cousin Francis Galton termed "eugenics" in 1883, just a year after Darwin's death (1883: 25).

In their accounts of how Darwin's thinking animated later social Darwinian and eugenic movements, historians of science and disability have traced the deployment of race and disability in his evolutionary writings. In *The Descent of Man and Selection in Relation to Sex* (1871a), Darwin attempted to account for the gaps in fossil records between human beings and primates by suggesting that there was no "missing link" in the records because these intermediate species took the living forms of "idiots" and "savages." Darwin derives this hierarchical model from developing racial science as represented by the work of anthropologist Carl Vogt, whom he cites for his views that the "abnormal forms" of "microcephalic and born idiots" were understudied opportunities to better understand humanity's lowly origins (Vogt, 1864:

194–195). As Steven Gelb has argued, Darwin "used intellectual disabilities to support the theory of evolution, and, in so doing, facilitated a reliance on heredity as definitive of persons with disabilities along with the view that they were not wholly human" (2008: para. 2). Cognitive disability signified for Darwin an enduring animality in human beings that would, like many other excesses of natural selection, be "eliminated" as natural selection continued to shape human variation for the better.

Darwin also found "idiots" to be compelling case studies because they embodied the "atavistic reversions to extinct forms whose study would reveal the characteristics of earlier stages of human evolution" (Gelb, 2008: para. 7). Much like the racist scientific claims that black Africans were the missing link in the evolutionary chain from primates to humans, the sub-human figure of the "idiot" contained humanity's evolutionary past in all of its failed forms. The "idiot" confirmed Darwin's theory of evolutionary gradualism by representing the basest form of human being: "we may trace a perfect gradation from the mind of an utter idiot, lower than that of the lowest animal, to the mind of a Newton" (Darwin, 1871: 106). "The idiot" seemed beneath even the barnacles and worms Darwin also studied that served as a humble reminder of humanity's more primitive past.

Yet, if "the meaning of disability functions as the unacknowledged Other in Evolutionary theory," acknowledging the presence of disability in Darwin's evolutionary writings is only the first step in "disability studies efforts to transform impairment from a presumed inferiority into unexpected adaptations within the origins of the species" (Mitchell, 2003: 695). While there is no denying the influence of Darwin's ideas on later eugenic projects that led to abuse and murder of thousands of disabled people well into the 1900s, I want to resist the reductive assumption that Darwin's evolutionary thinking must necessarily lead to what Banu Subramaniam identifies as a systematic conversion of the "benign language of variation" into "the profoundly political language of difference … inferiorities, pathologies, deviance, and perversion of others" after Darwin (2014: 14). Gelb takes Darwin to task for his dependency on and perpetuation of ableist stereotypes about intellectually disabled people as incapable of language and reason, but Gelb confines this reading of disability primarily to *The Descent of Man*. I argue that Darwin's other writings offer a far more capacious understanding of life that undermines the otherwise deterministic claims Darwin makes later about "idiots" as hereditary failures.

One of the more ironic absences in Darwin's *On the Origin of Species* is the very issue of origins themselves. What Darwin presents is "the genealogy, the historical movement (for we cannot even call it progress) of species, the movement from an earlier to a later form, a movement that presupposes an origin that it cannot explain, which perhaps is not an origin except in retrospect," all of which denies the possibility of an "origin of species because there is no unity from which descent is derived" (Grosz, 2004: 21, 25). Darwin admits that attempts at species classification can only be provisional since they are derived retrospectively through the analysis of often the minutest of differences that distinguish living forms. These taxonomies, which attempt to freeze life into a series of snapshots based on known organisms, can never fully account for how individual organisms are constantly undergoing micro- and macro-level changes that may not be perceptible or significant at the moment of classification. The "origin" of a species is not a singular point but multiple continua of contingent divisions, and deviations instead of fixed categories constituted by essential features, abilities, or forms. The issue of origins thus becomes "a nominal question," a "consequence of human, or rather, scientific taxonomy, a function of language" (Grosz, 2004: 23). That which defines a species is wholly arbitrary depending on which characteristics are valued over others and which degrees of differentiation between individuals and groups are brought selectively into focus. From a Disability Studies standpoint, that defining characteristic has all too often been physical or mental ability.

The etiological impulse to locate and isolate the root causes of disability and illness also bears with it the promise of "rehabilitative futurism," a term Anna Mollow uses to describe how biomedicine tends to "fantasize the eradication of disability" in its imagination of better, healthier futures achievable through technological innovation (2012: 288). The prospect of rehabilitation depends on what disability scholars and activists have called the medical model of disability, which frames disability as a defect inherent to the individual and a problem that urgently needs to be, and can only be, solved by medicine. The medical model facilitates what Alison Kafer has described as a "curative imaginary" that "not only *expects* and *assumes* intervention but also cannot imagine or comprehend anything other than intervention" (2013: 27). Disabled people, especially those with unmanageable, chronic, or incurable conditions, are often seen as displaced from developmental trajectories and linear, curative timelines that move seamlessly from diagnosis to treatment to healthy resolution. At odds with the expectations and demands of normative time, disabled people instead operate on crip time. On the most basic level, crip time acknowledges that disabled people may require more time to complete tasks or to move in space. But, more radically, crip time is a complete "reorientation to time" that requires "reimagining our notions of what can and should happen in time, or recognizing how expectations of 'how long things take' are based on very particular minds and bodies .... Rather than bend disabled bodies and minds to meet the clock, crip time bends the clock to meet disabled bodies and minds" (Kafer, 2013: 27).³ The temporal openness that characterizes Darwin's theory of evolution embodies crip time because of its emphasis on contingency over certainty. Rather than a perfect progression toward increasingly more able organisms, evolution may deviate toward intermediate, partial, even regressive forms that are no less capable of surviving.

In the case of "idiocy," the cultural overvaluation of reason since the eighteenth century became increasingly naturalized by Victorian medicine and science as a primary indicator of human development (and of humanness). But Darwin himself suggests it is impossible to know whether or not cognitive disabilities like "idiocy" could have purposes beyond mere survival, such as those that might sustain the "mutual relations," or in terms of disability, *interdependent* relationships among species (1859: 6). Darwin's evolutionary theory remains radically open to the possibilities of polymorphous lifeforms whose bodily capacities cannot be reducible to reproductive "fitness," a capacity inflected by cultural values that cannot be determined in isolation but only in terms of the shifting contexts of that organism's relationship to its environment. A disability, in this case, cannot be assumed to be an intrinsic flaw of an individual organism but potentially a response to environmental pressures or part of a series of adaptations necessary for survival. "No one supposes that all the individuals of the same species are cast in the very same mould. These individual differences are highly important for us, as they afford materials for natural selection to accumulate," Darwin declares in *Origin*'s second chapter (1859: 45). The purpose or value of these "individual differences" may not yet or ever be clear beyond the simple fact that "forms of life are now different from what they formerly were" (84). Darwin ultimately defines natural selection as a force that not only culls but also *creates* as it "incites the living to transform themselves, to differentiate themselves by what they will become" (Grosz, 2005: 40). Different – not necessarily better, more successful, or more fit, but always "open to recontextualization and reevaluation" (29).

Darwin at one point tempers his argument about the inevitable need to eliminate those "weak in body or mind" by suggesting that human civilization is constituted of an inherent "instinct of sympathy" to "do our utmost to check the process of elimination; we build asylums for the imbecile, the maimed, and the sick; we institute poor-laws, and our medical men exert their utmost skill to save the life of every one to the last moment" (1871: 168). To "neglect the weak and helpless," Darwin argues, garners only a "contingent benefit, with a certain and great present evil" (1871:

169). Within a Darwinian system of unknowable futures, such benefits are indeed "contingent," as is any form of life. Darwin ultimately makes the claim that "savages" (and presumably "idiots") are incapable of such sympathy and that civilization is measured by the higher capacity to extend sympathy to all members of a nation and ultimately all human beings.

I do not seek to diminish the racialized quality of Darwin's account of sympathy, or the way it fed beliefs in Western cultural and moral superiority, but I want to consider a question posed by Kenny Fries in his intertwined disability memoir and history of Darwin's evolutionary thinking. Fries speculates that this passage from *The Descent of Man* represents Darwin's suggestion that the practice of caring for the disabled exemplifies "the importance of interdependence, of community," sustained only by the faculty of human sympathy (Fries, 2007: 163–164). While disabled activists and scholars have rightly resisted sentimentalized views of disabled people as only objects of pity, I take seriously Fries's more generous reading of Darwin as invested in mutual care, especially for the most vulnerable, as a collective good that benefits the species as a whole. Darwin here surprisingly eschews what would have been a predictable Malthusian calculus of scarcity and population checks in favor of an evolutionary justification for interdependence. Darwin instead cautions against a neglect of disability's unique ways of being and knowing – cripistemologies – born out of learning to survive in an individualistic, ableist world.[4]

6.3 Darwin's Interdependencies

To illustrate the breadth of life's different forms, Darwin famously introduced the image of the "Tree of Life" in *On the Origin of Species*, which "fills with its dead and broken branches the crust of the earth, and covers the surface with its ever branching and beautiful ramifications" (1859: 130). An image associated with the mythical and the biblical, the tree provided Darwin a way to substantiate his evolutionary theory with a metaphor that could also be diagrammed, visualizing species as forms shifting over and through time. Refusing the older metaphor of the "great chain of being" with forms of life fixed in their strata, Darwin's "tree" depicted life as defined by unceasing change and potential.

In her readings of Darwin's illustrations, Julia Voss reads the "tree" as the visual representation of Darwin having "broken with this teleological conception of nature" in favor of a "history of living things that can take random turns as the countless small variations preserved by selection accumulate" because "Darwin's evolution did not follow a goal" (2010: 124). The published image of the evolutionary diagram produced a great sense of anxiety for Darwin, who was reluctant to designate a singular point of origin and ultimately "avoided giving his picture of evolution a clear form" in spite of "the impression of regularity that standardized printing processes forced upon the printed versions of his diagrams, in contrast to the drawings he had done by hand" (Voss, 2010: 118). Darwin struggled with the reductionism and reproducibility of the diagram form, which compressed what were really millions of years of change into small, neat marks that contradicted what he saw as disorderly, chance variations that yielded infinite transformations – life's multitude of crip forms emerging in their own crip time.

Yet before the "tree of life," Darwin first articulated the theory of natural selection in *A Monograph on the Sub-Class Cirripedia with Figures of All the Species* (1851), which focused on the barnacle. The barnacle defied taxonomy and nomenclature because its sexuality and life stages were explicitly non-teleological: larvae could metamorphose into a series of possible forms without clear order and adult barnacles could interbreed among different barnacle varieties based on different environmental contingencies. As Justin Prystash has argued, the barnacle problematizes formal and taxonomic divisions because its development eludes predictable, progressive linearity (2012: para. 11). The plasticity of barnacle development, from its unification and separation into half-living and half-dead barnacle assemblages to its "sexual continuum running from hermaphrodites to bi-, tri-, and poly-sexual species" exemplified, in Darwin's observation, life's perpetual, unpredictable state of becoming (para. 15). The barnacle's metamorphic liminality eluded any clear sense of developmental progress – "more rhizomatic than arborescent" in its multiplicity (para. 6). What becomes clear by the conclusion of the *Monograph* is that the "coral of life" first hinted at in Darwin's 1837–1838 "B" notebook as a "horizontal history" of life (rather than vertical and hierarchical) not only decenters a primarily anthropocentric view of nature but also embraces the possibility that biodiversity challenges an insular conception of the human somehow disconnected from the "innumerable inhabitants of the world" (Darwin, 1859: 6).

Darwin himself understood the fundamental interdependence of life on a personal level, as a sick and disabled man. He opens *On the Origin of Species* with a frank admission that his "health was far from strong," which created a sense of personal urgency for him to finish and publish his work (Darwin, 1859: 1). Despite the investment in fitness in his evolutionary writings, Darwin struggled with multiple gastrointestinal conditions among many other chronic illnesses for most of his life. Three of his ten children died in childhood, while many of them struggled with chronic illnesses that required constant care. Annie Darwin experienced increasingly severe bouts of fever and gastrointestinal distress, and the youngest of the children, Charles Waring Darwin, was believed to have had a significant cognitive disability. I am less interested in retrospective diagnosis or speculative biographical readings of Darwin that seek to reclaim him and his family as disabled. Instead, I believe disability and chronic illness shaped Darwin's articulation of evolution as a set of processes that did not function solely to weed out his family and him. For a naturalist who felt so intensely the limits of his own body and mind, Darwin necessarily confronted the ironies of his own theories of selection as he imagined them on a planetary scale.

In his correspondences with Joseph Hooker and J. S. Henslow, Darwin was forthcoming about the vicissitudes of his health. He was incapacitated daily by incessant retching and vomiting, which prompted Darwin's colleagues and family to suggest he seek medical attention. Darwin, like many of his contemporaries, went to numerous physicians who variously diagnosed him with everything from dyspepsia to "suppressed gout" to nervous disorders, for which he sought therapies as extreme as hydropathy and galvanism. As Janet Browne has suggested, "many of Darwin's disabilities were ... socially relevant ones" in their "diversity, applicability, and lack of diagnosis" because they in fact enabled him to control when others could have access to him (1998: 248). Disability and chronic illness shaped Darwin's day-to-day life to the extent that his scientific work and public life happened around the very conditions he lived with and that his caregivers could help him address.

While it is difficult to make any argument about the veracity of Darwin's many sicknesses and whether or not he invoked them to suit his needs, Darwin developed an idiosyncratic working life determined by the ebb and flow of his chronic conditions: he knew he could work only a few hours at a time before his intensifying symptoms required long periods of idleness to mitigate.[5] The composition of the multiple editions of *The Origin of Species* and *The Descent of Man* was consistently punctuated by Darwin's meticulous documentation of his conditions in a health diary, which he used to track the progression of his illnesses and to provide a record to his caregivers. In this sense, Darwin's evolutionary writings were produced *in crip time* – hardly in alignment with the productive, regimented time of professional science but rather with Darwin's own sick body, whose chronicity and arrhythmia refuse any consolation of a linear path to recovery. Despite his urgency to publish, Darwin could only do this work at the pace his body could allow. Darwin's crip time is also evolutionary time: *recursive, unpredictable, contingent.*

Throughout his correspondences, Darwin noted repeatedly how much he depended upon others to complete his life's work. While biographers and scholars have celebrated Darwin's independent genius as a man of science, I want to emphasize how much Darwin's work depended upon his many ongoing relationships with caregivers who made possible the very embodied process of writing itself. I return to Darwin's praise of human sympathy in *The Descent of Man* to think about how Darwin's evolutionary theory was the product of interdependence: a work of science coproduced by a necessary reliance upon family, friends, and associates to help do his experimental research and upon the thinking of fellow collaborators like Charles Lyell, Joseph Hooker, and Alfred Wallace to develop his evolutionary theory (Fries, 2007: 163).[6] The erasure of Darwin's disabilities (as that which he "overcame" to do the great work of evolutionary science) signals not just the ableism of a historiography that refuses to believe disability could enable science or that "good" science could ever be done by (and not just on) disabled people, but also diminishes the wider communities of care that made possible Darwin's evolutionary project. If nineteenth-century science was increasingly the work of collective knowledge-making, what might it mean to reclaim Darwin as a disabled scientist who fostered intimate and intellectual communities because he knew it would be the only way to make this massive work possible? Darwin's own adaptations to his worsening conditions proved that neither fitness nor independence were prerequisites for his productive contributions to science and society. The work of evolution was the work of living with disability.

Notes

1 For a succinct overview of the various applications of Darwinian thinking from social Darwinism to Nazi eugenics, see Paul (2003).
2 Stephen Jay Gould (2002) later terms the potential for any given trait to be functional either in the present or in the future as "exaptation," which Darwin himself develops in later plant studies like *On the Movements and Habits of Climbing Plants* (1865) and *The Power of Movement in Plants* (1880). See also Wai Chee Dimock's account in Chapter 10 of how the twenty-first-century novel realizes Darwin's intuition about the possible flourishing of disabled life, as well as Kathleen Frederickson's critique in Chapter 8 of Grosz's reinterpretation of Darwinian evolution.
3 For more on crip time, see Samuels (2017); Price (2011); and Kuppers (2014).
4 For more on cripistemology, see Johnson and McRuer (2014).
5 For an extensive account of Darwin's conditions over the course of his life and the different treatments he pursued, see Colp, Jr. (2008).
6 For more on disability and interdependence, see Taylor (2019); and Piepzna-Samarasinha (2018).

CHAPTER 7

Race after Darwin

B. Ricardo Brown

In the histories, sociologies, and genealogies of race, Darwin's *Origin of Species*, *Descent of Man*, and *Expression of Emotions in Man and Animals* stand a Janus-like vigil over our past, present, and future notions of human variation (1859, 1871a, 1873). They arrest us with the question, "Darwin's trilogy argued for humans as a single species (monogenism), so then what are we talking about when we talk about race?" To attempt a comprehensive answer requires the simplification of a complex object of knowledge and everyday life; a landscape which one can only survey from a distance. To briefly essay race after Darwin is to knowingly confront the inevitable failings of monumental and systematic efforts. On the other hand, to narrow one's view to a specific place or period – with the assumption that its singularity somehow crystallizes in miniature the social totality – inevitably results in overlooking many of the lines of descent that race has passed along since Darwin's shadow fell across the sciences of life.

While his work is often cast as a decisive break with the past, Darwin did not achieve his goal of ending the Enlightenment debates on the origin of humans as a single species ("monogenism") or as multiple, distinct species ("polygenism"). Instead, his long shadow obscures the continuities of the concept of race, polygenism, the fixity of species, and the origin and meaning of variation in nature – often referred to as "the Species Question" – before and after the publication of the *Origin*. After Darwin's intervention and despite his own abolitionist sentiments, race remained at the center of scientific reasoning about variation in humans. From the threat of degeneracy to so-called Social Darwinism and, later, in the social reformism of eugenics, race remained a consistent object of study. Angela Saini notes that Darwin did not end race science; if he had, it would today be merely a historical curiosity (2020). Instead, race has functioned as an organizing principle of knowledge production and as a foundation of technologies for the management of populations and societies. Parallel with transformations in this apparatus of race during

Darwin's time was the professionalization of the scientist along with the institutionalization of new disciplines such as the new sciences of life: biology, ecology, and sociology.

In the first half of the nineteenth century many naturalists were consumed with three aspects of the Species Question: First, what is the meaning of variation in nature – how are we to understand the meaning of species difference and even the apparent extinction of species? Second, are species fixed and unchanging or can they change? Third, can the variation that we find in humans give us insight into the first two questions? It was believed that if we could understand the meaning of variation in humans, we would be able to understand why nature itself is so varied. Once Linnaeus placed humans into nature and classified them by the physical and cultural differences that today define racial categories, naturalists such as Johan Friedrich Blumenbach, James Prichard, and Georges Cuvier asked whether human races constitute different species, and whether racial characteristics – like all things in a created and designed nature – are fixed and unchanging, perhaps even designed.[1]

Darwin, a convinced monogenist and abolitionist, argued that "change over time" via natural and sexual selection only makes sense if one accepts that humans are a single species with a common genealogical past: "we may conclude that when the principles of evolution are generally accepted, as they surely will be before long, the dispute between the monogenists and the polygenists will die a silent and unobserved death" (1871: 235). As a deeply materialist observer, Darwin is comfortable with the antithesis to determinism: the view that chance is an essential aspect of nature itself. Darwin's "tangled bank" offers no sense of certainty, but only a vivid demonstration of ecological interdependence and systems of relations. And certainly "the oversimplified model of heredity established in the early 20th century has been dismantled by scientific developments" (Leung, 2014) while "its legacy remains embedded in popular culture" (Bowler, 2019).

How is it that theories of race predating the Darwinian revolution moved from a relatively minor position within natural history to a central position within the new sciences of life? The persistence of these scientific ideologies – theories and practices that verge on but never fulfill the requirements of scientific theory (Canguilhem, 1988) – raise questions about the extent of the "revolution" in our understanding of human variation initiated by the publication of the *Origin of Species*. Indeed, from their beginnings, biology and sociology staked their legitimacy as the new sciences of life on their ability to finally unravel the origin of human difference and so produce knowledge for effectively governing those newly racialized – and increasingly urbanized – populations. The persistence of the concepts of race and polygenism complicates any study of Darwin, Darwinism, and race, from everyday speech – such as the uncritical use of terms such as "native," or "Indigenous" without acknowledging earlier uses in polygenist works such as Nott and Gliddon (1857) – to scientific discourses, including multiregional theories of human origin and the persistence of genetic determinism.

Race never became a discarded paradigm or a mere anachronistic scientific error. In the wake of the *Origin of Species*, race – often with a barely disguised revision of polygenism – became an object of scientific study and a force whose sociological significance only intensified within the relations of modern urban everyday life. Of course, Darwinism – in the form of Social Darwinism and eugenics – produces its own theories of race as a means of classifying human difference, but the racialist aspects of Darwin's legacy only suggest the extent to which these scientific ideologies, which were once comfortably housed within the fixity and systems of classification of natural history, found a place within the new sciences of life (Canguilhem, 1988). Establishing the meaning of race and human variety provided not only knowledge, but also legitimacy and social/political relevance to the emerging disciplines of biology and sociology. It is almost impossible to examine either of these sciences of life without noting their relevance to government and to the health of the governed populations (Faris, 1968 [1956]; Foucault, 2001). Race categories remain central for the classification of human variation, from the organization of scientific knowledge, to the legitimization of governmental authority and the formulation of social policy. Because race is "malleable, fluctuating, and contested," (Ford, 2001: 807) it can be poured into any mold.

Despite Darwin's intervention into the Species Question debates, his acolytes and popularizers worked diligently to adapt racial classifications to the needs of the newly emerging sciences of life. Saini (2020) maps the locations where the continuities of race science can be found today. Race as a means to classify/understand variation in humans now takes on greater importance in biology and sociology than it had under the *regime* of natural history and political economy. Darwin proposed that we have modified ourselves and are not the result of special creation, catastrophes, or separate origins that produced our variation. Difference is the result of subtle variations across relatively few attributes, something that Pliny the Elder, who lacked any conception of race, long ago marveled upon. In Darwin's work, natural selection, sexual selection – the latter as the site of an intersection of power, reproduction, gender, and a constellation of sexual relations – together with chance and contingency, produce the variation and difference we find in nature and so, too, in ourselves: "The diversity generated by sexual reproduction among individuals in a human population is seldom seen as what it is: one of the main forces driving evolution, a natural phenomenon without which we should not be here .... It gives the species all its wealth, all its versatility, all its possibilities" (Jacob, 1982: 75).

Saini's notion of a recent "return of race science" (2020) coincides with current manifestations of the return of an authoritarianism that wants to intervene in the production of difference through laws, regulations, and the state's monopoly on the legitimate use of violence. And it is the domain of the law that demands the certainty of knowing who is speaking, their identity, their elective and/or natural affinities, their "defects," and so on. The constant reinscription of race in government, law, medicine, and public health demonstrates the social fact of systemic racism as a means to organize our understanding of everyday life, often as the subject of a public "national discussion": "the 'coping' of people within a racialized social reality is an everyday accomplishment, constantly renewed" (Alleyne, 2002: 8). Indeed, to observe the multiple currents of race after Darwin is to repeatedly encounter descriptions of a "return" or "re-emergence" of racism, racialism, and race science. The seeming eternal return of race science cannot be reduced either to the return of the repressed – since our interest in the explanatory power of race has never been repressed – or to a cynical scheme imposed by some authority, though both of these have their obvious roles in the propagation of racialism, violence, and terror. A common belief in the explanatory power of race is obvious "in the use of racial categories in case law, statues, and constitutional texts .... in racial criteria for immigration" (Ford, 2001: 807), segregation and Jim Crow laws, and today from Guantanamo to the Uighurs to the prisons of Brazil and New York, where incarceration and racialism walk hand in hand.

7.1   Critical Race Theory and Critiques of Science, Race, and the State

Critical race theory (CRT) and race science after Darwin develop together within a context of continued contestation of both the role of science in society and the nature of science, scientific validity, and variation in humans. CRT, which first appeared in elite law journals, points to the unspoken racial biases in the American legal system while noting that this same system pays little attention to the effects of race and racism in its administration of the law. Far from offering a general critique, the origin of CRT lay within the bounds of the law and legal theory. Its early law review articles, written for the most part by Black legal scholars, demanded CRT's inclusion in the discussion of civil rights law because "courts do quote [law] review articles ... [and] judges ... read and [are] informed by them" (Delgado, 1984: 573). The then-current legal theory of civil rights itself "demonstrated the exclusion of minority writing about key issues of race law, and that this exclusion ... causes blunting, skewings, and omissions in the literature dealing with race, racism, and American law" (573). In response, CRT "not only challenged the basic assumptions and presuppositions of the prevailing paradigms among mainstream liberals and conservatives in the legal academy, but also confronted the relative silence of legal radicals – namely critical legal studies writers – who 'deconstructed' liberalism, yet seldom addressed the role of deep-seated racism in American life" (West, 1995: xi). The specificity of its origins and demand for recognition are important in helping locate the concept of intersectionality, which soon emerged from the early CRT arguments and demanded the recognition of the interrelation of class, gender, and race.

CRT has several overlapping assumptions or themes. The first is that racism is "ordinary, not aberrational – 'normal science'" as Delgado and Stefancic write, invoking Thomas Kuhn's (2001) notion of paradigms in the history of science in order to present racism as a paradigm for everyday life: it is "the usual way society does business ..., common, everyday experience" (Delgado and Stefancic, 20001: 7). This everyday experience of supremacy has psychological effects and material consequences that are simultaneously the consequence of and the foundation for the social construction of race. CRT thus echoes Darwin's view in *Descent* that human differences are superficial and dwarfed by what is shared in common. In this sense, Darwin's insights can serve as a basis for CRT:

> People with common origins share certain physical traits, of course, such as skin color, physique, and hair texture. But these constitute only an extremely small portion of their genetic endowment, are dwarfed by that which we have in common, and have little or nothing to do with distinctly human, higher-order traits, such as personality, intelligence, and moral behavior. That society frequently chooses to ignore these scientific facts, creates races, and endows them with pseudo-permanent characteristics is of great interest to critical race theory. (Delgado and Stefancic, 2012: 7)

The current attention to intersectionality, as originally expressed by Kimberle Crenshaw (Crenshaw et al. 1995), developed out of a demand for recognition in the law and in the courtroom.

Crenshaw's insight was that you can't look at injustice along a single dimension. Injustice, to put it one way, is not monolithic .... A black woman experiences racism differently than a black man, such as when the mistreatment she suffers blends both racism and sexism, and she experiences sexism differently than a white woman, such as when the sexism she faces has a racial component the white woman does not have to endure. (Keita, 2019)

Emerging from a demand for legal recognition and inclusion, CRT's success stems in part from its reformist goals remaining "eternally normative," but the very location of its emergence lays bare the systematic deployment of race and the political commitments of "CRT, as an attempt to legitimate the perspectival lived-realities of differently situated persons" and as "a humanism for not only racial, but also global, justice" (Gordon, 2019).

Intersectionality at once makes plain the social construction of race, gender, and class while running the risk that disputes over its meaning may reinscribe classifications of difference and value. Recent attacks on CRT illustrate the eternal return of race. Politically, the reaction against CRT coincides with the overt supremacy and racialism of contemporary populism, which threatens a violent reaction against those who might dare to protest such injustice. A recent example of this is expressed by the theologians of the Southern Baptist Convention (Schroeder, 2020), who declared that "critical race theory and a new framework called 'intersectionality' are 'antithetical to the Bible and the only Gospel that can save.'" (Bailey and Boorstein, 2020).

While the critique of race is fundamental to the critique of race in law and social policy, it often shares the fraught assumption that scientific critiques of racial ideologies long ago caused "race science" to suffer that "silent and unobserved death" that Darwin anticipated (1871: 235). Many works in CRT begin with the declaration that scientific inquiries such as the human genome project provide sufficient justification for understanding race as a purely social construction. But this casual acceptance of scientific authority as proof of the social construction of race suggests the limited degree to which the many sociological and historical critiques of science have contributed to CRT, and more broadly to our understanding of race and racialism. Ironically, had CRT taken the critique of science after Darwin more seriously, it might have avoided leaving the door open to recent political and theological objections that are leveraged on a critique of the objectivity of scientific facts.

CRT accepts the scientific critique of race but often ignores how racialism has continued to permeate the history of the sciences of life. CRT argues that the authority of science establishes the social construction of race as "not objective, inherent, or fixed, they correspond to no biological or genetic reality; rather races are categories that society invents, manipulates, or retires when convenient" (Delgado and Stefancic, 2001: 7). Yet the persistence of race science is itself an indication that science is not removed from the forces of society but embedded within them. "Unfortunately, few in this society seem prepared to relinquish fully their subscription to notions of biological race. This includes Congress and the Supreme Court" (Lopez, 2000: 168).

Simply put, the history of science is not the critique of science. CRT often treats race science as a relic of early errors of knowledge or as ideologies long ago banished from the domain of science and reason, surviving only in the social relations of everyday life (e.g., police violence and brutality). However, historical and sociological critiques of race science have rarely given such assurances. As authority is embedded in the social relations of capital, so too are the sciences of life, but to accept this would cause CRT to engage not only in a critical evaluation of the domain of law and sociology, but of science and medicine as well.

The fault lines separating critical race studies and critiques of science outline how race after Darwin has been persistently and continuously deployed across multiple disciplines and systems of knowledge. In the sciences of life (sociology, biology, and ecology), it is found in scientific ideologies, taxonomies, social policy, technologies of government, and experimentation on humans and primates. In law, race – along with gender, sexuality, and class – unites courtroom rhetoric, verdicts, sentences, Constitutional criticism, and concepts of social construction (Delgado and Stefanic, 2001: 8). The adoption and refining of Thomas Kuhn's paradigms and normal science uses the authority of scientific knowledge for intellectual support, but ignores his critique of this authority's stability.

7.2 Homelands, Diasporas, and Being

A further manifestation of race after Darwin demands attention: ongoing attempts to hold onto race, to understand human variety in terms of race, and to find value in racialized difference – to find the reality of race "in truths that can only speak for themselves" (Gordon, 2019). In this sense, race is taken to be something internal and personal that is always being expressed in everyday life. It is that which is always speaking and demands that we speak. The constant production of race as an object of knowledge reproduces race as a source of solidarity, identity, authority, consciousness, and authenticity. It becomes both a psychological and a physical marker of a community, of a common origin and history, and even of a diaspora from a homeland. Thus, race serves as justification for supremacy, exclusion, and the dehumanization of those outside of the community, as well as a motivation for resistance, liberation, and emancipation. It is found in "the unique voice of color" whose foundation in race gives it the authority to speak as a collective of singular voices (Delgado and Stefanic, 2012: 8).

Rhonda Sharpe has shown how the term "women of color" began as a political expression of solidarity and recognition only to be transformed into a biological term allowing "the aggregation of Asian, Black, Hispanic, Native American and multi-racial women as a homogeneous group despite their distinct differences .... '[W]oman of colour' or 'people of colour' erases identity and ignores ... the unique experience of each group of women" (2019). Sharpe suggests that the acknowledgment of race as a biological or statistical reality is necessary for anyone committed to inclusion and antiracism. Others from sometimes very different political locations go further to argue that far from being a social construction, race is a biological fact, and that the "biological concept of race" validates "attempts to rehabilitate race that are scientifically respectable and genetically informed" (Sesardis, 2010: 161).

Social construction also rests uncomfortably beside Arun Saldanha's Deleuze-inspired attempt to reinscribe race as a natural and ontological artifact of phenotypes: "Race should not be eliminated but instead its energies harnessed through a cosmopolitan ethics which is sensitive to its heterogeneous and dynamic nature" (2006: 9). This harnessing is to be accomplished through "a serious engagement" with the "biological dimensions" of race. Saldanha's cosmopolitan "race realism" returns race to the materiality of the body as an "immanent process" because "though contingent, race can not be transcended, only understood and rearranged" (2006: 9). The seemingly liberatory prospect of revolt through race that Saldanha proposes (the right wing often embraces a similar goal of a naturalized revolt) is also a means to dominate and control the same natural "energies" that flow through specific racial phenotypes. Saldanha wraps phenotypes in Deleuzian vitalism and his materiality of racial phenotypes evaporates into the ether. Race functions for Saldanha just as it did for the early naturalists: as the key to the meaning of variation in nature. The supposed "limited plasticity" of "the creative materiality of race" is the foundation for his concept of the racial phenotypes: "the body melts into a silhouette and is replaced by the genotype and its expression, the phenotype" (Gudding, 1996: 527). To preserve race within a cosmopolitan ethics, Saldanha sets up camp in the impregnable refuge of ontology, a place within an administered nature for homelands, diasporas, phenotypes.

In a different register, Kwame Anthony Appiah (1986, 1996, 2006) asks that we be concerned with the truth of race. What about the evidence of our own eyes? Racial difference is obviously inscribed in the skin, hair, and bones. While Saldanha actively embraces racial phenotypes and categories, for Appiah the truth of race balances its rejection as a scientific concept and acceptance as a cultural marker of variety. But one must join with Stuart Hall in asking whether the discourses on race were overdetermined by the search for the truth of race. Hall argues that "racial discourses constitute one of the persistent classificatory systems in human culture" (2017: 46). A biological concept of race remains necessary to any discourse of racial difference, even critical ones.

Appiah follows DuBois' two notions of race as first physiological, and second a badge of slavery's history. To Appiah, DuBois never escapes the constraints of the physiological classifications of race, even though he comes to adopt the second perspective that what is important is "a common history, have suffered a common disaster and have one long memory ... the social heritage of Slavery" (Hall, 2017: 38). And like DuBois, Appiah focuses on "the grosser physical differences of color, hair, and bone which despite the fact that they remain anomalous to actual populations and 'transcend scientific explanation' are what finally come to underpin the division of the great families of human beings into races in our common sense understanding of the word" (2017: 60).

Hall describes the ephemeralization of race not as biological or genetic but as another sliding/floating signifier of power relations within which physical markers become "signifiers of difference," carrying meanings that are not inherent in the markers themselves. As humans, we internalize and naturalize these marks: they are burned into us, as Nietzsche (1967) said. Hence, Appiah rejects the view of race as a mere term of difference, though Hall argues that Appiah does not account "for the way race is so tenacious in human history, so impossible to dislodge" (2017: 43), because he does not directly engage critiques of scientific ideologies of race. Hall reads Appiah's appeal to "the truth" of race as an attempt to find how nature explains race and how race can be an explanation for the nature of social difference (Hall, 2017: 43). The "truth" of race becomes the "basis [for] the operation of power-knowledge-difference" (Hall, 2017: 60). From Hall's perspective, the search for, or insistence on the truth of, race serves the same social relations of authority, logics of domination, and systems of classification that, in the early Enlightenment, created race as a means to understand and give meaning to human variation.

Before Darwin, early classifications of human difference, such as those of Linnaeus and Blumenbach, used racial categories to describe a racialized nature. After Darwin, these categories remained ubiquitous in law, social statistics, and so on. On close examination these categories as well as Saldanha's cosmopolitan phenotypes collapse not because they are immoral or provincial, but because they have no existence in nature. However, as scientific ideologies they continue to organize our knowledge of human variation and difference. Ironically, Darwin's critique often remains on the margins of the discussion of race, his name and work rarely referenced except as a call to authority, an example of iniquity, or a mere passing reference. Any posthuman or transhuman dominant class will find better justifications for the progress that they desire in the mysticism of the late teleological speculations of Alfred Russell Wallace (1908) and the *laissez-faire* dreams of Herbert Spencer (1871) than they will in Darwin's works.

7.3   Race and Technology

"The truth of race" is also found in a more material inscription. As J. Jesse Ramirez notes, writers engaging with genetics and technology (for example, Wailoo et. al. 2012) are advancing the critiques of science by describing how racialism becomes embedded in the physical body of the robot and in the code that allows it to function (Ramirez, 2020). The robot simultaneously exists for the benefit of its human masters, and, as in all the slave states of the past, instills a constant fear of rebellion and need for control.

These concerns are not just academic. A recent white supremacist terrorist justified his violence as fear of "white replacement" through automation and immigration (Ramirez, 2020: 291). Despite the promises of AI companies and utopian science fiction, there is the fear that in the United States "working class whites will not be able to reap the benefits of the new automated technologies because they will be overrun by poor, unemployed, government-dependent Latinxs" (291). This fear of an automated/robotic future reminds us that "robots, as products of US history and culture, are cast from a substance that is simultaneously more immaterial and more real than their sensors and actuators: race" (291). The dehumanization of work and workers is compensated by investing the automaton with "human" or "natural" physical and linguistic characteristics. One finds a continuity from the "The Turk," a nineteenth-century chess-playing automaton complete with turban and pipe, to Westinghouse Electric's "Rastus the Mechanical Negro," robotic hotel clerks in Japan, and the robots of companies like Boston Dynamics, which released a holiday commercial featuring their creations dancing together to the Motown song "Do You Love Me?" (Boston Dynamics, 2020). The social media reaction to the video was a mix of awe, anticipation, dread, and terror.

It is not only in the anthropomorphizing of robots that we can see the functioning of racial ideologies. Ruha Benjamin and others have shown how race is embedded in robots from the early stages of design and architecture, yet concealed behind a veneer of objectivity and impartiality that are supposed to replace human bias. Likewise, racialism in coding/programming is shielded from scrutiny behind an assumption that code is colorblind, when in fact these new technologies "reflect and reproduce existing inequalities" while they are "promoted and perceived as more objective or progressive" (Benjamin, 2019: 5–6). However, as we know from the various critiques of science, race is not only a means of organizing scientific knowledge; it also functions as a technology as well "designed to sanctify and sanitize social injustice as part of the architecture of everyday life" (Benjamin, 2019: 17). For example, facial recognition software has been shown to have racial assumptions coded into its systems. Just as Kodak's "Shirley Cards" privileged whiteness and accentuated the darkness of others (del Barco, 2014), so too did early facial recognition programs have difficulty recognizing the faces of darker-skinned humans. Designers and programmers recoded the software, tweaking the programs to recognize "difference" (Ramirez, 2020: 299). In this way we also see how these assumptions about phenotypes and races are coded into systems. The "sciences" of physiognomy, phrenology, and degeneracy all find a place in technology that simultaneously naturalizes and fixes social phenomena as biological categories.

These technologies have profound implications for any notion of a "truth" of race. To make us comfortable with automation and technology, we use race and gender to humanize it, and ultimately we further the domination of nature through racialized technologies. This domination is also internalized through medical technologies, especially genetic testing and reproductive interventions that now allow one to literally reproduce the complexities of race, gender, class, and physical variation in the bodies of "designer" children. Perhaps by examining how racial assumptions are embedded in our technology – in something we have externalized and alienated – we will be better able to see how we produce it in everyday life.

7.4   Conclusion

In the *Origin*, Darwin asked his readers to imagine:

> [an] entangled bank clothed with many plants of many kinds, with birds singing on the bushes, with various insects flitting about, and with worms crawling through the damp earth, and to reflect that these elaborately constructed forms, so different from each other, and dependent on each other in so complex a manner, have all been produced by laws acting around us. (Darwin, 1859: 489)

This entangled bank is an apt metaphor for race after Darwin, as a tangled complex of scientific ideologies, systems of knowledge, techniques and technologies, politics, policies, "private" morals, and prejudices.

A version of the Species Question remains at the center of racialism, and for those who believe in its significance, race has an explanatory power that subsumes all difference into a dominated and administered nature. The science of race has always been disputed and its significance varies from author to author, much as the number of races varies with the era and the author's "narcissism of minor differences" (Freud, 1961: 72). Human variety and variation are today enveloped in and defined by the complex shackles of race, racialism, and racism as keys to difference. At the start of this chapter, we referred to race after Darwin's *Origin of Species*, *Descent of Man*, and *Expression of Emotions in Man and Animals* as Janus-like, standing in the space between a contested past and an ambiguous future, markers of the passing meanings of what it means to be human. Standing in the doorway, Janus was often depicted holding both a key and a stick.

Note

1   Cuvier, Samuel G. Morton, Josiah Nott and George Gliddon, and Louis Agassiz argued that the fixity of race proved the fixity of species, and the fixity of species proved that the variations of humans are fixed racial differences. The fixity of species as expressed by the fixity of "human races" allowed the creation of scientific classifications. In the first half of the nineteenth century, most naturalists believed the fixity of race proved polygenism, or the separate temporal and geographical origin of the races. The theory of polygenism dominated natural history and was promulgated by American naturalists and intellectuals eager to find a rational justification for slavery in the science of natural history. Only a small minority – Blumenbach, Prichard, and John Bachman – espoused monogenism, or the single origin of all humans.

CHAPTER 8

Darwin under Domestication

Kathleen Frederickson

Domestication has generally fallen by the wayside in scholarship that seeks
to orient Darwin toward queer and trans theory. In some sense, this lack
of interest in domestication is unsurprising. To a field that aspires to be
subversive, domestication sounds lamentably, well, *tame*. Worse, domestication is a cognate of domesticity, and many queers have often prided
themselves on developing alternate sexual publics to combat the problems
of privatized familialism. Nevertheless, I would argue that domestication
should fare better in queer theory. According to Darwin, domestic races
of animals and cultivated races of plants often exhibit an abnormal character as compared with that of natural species (Darwin, 1868a: 4). A partial
abatement of the pressures of natural selection, Darwin suggests, can open
up more options for domesticates, although these domesticates must also
contend with the sometimes near-total control of their domesticators. This
abnormality could assume a central place in a field that often organizes
itself around challenging norms associated with gender and sexuality.

In this chapter, I turn to domestication as a way of resolving some problems that have emerged as queer and trans studies scholars have responded
to Darwin's theory of sexual selection. For Darwin, sexual selection acts
as a "less rigorous" alternative to natural selection that comes into play as
the males of a sexually dimorphic species compete with one another for
the attentions of females who will choose with whom to mate. Darwin
argues that there are many "structures and instincts which must have been
developed through sexual selection," including weapons to drive away
rivals, bodily ornamentation, the ability to make music, and glands that
emit odors (Darwin, 1871a: 1:257). This description of sexual selection has
presented queer and trans theorists with a number of stumbling blocks,
in that it centers heterosexual reproduction orchestrated between aggres-
sive males and coy females.[1] In light of this problem, Joan Roughgarden
suggests that "the time has come to acknowledge the historical value of
Darwin's theory of sexual selection and move on" (2013: 6). Similarly,

Banu Subramaniam notes that that Darwinian evolution is "modeled on the primacy of human heterosexuality" and thus leads to science that centers "the vertical transfer of genetic material as the exclusive focus of biology" (2019: 89). To some critics, bracketing vertical genetic transfer from sexual selection has seemed like a viable way out of this conundrum. Most famously, Elizabeth Grosz has offered an analysis of sexual selection that accommodates homosexual object-choices by identifying sexual selection only with the pursuit of pleasure and aesthetics, while aligning sexual reproduction with natural selection. Because Grosz believes that natural and sexual selection are "two separate forces" (2011: 129), she can maintain that sexual selection produces variation while natural selection constrains it: natural selection accounts only for which variations will survive and be passed down.

But because it severs sexual selection from the "economy of nature," this split is not able to offer a robust theory of how sexual object choices come into being or circulate. We might instead, I suggest, turn to domestication to resolve this dilemma. In Darwin's work, domestication shares the concern with aesthetics that Grosz identifies with sexual selection while simultaneously illustrating, by analogy, how it is that natural selection speciates. When Darwin describes the work of breeders of fancy pigeons in the chapter on domestication in *Origin*, he does so in terms that are reminiscent of the females selecting mates in *Descent*. In *Origin*, Darwin quotes Sir John Sebright who boasted that "he would produce any given feather in three years" (quoted in Darwin, 1859: 31), just as female birds in *Descent* choose the feather they want when selecting a mate from among the males who pay court by displaying their plumage (Darwin, 1871a: 1:272). But in *Origin*, these illustrations are geared toward explaining natural selection, as breeders generate new varieties "by the accumulation in one direction, during successive generations, of differences absolutely inappreciable by an uneducated eye" (Darwin, 1859: 32): it is in this process that he finds the mechanics of speciation to be easiest to witness and understand. The changes wrought by the "economy of nature" function in the same way but are harder to apprehend, occurring, as they tend to do, over longer timespans and broader geographical expanses. Domestication thus encompasses criteria pertinent to both sexual and natural selection. It therefore demands that we theorize how it is that aesthetic criteria matter within the economy of a world in which an organism finds itself.

I begin by charting debates over how best to define how domestication differs from "nature," before turning to a response to Grosz's work on sexual selection. At the end of the chapter, I return to Darwin's engagement with the pigeon fanciers to assess what domestication might allow us to see about how the demands of reproduction and survival inflect aesthetics, pleasure, and sexual object choice.

* * *

On one level, it is hardly clear why domesticates should be easily distinguished from wild species. Based on the observations she made during her fieldwork in Indonesia, Anna Tsing suggests that it can be difficult to assess what should count as properly domesticated. In the Meratus Mountains, she points out, people place baskets under their raised houses for hens laying eggs, even though those hens otherwise live in the wild. Humans may also supplement the newly hatched chicks' diets until they can wander off and fend for themselves in the forest. As adults, the chickens will choose their own mates in the wild but are likely to return to the ridge of the house roof to roost (Tsing, 2018: 235–236). "Is this domestication," Tsing wonders (2018: 236), or something else, neither wholly wild nor wholly domestic? In highlighting the porous borders between the wild and its others, Tsing draws attention to the myriad and often partial ways in which humans involve themselves in sustaining and shaping the lives of plants and animals.

The borders between the wild and the domestic were hardly more secure at the moment Darwin was writing. That wildlife conservation emerges as a social movement at the end of the nineteenth century attests to the extent to which humans had already intervened in nonhuman worlds. British naturalists transported plants and animals across the globe in efforts to raise species they desired in the "wilderness" of territories they controlled. Darwin's time aboard the *HMS Beagle* constituted part of that endeavor – and, indeed, his insistence on the importance of variations in climate to a theory of speciation results, in part, from his firsthand experience attempting to raise organisms in nonnative environments.[2] From that perspective, most species are a little bit domestic, if we follow Tsing in understanding "domestic" to mean subject to human involvement. On the other hand, even "domestic" species are not subject to complete human control. In spite of breeders' best efforts, for instance, the merino sheep never could adapt to the English climate, becoming, as Rebecca Woods puts it, "an object-lesson on the power of climate and the limits of human virtuosity"(Woods, 2017: 17). Climate is just one register in which domestic species remain subject to "nature."

Given this intertwining of the domestic and the natural, it is surprising that Darwin was so unusual among nineteenth-century naturalists in arguing that domestic species demonstrate the mechanism for how variation can lead to lasting speciation. In contrast, Alfred Russel Wallace's famous Ternate paper had adopted the far more prevalent position that "domestic varieties, when turned wild, must return to something near the type of the original wild stock, or become altogether extinct" (Wallace, 1859: 60). Wallace's Ternate paper and Darwin's 1842 sketch of his theory of natural selection are generally regarded as sharing essentially the same argument, so much so that Darwin himself notes that "if Wallace had my M.S. sketch written out in 1842 he could not have made a better short abstract!" (Darwin, 1858). But they nonetheless took radically different lessons from domestication. Darwin asserts that, unless changed conditions of life necessitate further variation, the modifications produced by domestication endure just as variations in nature do (Darwin, 1859: 15). On this basis, he is able to develop the analogy between breeders and nature that organizes *Origin*'s argument about natural selection.

When it comes to sex, the lines between domestication and nature are no less blurry. In *Descent*, Darwin notes that he has to turn to domestic animals to speculate about wild ones: "as so little is known about the courtship of animals in a state of nature, I have endeavoured to discover how far our domesticated quadrupeds evince any choice in their unions" (Darwin, 1871a: 2:270). He cites evidence from a number of veterinary experts, who list examples of attachments that Darwin deems incompatible with either evolutionary fitness or the wishes of human domesticators: a terrier's unrequited love for a retriever so intense that she refused all other mates, a stallion who refused the mares that a racehorse breeder most wished him to impregnate, dogs that "fling themselves away on curs of low degree" (Darwin, 1871a: 2:270). A significant portion of Darwin's theory of sexual selection in the wild thus derives from domestic animals that did not do what their breeders or owners wanted them to do, and whose choices seemed irrational from the vantage point of either natural selection or the domestic aims of the breeder.

The ease with which the domestic/natural binary unravels may help explain what the zooarchaeologist Melinda Zeder describes as "a surprising lack of consensus on how to define domestication" (2015: 3191). Derived from *domus*, the Latin word for house, the word "domestication" usually evokes settlement, familiarity, home, and civilization – indeed, these connotations undergird Tsing's analysis. Zeder, however, recommends a different definition:

> Domestication is a sustained multigenerational, mutualistic relationship in which one organism assumes a significant degree of influence over the reproduction and care of another organism in order to secure a more predictable supply of a resource of interest, and through which the partner

organism gains advantage over individuals that remain outside this relationship, thereby benefitting and often increasing the fitness of both the domesticator and the target domesticate. (Zeder, 2015: 3191)

Humanists might find the mutualism claim surprising. After all, domestic chickens crammed into poultry farm cages seem unlikely to praise the humans who breed them. But it is worth remembering that evolution and ecology understand mutualism in terms of evolutionary advantage: it matters less that the chickens are happy and more that, as of 2018, there were 23.7 billion of them alive. Moreover, while human activities such as chicken farming loom large in analyses of domestication, Zeder reminds us that domesticators needn't be humans. We might just as well invoke leaf cutter ants and fungi (Zeder, 2015: 3191–3192) or a bevy of other pairings. Furthermore, not all resource management practices yield domesticates. It is, after all, possible to breed and care for a species for only a generation. By highlighting these essential features, Zeder seeks to avoid debates over, for instance, how much genetic or plastic difference a domestic species should show relative to its wild ancestor in order to be considered domesticated.

For Darwin scholars, Zeder's definition can help reframe Darwin's efforts to blur the distinction between nature and domestication. In Zeder's analysis, "nature" is no more interested in the welfare of a species than humans are. After all, red junglefowl – the wild species from which the domestic chicken is descended – are scarcely likely to see their interactions with leopards as for their own benefit. Rather, what distinguishes domestication from natural selection is the extent to which a domesticate is controlled by a single species and, concomitantly, shielded from other kinds of interactions, both good and bad. The significant degree of influence exerted by domesticator over a domesticate accounts for why domestication looks like unfreedom to most critics. Under domestication, it becomes possible to identify humans as responsible for changes to a species. Nature may not be friendlier than human domesticators, but the number and variety of interactions that a species encounters in a "natural" state means that it's hard to lay responsibility in any one quarter. In the wild, the presence of leopard predators might have been partially responsible for the modifications to red junglefowl, but so too might other factors, from the availability of bamboo as food, for instance, to changes in weather patterns.

When it comes to the increase in "abnormalities" among domestic species, Darwin argues both that humans have bred domestic animals for human interests (giving them potentially harmful traits) and that humans have sheltered domestic species so much that malign variations occur (rendering them unable to survive in the wild). The Polish chicken, he points out, has a crest of feathers and protuberance of skull so large that it can barely pick up its food. "Monstrous structures of this kind," he opines, "would thus be suppressed in a state of nature" (Darwin, 1868a: 254). But the relative absence of natural selection under domestication is not the only way that domesticates differ from natural species. In *Variation*, Darwin argues that, unlike natural species, domestic varieties are likely to remain fertile when crossbred. This fertility comes from domesticates' superior ability to tolerate change. Species in the wild, he maintains, "owing to their struggle for life with numerous competitors, must have been exposed to more uniform conditions of life during long periods of time, than have been domestic varieties" (Darwin, 1868b: 190). The simple fact of domestication, that is, shows that domestic varieties can tolerate altered conditions – indeed, that capacity is what allowed them to be domesticated in the first place.

Darwin makes the case that natural varieties differ from domesticates because he believes they inhabit distinct lifeworlds – one characterized by stasis, the other by change. But this view hardly gets at the question of the supposedly increased prevalence of monstrosity under domestication. Gillian Feeley-Harnik argues that Darwin had long thought of "the qualities of creatures as relative to their circumstances; what might be monstrous in one place or time might be adaptive in another" (2007: 157). In this sense, Darwin's view that domestication yields more monstrosities might simply designate creatures that are out of sync with the worlds in which they live. We might, from this vantage, think of the concept of monstrosity as a form of life that has not been able to build a world for itself. Nevertheless, it remains unclear if domestic monstrosities are out of sync with the lifeworlds of nature or with those of domestication. If people breed Polish chickens for their heavily feathered crests, does the monstrosity remain monstrous? Is domestication providing new lifeworlds in which adaptations that would not survive well in the wild can thrive?

* * *

The small, often aesthetic, variations that are so crucial to breeders are also integral to Elizabeth Grosz's theory of sexual selection as she seeks to rescue Darwin's sexual selection from a sociobiology that sees it as tied to reproductive fitness and the primacy of the gene. Unlike natural selection, she maintains, "the function of sexual selection is to maximize difference or variation, and it succeeds in doing this by maximizing sexual interests as much as bodily types or forms" (Grosz, 2011: 129). Grosz positions sexual selection as a primarily aesthetic force that works independently of fitness and survival. In Grosz's view, Darwinian sexual selection is fundamentally irrational and aleatoric. "Sexual selection," she tells us, "unhinges the rationality of fitness that governs natural selection" (132). Her tone throughout her analysis is laudatory. Sexual selection is "creative" and "a mode of enhancement," a process that "provides the energy, impetus, and interest in the production of excessive qualities," and "erupts massive variation and difference into the world of the living" (132–133). It is easy to understand the appeal of sexual selection rendered in this way for those queer radicalisms that see in queer kinship, intimacy, and sexual encounters the potential for remaking lived worlds into more just and more pleasurable forms. Compared to the struggle for existence and the pressures of natural selection, the excess and creativity of sexual selection sound far more enticing.

While Grosz follows Darwin's analysis of sexual selection in many ways, her version of sexual selection nonetheless encompasses a shift in emphasis from the one that appears in *Descent*. First, the distinction between natural and sexual selection is sharper in Grosz than it is in Darwin. Second, she does not attend to the social norms that Darwin invokes in setting the scene for sexual selection. When Darwin writes about sexual selection as male competition for female preference, he describes animals living in societies that have developed aesthetic norms: "The females are most excited by, or prefer pairing with, the more ornamented males, or those which are the best songsters, or play the best antics; but it is obviously probable, as has been actually observed in some cases, that they would at the same time prefer the more vigorous and lively males" (Darwin, 1871a: 1:254). In Darwin's eyes, many of these qualities (ornamentation, song, and play) cannot be explained by natural selection, though he admits that vigor and liveliness may be exceptions, in that they are attributes that Darwin imagines will fare well in the struggle for existence. Grosz, in contrast, excises connections between natural and selection altogether. Gone too in Grosz's analysis are the social norms that govern Darwin's description. Darwin speaks of the "best" songsters and the "best" antics, as though some kind of communal conventions exist that allow a group of females to rank the males vying for their attention. For Darwin, sexual and, relatedly, aesthetic culture undergirds sexual selection. Rather differently, Grosz writes that "sexuality is not about the production of a norm but about the eruption of taste" (Grosz, 2011: 130). Unlike Darwin, she writes that "sexual selection is itself the bizarre and incalculable appeal of objects, whether other members of the same species, other members of the same sex, members of different species, or inanimate objects that induce pleasure rather than progeny" (Grosz, 2011: 130).

I suspect Grosz introduces these shifts in focus because she wishes to make space for a multiplicity of possible selections, such that not all animals need to choose the same sexual objects. Part of her goal in doing so is to use sexual selection to account for homosexuality. "Homosexuality," Grosz writes, "… is one of the many excesses that sexual selection introduces to life, like music, art, and language, excesses that make life more enjoyable, more intense, more noticeable and pleasurable than it would otherwise be" (131). This mode of introduction, note, thus differs from sexual reproduction which, she maintains, "is part of natural selection" (128). Instead, homosexual object choices form a core part of sexual selection's orientation to excess and irrationality: "sexual selection," she suggests, "may be understood as the queering of natural selection, that is, the rendering of any biological norms, ideals of fitness, strange, incalculable, excessive" (132). If sexual selection is queer because excessive and incalculable, Grosz is identifying queerness with an aestheticized pleasure-seeking that occurs outside of the natural selection's economic quasi-rationality.

It is, however, worth putting some pressure on Grosz's argument that homosexuality is aligned with sexual selection but not the reproduction that belongs to natural selection. This claim is at odds with parts of Darwin's analysis in *Origin*. Darwin thinks of reproduction as occurring at the level of the population and not that of the individual. In *Origin*, Darwin puzzles through how it is that "neuter" insects can transmit instincts to future generations, given that they do not breed. In doing so, he becomes able to theorize, as Robert Richards observes, how "selection could act on units larger than the individual" (1987: 150). Worker ants without their own offspring are still involved in the reproduction of the conditions that allow for future generations of worker ants. As I have argued elsewhere, this understanding of selection in relation to neuter insects was adopted by homosexuals in the late nineteenth century who sought to understand how their lives participated in the reproduction of social worlds in which they lived (Frederickson, 2014: 85–90). At the turn of the twentieth century, the gay rights activist Edward Carpenter theorized his "homogenic instinct" by noting that "as at some past period of evolution the worker-bee was without doubt differentiated from the two ordinary bee-sexes, so at the present time certain new types of human kind may be emerging, which will have an important part to play in the societies of the future" (1921: 11). In the early twentieth century, theories of sexual "inversion" entailed collapsing what today are routinely separated into sexual orientation and gender identity. Carpenter is thus able to identify the worker bees as analogues for inverts who are core parts of the reproduction of bio-social worlds.

Grosz responds negatively to a related version of this argument when she faults E. O. Wilson for his view that homosexuals in early societies "may have functioned as helpers" (quoted in Grosz, 2011: 129), a claim that she dismisses for both desexualizing homosexuality, and for casting homosexuality as "a socially useful form of altruism (!)" (129). There are good reasons for criticizing the "helper" model, to the extent that it suggests that homosexuals are only involved in natural selection in a supporting role, with the leading actor being sexual reproduction. But shifting attention to population-level reproduction needn't cast homosexuals as altruistic bit players. Many models for intergenerational kinship exist. Some homosexuals might, after all, see themselves as reproducing a world for future homosexuals. There is no reason that sharing genes with offspring should be "selfish" but other kinds of kinship forms "altruistic." Homosexuality only looks altruistic if we assume that a "selfish" interest in reproduction must center individualized genetic transfer as opposed to an investment in the reproduction of the population writ large, a process that includes making sure the population stays safe and fed.

Thinking about queerness in terms of this kind of reproduction is one way of drawing sexuality back into the realm of the social, something that Grosz's identification of homosexuality with "bizarre and incalculable" sexual selection leaves to the side. This attention to incalculability is one of the reasons that Jordy Rosenberg includes Grosz among queer theorists who practice a problematic "de-suturing of objects from the social world, [and] an unloosing of the socius from historical time" (2014: np). Writing about Timothy Morton's argument that queer theory and ecology are one and the same, Rosenberg suggests that Morton figures his "fantasies about 'queer ecology'" as "fantastically aleatory and seemingly essentially resistant to discipline" (2014: np). This characterization applies equally well to Grosz's claim about the "bizarre and incalculable" nature of sexual selection. In Rosenberg's eyes, the removal from social determination renders this kind of account of queerness "a primitivist fantasy that hinges on the violent erasure of the social," one that "drive[s] toward the occlusion of the dynamics of social mediation" (2014: np). The alternative, Rosenberg suggests, is to theorize how sexual encounters participate in social reproduction. For Rosenberg, queer theorists would do well to return to Stuart Hall's argument about social reproduction as a critical site of politics, one "both material and symbolic, since we are reproducing not only the cells of the body but also the categories of the culture" (Hall, 1996: 234).

I have paused to connect homosexuality with reproduction because it is part of my wish, first, to see queerness as something other than a spontaneous variation or aesthetic choice and, second, to understand how sexual selection depends on a set of considerations that are at work in natural selection (of which reproduction forms a part). A consequence of Grosz's language is that the "eruption of taste" that "introduces" homosexuality comes out of nowhere and seems to imply that seeking determinants for this queer, bizarre pleasure-seeking is either futile or beside the point. Nowhere does Grosz ask questions about how these object-choices come to be. How does an organism learn how to choose any sexual object? What conditions those choices? How free or spontaneous are they? Are these choices categorically divorced from ones about material welfare?

To be clear, I am not suggesting that aesthetics and pleasure are wholly irrelevant to sexual object-choice, merely that the danger of separating sexual from natural selection is that it positions sexual selection as a ludic outside to the economic considerations of the struggle for existence. Natural selection, after all, is the space in which economic considerations appear most forcefully in Darwin's philosophy. Many critics have argued that Darwin's theory of natural selection embodies principles of political economy, although commentators do not agree on what these principles are. For Sylvia Wynter, Darwin's theories are enabled by "the wider context of the intellectual revolution of Liberal or economic (rather than civic) political humanism that is being brought in from the end of the eighteenth century onwards" (2003: 322). In contrast, Marwa Elshakry argues that "for many Arab intellectuals, as with many colonial intellectuals elsewhere, socialism was at first tied more strongly to evolution and to Darwin than to communism or to Marx" (Elshakry, 2013: 224). I am here less invested in entering into debates about which economic models are most Darwinian than I am in simply noting that scholars have tended to identify natural selection and the struggle for existence with political economy.

In light of this identification, we might think about the relationship between natural selection and sexual selection in terms of Karl Marx's base/superstructure model. To the extent that natural selection favors variations that enhance a population's ability to obtain or produce its material needs, natural selection concerns itself with the base. In contrast, both aesthetics and sexual selection would belong to the superstructure, which Marx designates as a broad sphere encompassing politics, culture (including sexual culture), art, literature, law, and ideology. Base and superstructure, however, are not independent:

> the sum total of these relations of production constitutes the economic structure of society – the real foundation, on which rise legal and political superstructures and to which correspond definite forms of social consciousness.

The mode of production in material life determines the general character of social, political and spiritual processes of life. It is not the consciousness of men that determines their existence, but, on the contrary, their social existence that determines their consciousness. (Marx, 1904: 11–12)

Marx argues that superstructures respond to the productive arrangements of the base: the base in some way "determines" them. Marxist cultural critics have debated how that "determination" works but agree that it makes sense to understand aesthetics and other superstructural phenomena as responsive to the forces and social relations that govern production. Such a model would thus suggest that sexual selection – with its affiliation to superstructural aesthetics – ought to respond to economic considerations at play in natural selection. As I will elaborate below, treating them as independent leaves sexual selection under-determined.

* * *

The problem with cementing a link between nature and a scene of queer and/or trans potential is that it risks positioning the many sexualities, sexes, and genders in nature as exempla of freedom – what humans could be were it not for the fetters of human society. On the other side, the argument that domestication yields "abnormalities" presumes that self-interested humans ruin what would otherwise be a free exercise of species self-development under nature. A domestic chicken bred for slaughter is hardly the go-to mascot for a movement for sexual and gender liberation. Nor, with the exception of enslaved people, are humans subject to the degree of domination and control faced by many domesticated animals. But the chicken is also a lens into how economic interest, constraint, and avenues of subterfuge, for starters, shape scenes of (im)possibility. Domestication thus marks the place where we can best see a base–superstructure model at work in Darwin's theory. That doesn't mean, though, that we should assume that sexual selection in nature is devoid of the economic forces that clearly govern selection of all kinds under domestication. Nor should we assume that the base "determines" the superstructure with a rigid and uniform lockstep; maintaining that capitalism in some way "determines" contemporary art does not prevent contemporary art from proliferating in a wide range of modes.

In this respect, the centrality of pigeons to Darwin's analysis of domestication offers a useful lens through which to understand both the similarities and the differences between domestication and sexual selection. "Believing that it is always best to study some special group," Darwin writes, "I have, after deliberation, taken up domestic pigeons …. I have associated with several eminent fanciers, and have been permitted to join two of the London Pigeon Clubs. The diversity of the breeds is something astonishing" (1859: 20–21). On the one hand, the similarities between domestication and sexual selection hold up. Fanciers deployed aesthetic criteria, breeding the birds for qualities that, in line with Grosz's account of sexual selection, might be called excessive or irrational.

On the other hand, however, Darwin's analysis of the "economy of nature" (1859: 62) finds an analogue in domestication, albeit one to which he gives scant attention. While, to be sure, fanciers were not breeding pigeons for qualities that would optimize their chances of survival in the wild, they were nonetheless breeding pigeons that would be desirable within human society and economy. Pigeons in cities were either kept at home, exhibited at popular poultry exhibitions, or sold at the bird markets to people who wanted any number of qualities: miners especially sought the birds for the newly popular sport of pigeon-racing (Feeley-Harnik, 2007: 162); breeders bought birds they thought would yield competition-winning offspring; others bought them as pets. This is all to say that political-economic considerations inflected the breeding of the birds: the criteria may have been aesthetic, but part of what links domestication to natural selection is that breeders, both consciously and unconsciously, picked attributes that would have value within the economic circumstances and social relations that governed the fancy.

It may be that sexual selection holds the key to variation. But the gay animals and the creatures who have fascinatingly unusual sex lives still had to survive in the world; to the extent that the forms of their sex lives persist over time, the conditions that make them possible have to be reproduced. The sexual choices you make in a large city full of gay bars may differ from ones you make in a remote location with only a dozen humans around for miles; they may also differ if you travel a lot for work versus if you seldom leave your community; if you suddenly find yourself working very long hours during the week but get weekends off, you may choose lovers that only want to see you once a week; you may like lovers with pink hair because, in our contemporary moment, pink hair signifies a counterculture with which you identify. To whatever extent you wish to see the conditions for your sexual object choices continue into the future, you will have a vested interest in reproducing the populations and material conditions that make them possible. When Darwin observes that many wild species will not breed in captivity – be it from fear, unfamiliarity, or loss of the company of former affiliates – he is nodding to the fact that material conditions underscore the sexual choices that animals make. Reading sexual selection as separate from the struggle for existence risks ignoring all the work it takes to sustain any of things usually understood as a sexuality. Inasmuch as Darwin's work on domestication is the place in which sexual choices are most clearly situated in relation to material conditions, we should not set it aside, distracted by the glow of a nature imagined as freedom.

Notes

1 For more on Darwin's theory of sexual selection and the history of feminism, see Carol Colatrella's Chapter 9 in this volume.
2 On how the *Beagle's* voyage participated in developing the "Anthropocene frontier" that was required for "perceiving nature as a single interconnected system," see Jesse Oak Taylor's Chapter 2 in this volume.

Feminism at War
Sexual Selection, Darwinism, and Fin-de-Siècle Fiction
Carol Colatrella

> Sexual difference is the question of our age.
> Elizabeth Grosz, *Becoming Undone*

Tumultuous political debates, fears of violent revolutions, and the rise of women's rights campaigns in Britain, the United States, and France in the nineteenth century provide a context for considering Charles Darwin's theory of sexual selection and its engagement with feminism. His theory of evolution by natural selection inspired radically different reactions as many writers responded to "the most disturbing question" of "what it meant to be human" rather than "uniquely privileged beings created in the divine image" (Otis, 2002: xxvi). Darwin's *The Descent of Man, and Selection in Relation to Sex* (1871a) provoked subsequent discussion in exploring sexual differences, male–male combat, and female choice in courtship as key elements of *animal* copulation, while insisting that male choice controls *human* sexual relations. Produced during a period marked in the United States and Europe by political conflicts and by developing reform movements calling for equality, *Descent* contributed to evolving cultural ideas of sexuality and gender roles and to new representations of women in popular media and fiction that in turn influenced social attitudes and gave rise to Darwinian feminism.[1]

Nineteenth-century feminists admired and even drew upon Darwin's theory of evolution by natural selection in *The Origin of Species* (1859) and his explanation of sexual selection in *Descent*, but they rejected the latter's assessment of women's inferiority and confinement to domestic roles. Instead, feminists advocated reforms related to suffrage, education, and marriage. Social Darwinists and eugenicists in these countries extrapolated from Darwin's theories to argue that woman's domestic roles would enable her to shape the course of human evolution, eventually improving individuals and society. Fin-de-siècle fiction writers Emile Zola and Guy de Maupassant responded to both Darwinism and feminism by highlighting women characters that resist patriarchal expectations, act patriotically, and experience varying degrees of success in battling legal limitations, social conventions, economic circumstances, and wartime dangers. Sex differences and sexual selection would continue to concern feminist politics, evolutionary biology, and realist fictions. Demonstrating the influence of Darwin's scientific theories on feminism, this chapter traces the long history of concepts of sexual difference and sexual selection in different responses to *The Descent of Man*, including social Darwinism, eugenics, naturalist and New Woman fictions, and feminist theories that propose a fluid understanding of sex and gender superseding the earlier two-sex model (Butler, 2007: 136).

9.1   Sexual Selection and Feminist Responses

Descent extends earlier work about evolution and sexual difference, incorporating Darwin's (and others') observations and experiments regarding animal attraction, male combat, female choice, and courtship behavior. Although fascinated with hermaphroditic and polysexual species in plants, Darwin built his theory of sexual selection on a two-sex hierarchical system developed before the nineteenth century. Historian Thomas Laquer explains two-sex differentiation as stemming from human anatomical comparisons ("discoverable biological distinctions") that writers extend into other dimensions: "By 1800 ... Not only are the sexes different, they are different in every conceivable respect of body and soul, in every physical and moral aspect" (1987: 2). Historian Londa Schiebinger agrees that anatomical differences were "used in the eighteenth century to prescribe very different roles for men and women" and to determine women's lower rank in the social hierarchy (1987: 46). The two-sex paradigm prevailed in the nineteenth century as biologists and botanists investigated how organisms thrive or fail in specific environments, expanded their understanding of heredity and reproduction, and developed a normative sexual politics, according to Michel Foucault's insight (LaFleur, 2018: 3–8).

Darwin's accounts of sexual differences in *Descent* generally concern animals, not humans. His theory of sexual selection notes aesthetic aspects of sexual choice affecting reproductive outcomes, looking at male display and female choice in animals as related elements of sexual attraction leading to copulation and reproduction. Males fight or display charms so that females select them, but female choice based on aesthetics does not overcome sex inequality. Darwin identifies the male animal's superior strength and combativeness; he remarks on "The law of battle for possession of females," noticing that females have rounder faces and bodies and a broader pelvis and are "the constant cause of war" (Darwin, 1981 [1871]: v. II, pt. II, 312, 323). Philosopher Elizabeth Grosz explains that Darwin's theory of "sexual selection privileges some males over other males (or less commonly some females over other females) not in the struggle for survival, but in gaining some advantages over other males in terms of sexual attractiveness and in the ability to transmit these advantages to their male, or male and female offspring" (Grosz, 2011: 124). Darwin notes that female animals choose males based on ornament or fitness but points to different factors among humans (money, power, status) that give men more leverage than women in marital arrangements. In this way, his theory of sexual selection aligns with patriarchal ideas of anthropologists of his era, as literary scholar Rosemary Jann argues (1994: 287).

Darwin posits that in some animal species "inequality between sexes might have been acquired through natural selection," although he regards such disparity as "a rarity" that "need not be considered" (Darwin, 1981 [1871]: v. II, pt. II, 312, 316). Instead, inequality, biological and cultural, is more apparent among humans. Men are taller, heavier, and stronger than women, and they have larger brows, more hair, and deeper and more powerful voices. Men are courageous, pugnacious, energetic, and have larger brains and beards. Darwin indicates women require more training to be raised to the level of men, whose "severe struggle in order to maintain themselves and their families ... will tend to keep up or even increase their mental powers, and, as a consequence, the present inequality between the sexes" (Darwin, 1981 [1871]: v. II, pt. II, 329). Pointing to consistent male superiority, he contrasts the two sexes: "The chief distinction in the intellectual powers of the two sexes is shewn by man attaining to a higher eminence, in whatever he takes up, than woman can attain – whether requiring deep thought, reason, or imagination, or merely the use of the senses and hands" (Darwin, 1981 [1871]: v. II, pt. II, 327).

Historians have pointed to the social and political ramifications of Darwin's theories of natural and sexual selection on culture, and to the cultural influences on his theories. G. J. Barker-Benfield explains that owing partly to Darwin's *Origin*, "the reaction to women's rights was linked to the erosion of male identity" (2000: 206). Erika Milam looks forward: "Seeking to understand the sexual behavior of humans thus raises fundamental questions about who we are, from definitions of masculinity or femininity to the nature of choice" (2010: 168). Darwin recognized male biological, intellectual, and cultural advantages in choosing sexual partners, which affected opportunities for sexual reproduction. Rosemary

Jann explains that Darwin "treated male competition as vital to human progress and female dependency as crucial to the forging of human society. Whenever Darwin imagines our semihuman ancestors, he envisions a patriarchal family group in which the males are already choosing, controlling, and jealously guarding their mates" (1997: 152). For Darwin, courtship, marriage, and bearing children benefit from shared family resources and social stability, conditions marking a society as civilized and demanding women's deference to others' needs.

Darwin's theories about natural selection and sexual selection relied on information gleaned from his and others' direct experimentation on plants and animals, field reports from valued correspondents, his observations of family and acquaintances, their observations, and research reported by other scientists (Browne, 2002: 360–361). He corresponded with a remarkable range of people, including many women, from a variety of backgrounds. Biographer Janet Browne describes Darwin's irritation with Clémence Royer, who inserted eugenic ideas into her French translation of *Origin*, and with Frances Powers Cobbe, whose antivivisectionist advocacy to limit biological experimentation threatened scientific research and knowledge acquisition (Browne, 2002: 331–332, 422). Darwin shared the gender biases of Victorian men of his generation, but these anecdotal examples should not overshadow the fact that he respected women's talents.

Historian Evelleen Richards acknowledges that "the major obstacle in Darwin's way to female choice was less a lack of information than his acculturated presumption of the predominance of male sexual preference in sexual selection"; she connects his personal beliefs with his difficulty developing the theory of sexual selection and finds that despite his "difficulty in naturalizing female choice, he was well on his way to normalizing male aesthetic selection as a major determinant in the divergence of the human races" (2017: 332, 334). Literary critic Pearl Brilmyer argues that Darwin's reference to the peacock becoming "more powerful and intelligent than the peahen" is similar to how "man had over time become more powerful and intelligent than woman. Thus woman appears a less-developed man, her anatomy more childlike or 'primitive,' her mental qualities (such as intuition and imitation) harkening back, as Darwin phrased it, to 'a past and lower state of civilisation'" (2017: 21).

In Darwin's day, many questioned the supposed inferiority of women as universal or permanent. Historian Cynthia Russett references feminist social scientists who claimed that "the alleged sex differences lacked proof ... and ... were unlikely to be innate, but were probably the result of social factors" (1989: 12). Brilmyer recognizes that women writers critiqued Darwin's comments about women's inferiority but did not reject his theories; instead they regarded his ideas as "an important touchstone for feminist activism and theory from the nineteenth century to today," particularly appreciating that cultural conditions evolve (2017: 19). She explains that, over time, "Darwin's understanding of matter as a fundamentally indeterminate and temporally conditioned phenomenon has been invoked by feminists to call into question biologically essentialist theories of sex and race, opening the door for the emergence of new, anti-essentialist accounts of the role of matter and the body in the human social world" (20). American women critics rejected being relegated to a "lesser status," as Russett argues, indicating that Antoinette Blackwell and Eliza Burt Gamble "did not deny the existence of innate differences themselves; indeed, they emphasized them," while regarding the sexes as having "equivalent strengths" (1989: 12). In *The Sexes Throughout Nature*, Blackwell offers a "critique of sexism in theories of evolution" and identifies the notion of women's inferiority advanced by Herbert Spencer and Darwin as "decided on both sides by inferences drawn from yet untested data" (1875: 12). Historian Kimberly Hamlin points out, "In contrast to natural selection, sexual selection suggested that human reproductive choices, conscious or otherwise, significantly shaped evolutionary development and could lead to vast social change" (2014: 152). Blackwell describes how women could work outside the home if females provided direct sustenance to young offspring and males would in turn prepare sustenance for female partners. Such reconfiguring of gender roles would relieve women of some domestic duties and allow them time for intellectual work.

Eliza Burt Gamble's *The Sexes in History and Science* (1916), a revision of *The Evolution of Woman* (1894), responds to Darwin's evolutionary theory in claiming that earlier societies offer examples of equality and that civilization makes women economically dependent on men. Science studies scholar Stacy Alaimo claims that *The Evolution of Woman* "depicts an ontology that radically departs from entrenched cultural notions of separate male and female principles and domains" (2013: 393). Gamble criticizes patriarchal notions of women's inferiority embedded in some scientific works: "So deeply entrenched has become the idea of women's subjection that it is impossible for many male writers to contemplate a state of society in which women are not dominated and controlled by men," for "all the avenues to success have for thousands of years been controlled and wholly manipulated by men while the activities of women have been distorted and repressed" (Gamble, 1916: 135, 79). Brilmyer sees Gamble's *Evolution of Woman* as endorsing female superiority in claiming "that woman is actually more highly evolved than man," for "Darwin's observations of animals showed that males were driven in their decision-making by sexual desire. Females, on the other hand, were more intellectually motivated and thus capable of greater thought and restraint" (Brilmyer, 2017: 22). If changing circumstances could increase women's status: "as Darwin claimed, 'human nature' itself is not a fixed constant but something constantly changing, then, some of Darwin's readers argued, there can be nothing natural or permanent about the subordinate status of women in society" (19). Exemplifying "the transformable quality of all matter," Brilmyer regards Darwin as recognizing "the two sexes had emerged over time in response to environmental shifts" (20).

Grosz considers the mechanisms of change identified in Darwin's theory: sexual choice related to beauty and aesthetics motivate sexual congress and affect reproductive outcomes. For her, "sexual selection ... may exert a contrary force to the pure principle of survival" (Grosz, 2004: 75). She disagrees with "feminist egalitarians who are wary of biological discourses," for "it is not clear how much Darwin himself succumbed to such assumptions" concerning "relations of superiority and inferiority between sexes and races" (Grosz, 2004: 71–72). Darwin's belief in sexual difference did not preclude his accepting "that woman can, in addition to her skills of procreation and nurturance become as educated, as civilized, and developed as man" (Grosz, 2011: 156). Darwinian feminists acknowledged that Darwin's account of sexual selection highlighted troubling social disparities between the sexes but argued that changing social circumstances would adjust educational and professional opportunities for women.

9.2 Darwinism, Eugenics, and the New Woman

Havelock Ellis also anticipated that social evolution would lead to sex equity (Ellis, 1926: 524). Yet Darwin's ideas about sexual selection attracted criticism from Alfred Russel Wallace, who in the 1870s objected to Darwin's idea that animals demonstrate aesthetic preferences, only to later retract this criticism. Richards characterizes Darwinism as being "in decline" at the end of the nineteenth century for "natural and sexual selection were in crisis" and "female choice was on the loose, dogged by its associations with the radical New Women, scandalous free love, secularism, and socialism" (2017: 515). In the United States, suffragists campaigned for voting rights, and Darwinian feminists, including Charlotte Perkins Gilman, published progressive essays and fictions illustrating educational, employment, and entrepreneurial opportunities for women.

Political scientist Diane Paul points to contradictory uses of Darwin's ideas, which were "invoked in support of the claim women's place was in the home, not the school or the workplace," and also used to support radical arguments of those who "argued that the continued subjugation of women thwarts sexual selection and thus endangers the future of the race" (2003: 226). Identifying eugenics as an outgrowth of social Darwinism, "an essentially conservative ideology and social movement, which appropriated the theory of evolution by natural selection to support unrestricted laissez-faire at home and colonialism abroad," Paul cites historian Richard Hofstadter's definition of social Darwinism as a belief that "the best competitors in a competitive situation would win," a principle affecting perceptions of race, class, and gender (Paul, 2003: 224). In 1840s Britain and Europe, fears of human degeneration accompanied "social turmoil and bitter class conflict" along with reports of "pauperism, violence, and crime" blamed on "rampant disease and disorder" (Paul, 1995: 22). Social Darwinists in the late nineteenth- and early twentieth-century feared deviance associated with immigrants and the lower classes. Historian Angelique Richardson identifies what she refers to as "eugenic feminism" (2003: 34–35); she argues that this was a repressive and authoritarian aspect of fin-de-siècle thought which claimed that sexual selection could bring about changes in the class make-up of British society. (2003: 34–35). These feminist eugenicists believed in sexual selection's powers to shape human heredity and evolution.

In this period, dramas, news accounts, and fictions presented new models of behavior for women and men of different classes and outlooks. The "New Woman," a phrase first employed in 1894 in Britain, was regarded, as literary scholar Sally Ledger explains, as "wild" and as associated with free love and socialism (1997: 12, 19). Ledger references periodical articles linking the New Woman to proposed reforms aimed to enhance women's lives. Popular New Woman novelist Eliza Hepworth Dixon regarded women's reduced rate of marriage as the result of her having better education and employment, and to the "gradual acceptance of unescorted single women in towns and cities" (Ledger, 1997: 22). M. Eastwood, in an 1894 article, applied "Socio-Darwinistic principles" in characterizing "the New Woman as a product of evolution, as a 'higher' type" (Ledger, 1997: 23). New Woman writers experimented with narrative forms, reworking the realist genre to convey reform arguments about sexual and social freedom, and connecting evolution and feminism within discourses referencing sexuality and reproduction as subjects affecting women's social, economic, and political prospects (Ledger, 1997: 184, 194).

Henrik Ibsen incorporated evolutionary ideas related to heredity, randomness, and lack of teleology in his dramas and provided audiences around the world with powerful examples of empowered, feminist women seeking independent lives (Aarseth, 2005: 3; Shepherd-Barr, 2017: 63–67). Considering an 1894 *Daily Telegraph* column questioning the value of marriage and many readers' responses to it, Margaret Gullette assessed the broad impact of this newspaper debate over whether the institution of marriage was a failure for men and women: "Women who didn't go see Ibsen's play or buy literary journals or George Gissing's *The Odd Women*, who didn't think of themselves as culturally advanced, could be caught up in *this* debate" (Ledger, 1997: 22). Similarly, literary critic Gillian Beer regards novels by George Eliot and Thomas Hardy as responses to Darwin's theory of sexual selection in reexamining "the role of women, whose progenitive powers physically transmitted the race" (2009b: 196). Realist and naturalist fictions highlighted dimensions of sexual selection and revised the novel's traditional treatment of relations between women and men, dispensing with "courtship, sensibility, the making of matches, women's beauty, men's dominance, *inheritance* in all its forms," which "became charged with new difficulty in the wake of publication of *The Descent of Man*" (Beer, 2009b: 198). Women characters manage sexual desire and reproduction while navigating, for better or worse, Victorian conventions demanding that sexual activity should be associated strictly with maternity (Ledger, 1997: 153). The sexuality of Hardy's characters Tess in *Tess of the D'Urbervilles* (1891) and Sue in *Jude the Obscure* (1895) transgresses social norms; these women are punished for straying from patriarchal expectations. Beer regards Hardy's depictions of natural laws and fecundity as "beyond the control of humankind" in contrast with Emile Zola's optimistic representations of female fecundity as ensuring progress (Beer, 2009b: 223).

9.3 Darwinism, French Fiction, and Womanly Power

Zola believed that literature could influence human behavior (Colatrella, 2011: 79–86). His fictions illustrate environmental forces and cultural attitudes affecting women's fortunes, and critics have noticed a nascent feminism in his empowered female characters. His diverse representations of women track with the up-and-down fortunes of French feminists, who, according to historian Claire Moses, "were concerned with winning political rights" in the nineteenth century, while "the majority of French men and women accepted the centuries-old patriarchal system that regulated sexual roles and rights" (1984: 1). Pierre-Joseph Proudhon and Jules Michelet endorsed conservative ideas about women's roles, although feminists promoted women's education and work opportunities to enable economic sufficiency, reduce poverty, and eliminate prostitution (Moses, 1984: 161). Historian Karen Offen explains French "familial feminism" as aiming "not to overthrow the economic basis of patriarchy but to reorganize the existing society to the greater advantage of women," noting French theatergoers' criticism of Nora, deemed suspicious for abandoning her children in Ibsen's *A Doll's House* (1984: 653). Historian Marilyn Boxer points to feminist socialist journalist Aline Vallette, who linked "her politics with evolutionary biology," promoted "a theory called 'sexualism' that promised to reorder societal priorities in favor of mothers and children," and "represented hope for that more child- and woman-friendly society of the future" (Boxer, 2012: 1, 12). French scholar Chantal Bertrand-Jennings understands ambivalences in Zola's fictions to be inspired by Darwinism, for these texts illustrated "beliefs, fears and anxieties concerning women and femininity ... of his own time and to a lesser degree of our own era," while also outlining new possibilities for women (1984: 26).

According to philosopher and biologist Jean Gayon, French scientists, unlike their counterparts in Britain and the United States, "resisted the penetration of Darwin's evolutionary ideas" (Gayon, 2013; 243). Scientists Claude Bernard and Louis Pasteur "were explicitly antagonistic to any biological research that aimed at explaining the phenomena of life in terms of origins," which they thought speculative, and "no significant French biologist before 1900 incorporated Darwin's major hypotheses into an active research program" (Gayon, 2013: 244–248). Nevertheless, Darwin's ideas did enter popular discourse and the social sciences in France, for, as historian Linda Clark explains, despite Jean-Baptiste Lamarck's sway over French biologists, others took note of "the entry of the Darwinian catchwords 'struggle for life' (lutte pour la vie or concurrence vitale) or 'natural selection' (sélection naturelle) into either journals of high culture or the daily press" (Clark, 1981: D1025). Literary scholar Rae Beth Gordon points to Darwin's 1878 election as a correspondent member of the French Academy of Science as leading to Darwinism becoming "one of the most popular subjects of conversation in France" (2009: 60). French anthropologists in the period adopted nuanced dimensions of social Darwinism referencing eugenics, and sociologist Gustave Le Bon used Darwinian terms to describe war in 1889 in *Les Premières Civilisations*: "The struggle for existence is the natural and permanent state of human races as well as animal species" (Clark, 1981: D1037–D1038).

Zola embedded references to Darwinism and to social Darwinism in his fictions and his literary manifestos about naturalism, describing his scientific study in literature in *The Experimental Novel* (1880), in which he indicated a novelist should observe and analyze social milieux much as a doctor studies human anatomy (Colatrella, 2016; Pagano, 1999: 48). He characterized his twenty-volume Rougon-Macquart series as detailing "the natural and social history of a family under the Second Empire" and claimed the first novel "should be scientifically entitled 'The Origin'" (Zola, 1871). Literary critic David Baguley remarks "Zola wrote very much in the spirit of Darwin's heritage, never a disciple but undoubtedly a 'darwinisant'" (2011: 211–212.)

Zola and his contemporary Guy de Maupassant reference hereditary differences and social competition between individuals of enemy nations in terms familiar to social Darwinists. The anthology *Les Soirées de Médan* (Zola, 1880) includes Zola's "The Attack on the Mill" and Maupassant's "Boule de Suif" as antiwar responses to the Franco-Prussian War (1870–1871). A "naturalist manifesto," the collection describes how selfish ambitions of French political leaders caused an imperial nation to lose a war and descend into chaos, and the stories underscore burdens placed on women (Zola, 1984: 356). Zola and Maupassant acknowledge the high costs of the war; they represent the failings of French soldiers who can only dream of Napoleon's heroic victories and contrast patriotic French women who confront the enemy. Maupassant's fictions feature courageous prostitutes whose integrity contrasts with the greed and self-interest of aristocratic and bourgeois French citizens. "Boule de Suif" identifies the costs of the German occupation during which "the conquerors demanded money" and subjugation, prompting "obscure acts of vengeance," "savage but justifiable, unknown acts of heroism" committed by French citizens on uniformed Germans (Maupassant, 2015: 189). Fellow passengers prevail upon a prostitute to accept the forced sexual advances of the officer who blocks their travel; however, the prostitute's generous self-sacrifice gains her no respect, as the story ends with those she protected scorning her. In "Mademoiselle Fifi," an enemy officer annoys the prostitute assigned as his dinner companion by blowing smoke in her mouth, pinching, and biting her, acting from "a vicious desire to ravage her" (Maupassant, 2015: 122). After the German officer insults all men and women in France, the prostitute stabs him, flees the scene, and finds protection by hiding in a church.

Characterizations, settings, and plots in these fictions reconfigure patriarchal assumptions about man's superiority and woman's inferiority to acknowledge the latter's courage and bravery and to appreciate that future gender equality could serve national interests. Unprepared male French commanders and soldiers in *The Debacle* mismanage the war, a failure represented by the soldier Maurice's thoughts: "The degeneration of his race, which explained how France, victorious with the grandfathers, could be beaten in the time of their grandsons, weighed down on his heart like a hereditary disease getting steadily worse and leading to inevitable destruction when the appointed hour came .... France was dead" (Zola, 1972: 322). Many female ordinary citizens in the novel play heroic, familial feminist roles during the war. Maurice's twin sister Henriette bravely scurries through fighting to look for her husband Weiss, finding him in front of a Prussian firing squad. Unable to save him, she asks the enemy to kill her too. After they refuse, Henriette spends the rest of the war compassionately nursing French and enemy soldiers. Seduced by the Prussian spy Goliath after her boyfriend Honoré joins the army, Silvine gives birth to the spy's son but remains devoted to Honoré even after his death and travels through grotesque scenes of dead soldiers and devastated villages to retrieve his body. Goliath's threats against her and the child provoke Silvine to arrange the spy's brutal murder by French brigands. Although constrained by the occupation, women navigate around the enemy's authority. Henriette's married friend Gilberte flirts with the enemy Prussian captain billeting in her family's home so that he will release Henriette's uncle from jail. Gilberte's straitlaced mother-in-law ignores Gilberte's love affair with a young Frenchman because she is relieved that her son's wife maintains an unconsummated flirtation with the Prussian captain, a relationship that allows her to seek favors for the townspeople.

Zola and Maupassant represent Frenchwomen who retrieve their partners' corpses, engage in relationships with the enemy to protect fellow citizens, and act as patriotic saboteurs who employ feminine ingenuity, flirting, and resistance to survive, rescue, and protect others. Fictional battlefields and bedrooms become competitive environments testing sexual differences and sexual relationships. Circumstances of war press individual women to cast off deferential submission and to adopt heroic, patriotic roles to preserve family and country. Female characters adapt to wartime circumstances, retaining femininity as they exhibit courage, intelligence, and generosity that belie assumptions about women's supposed inferiority. Their intuitions, capacities, and actions are inspirational: they rely on their knowledge, intelligence, and networks to navigate wartime hazards. Female characters employ deceit to protect loved ones and show compassion for the weak. Their stories demonstrate that social circumstances and cultural values concerning the appropriate roles for women change over time, requiring individuals to summon whatever resources they have to protect themselves, their families, and their nation.

9.4 Conclusion

Darwin's theories of natural selection and sexual selection provoked feminist responses and shaped how naturalist and realist fictions applied, reconfigured, or resisted what social Darwinism had to say about sexual attraction and reproduction and women's status in relation to men's. Scholarship about Darwinism and feminism aligns principles of sexual difference and sexual selection with shifting cultural formations affecting gender equality. Alaimo praises Grosz, who "has asserted the value of Darwinian theory for feminism as well as for the humanities more generally, emphasizing this 'new and surprising conception of life' as 'dynamic, collective, change'" (Alaimo, 2013: 391). Brilmyer notes Simone de Beauvoir's claim in *The Second Sex* (1949: 301) that "one is not born, but rather becomes, a woman"; she resists the idea of "sex as a rigid, stable biological phenomenon, emphasizing instead the socially constructed nature of sexual subjectivity" (Brilmyer, 2017: 24). Species transform over time, according to evolutionary theory, and prospects for gender equity also evolve depending on social context.

As a social construct, gender fluctuates depending on individual behaviors and social conventions. From early modern to recent times, observed anatomical differences have structured biological theories and social roles, but anatomy does not determine social destiny. Judith Butler's *Gender Trouble* (2007) asserts "the fluid nature of gender": "what appears to be a biologically given binary is actually a dynamic set of social behaviors that, taken together, produce the appearance of a rigid or stable sex" (Brilmyer, 2017: 24). Human beings adapt our bodies, and we build and reconfigure our environments. Individuals manage significant bodily transformations, including augmentations and other surgeries, as well as hormone and other drug treatments undertaken for personal and medical reasons. Such adjustments produce a variety of bodies, sexualities, and sexual orientations, and demonstrate gender fluidity.

Darwin was fascinated with hermaphroditic plants, including those that adopt a sex, an action indicating that sex distinctions are not fixed. According to John Pannell, Darwin appreciated that there might be evolutionary advantages for plants being male/female or being hermaphrodite: "He was puzzled about why hermaphroditism should ever have evolved towards separate sexes but realised that hermaphrodites might benefit by becoming specialists in one sexual function or the other" (Pannell, 2009). Humans manage their embodiment, choose their sex, and design sensuous environmental experiences. Eva Hayward draws on Darwin's account of the aesthetics of sexual selection in "Spider City Sex," which contemplates how environment matters to those changing sex. Hayward discusses "the conditions of transsexual transitioning, or trans-becoming, what makes transsexuality possible," reminds us that "the animal has always been present" in transitioning, and finds a powerful symbol of a self-architect in Louise Bourgeois's bronze *Crouching Spider* sculpture overseeing San Francisco's Embarcadero (Hayward, 2010: 226, 228). Hayward draws on Darwin's ideas about the aesthetics of sexual selection to link organism, environment, and creativity in a discursive nexus connecting spiders, streets, and trans-selves. Instead of dichotomies, binaries, and hierarchies of a Linnean classification system or a two-sex paradigm, we have a new version of the entangled bank: entanglements linking transitioning and transitioned bodies mobilizing in urban networks. This scene of transforming, with its variant organisms and environments, is an exuberant image of what literary critic George Levine terms "the extraordinary richness and diversity of … life" represented by Darwin (Levine, 2011: 220).

Note

1 For further discussion of the relation between Darwin, later feminisms, and the interpretation of gender, see Chapter 14 by Angelique Richardson.

CHAPTER 10

The Survival of the Unfit

Wai Chee Dimock

In the fifth (1869b) edition of *On the Origin of Species*, Darwin added a subtitle, "The Survival of the Fittest," to his pivotal chapter 4, "Natural Selection." Taken from Herbert Spencer's *Principles of Biology* (1864), this muscular phrase gives the impression that evolution is also a muscular reflex, a straight path from effortless strength to effortless victory. Featuring sure winners trailing superlatives, it allows for no surprises. Those who are the fittest – most equipped to survive – survive.

It's a ringing tautology, but there would have been no need for *Origin* if things were that simple. Complications arise right away, for evolution doesn't seem to be a straight path for anyone, not even those who survive. Survival is chancy, circuitous, the effect of complex adaptation, and by no means guaranteed. It doesn't seem to be an autonomous process, and it's never without its ugly twin. Darwin insists there can be no survivals without extinctions, a volatile endgame making evolution not the self-evident triumph of those destined to come out on top, but endlessly fluctuating, with winners and losers continually recalibrated, their fates tangled up to the end.

That tangled fate is clearly in play in a section of chapter 4 titled "Extinction Caused by Natural Selection." In it, Darwin says: "as new forms are produced, unless we admit that specific forms can go on indefinitely increasing in number, many old forms must become extinct" (Darwin, 2003 [1869]: 326). Extinction is a correlated development, the system-wide housekeeping done by a planet with finite resources. It is integral to the workings of any ecosystem, indeed the only thing we can count on. Darwin returns to it, with great eloquence, in the penultimate paragraph of *On the Origin of Species*:

> Judging from the past, we may safely infer that not one living species will transmit its unaltered likeness to a distant futurity. And of the species now living very few will transmit progeny of any kind to a far distant futurity; for

the manner in which all organic beings are grouped, show that the greater number of species in each genus, and all species in many genera, have left no descendants, but have become utterly extinct. (459)

In this and scores of other similarly haunting passages, Darwin depicts the future as a closed door to most of Earth's inhabitants. He could not have known about the mass extinctions of the twenty-first century, but he would have been unsurprised – if also horrified – by the May 2019 UN report predicting that one million species will go extinct within the next decades (Leahy, 2019). Writing before the full impact of climate change has set in, and unduly sanguine about extinction because he couldn't foresee its pace (see Chapters 2 and 5), Darwin seems nonetheless to have anticipated some of its stark reality. So he is with us again today, speaking with eerie prescience not of the fossil records from the distant past, but in the daily headlines from our immediate present. Still, things are not altogether hopeless. What Darwin says, after all, is that "not one living species will transmit its unaltered likeness to a distant futurity." *Unaltered likeness*, it seems, is the problem, the dead end. For those that manage to evolve and adapt, a path to the future is not out of the question.

What might this stern but sometimes forgiving prophet have to tell us about the fate of the novel, looking ahead to a century of great turmoil, with outsized unknowns greeting us at every turn? Gillian Beer (2009b) and George Levine (1988) have alerted us to the many overlaps between Darwinian evolution and narrative fiction. Adam Gopnik points out that this naturalist writes like a novelist, raising the possibility that literary observations about humans might have something in common with scientific observations about the nonhuman world (Gopnik, 2006). I'll be exploring the contemporary novel through this lens, drawing especially on Darwin's insight that life forms are correlated and coevolving to argue that the novel, faced with the specter of extinction, can also go forward by reclaiming a past genre – specifically, the epic – as a companion lifeline to the future. Merging with that ancient genre to become a new epic realism, an update on Georg Lukacs' (1974) genealogy of these two terms, this elemental form puts in the foreground a super-realistic group of characters – those with disabilities – as an experiment in the survival of the unfit. "Unfit" is an inverted term here, used affirmatively, not to designate a lack but to challenge the very premise of ablebodiedness (Grosz, 2011; Lau in Chapter 6 in this volume). That inversion will have wide implications both for the novel and for the human species as a whole, as each faces the exploding calamity of climate change.

*

In an unintentionally prescient moment in *Origin,* Darwin writes that in "the case of a country undergoing some slight physical change, for instance, of climate, some species will probably become extinct" right away (2003 [1869]: 90). But "from what we have seen of the intimate and complex manner in which" all life is "bound together," we may predict that "any change in the numerical proportions of the inhabitants, independently of the change of climate itself, would seriously affect the others" (90).

Darwin is speaking, of course, only of biological species. However, biology for him is also a conceptual template, a way to think about evolving forms. Languages, for instance, are much like biological species in their nested classifications, their correlated flourishing and decline, as he takes pains to emphasize in *The Descent of Man:*

> Languages, like organic beings, can be classed in groups under groups, and they can be classed either naturally by descent, or artificially by other characters. Dominant languages and dialects spread widely, and lead to the gradual extinction of other tongues. A language, like a species, once extinct, never, as Sir. C. Lyell remarks, reappears. The same language never has two birth-places. (Darwin, 2004 [1871]: 111)

So far, a strict zero-sum game is in play in both the biological and linguistic realms. Yet, while the extinction of languages is well known and well documented, the extinction (or not) of other classes of linguistic objects – for instance, the "artificial" class called the novel, or the epic – is not so clear-cut. How fixed and long-lasting are these genres? Are they here for good, or are they mutable, ephemeral? And is there a built-in end date for these narrative forms, making extinction inevitable at some point? By his own example, Darwin seems to suggest that there is considerable fluidity here, evidenced by the low-probability survival of certain linguistic objects that, on the face of it, might not seem the fittest.

Darwin's own "Abstract" (that's how he referred to *On the Origin of Species*) is an example of such a low-probability survivor. He had not meant to publish it in this guise. But as the full treatise "will take me many more years to complete," and as "my health is far from strong," he had been urged by Charles Lyell and Joseph Hooker to get it out even in an "imperfect" form, especially since another naturalist, Alfred Russel Wallace, "who is now studying the natural history of the Malay archipelago, has arrived at almost exactly the same general conclusions that I have on the origin of species" (Darwin, 2003 [1869]: 27).

Published under duress, the resulting volume is hardly optimized for survival. Fortunately, unlike languages that go extinct thanks to a strict zero-sum game, his own linguistic creation seems subject to a different calculus. Darwin is not without hope that it would have a future, though reached through a peculiar process:

> I can here give only the general conclusions at which I have arrived, with a few facts in illustration, but which, I hope, in most cases will suffice. No one can feel more sensible than I do of the necessity of hereafter publishing in detail all the facts, with references, on which my conclusions have been grounded; and I hope in a future work to do this. (2003 [1869]: 28)

The existing weakness of *Origin* turns out to justify its bid for a future. Rushed into print by the actions of others – including the unwelcome but crucial input of Wallace – it adapts by claiming time as a medium of remediation. Not entirely fit at the moment, it promises to do better the next time around. The second try is an evolutionary necessity. Variants are a must, since the only way *Origin* could survive is as a long-term project, a work-in-progress kept afloat by future editions, with gaps to be filled, new information to be added, and shaky points to be shored up. The survivors here don't have to be the fittest, for the so-called unfit, with ongoing adaptation, can beat the odds and gain traction over time. Such adaptation turns the zero-sum game into a statistical unknown, with the future anyone's guess.

*

It is this statistical unknown that I'd like to bring to bear on Mikhail Bakhtin's account of the rise of the novel, a zero-sum game correlated with the demise of the epic. We come upon the epic "when it's already completely finished, a congealed and half-moribund genre," Bakhtin writes (1981: 14). Because "it is walled off from all subsequent times, the epic past is absolute and complete. It is as closed as a circle. Inside it everything is finished, already over. There is no place in the epic world for any openendedness, indecision, indeterminacy. There are no glimpses in it through which we glimpse the future"

Fans of "epic" science fiction novels, movies, TV shows, and video games would have no idea what Bakhtin is talking about. This supposedly extinct genre is not behaving like one. Morphing from noun to adjective, it is everywhere, showing up on every platform and in every shape and size, a variant-rich survivor with a future stretching far into the distance. No longer simply a genre, it has become a measure of vastness: a scale or an impulse that defies containment. Transposed and repurposed in count-less ways, it is versatile and tenacious, responsive to crises thanks to its continual updating. At once the most ancient and most recent, it is able to offer glimpses of the monstrous, elided in other genres but given full expression here, keeping company – as Amitav Ghosh has noted – with the nonhuman from the first.

In *The Great Derangement: Climate Change and the Unthinkable*, Ghosh pays tribute to the "awareness of nonhuman agency" in ancient epics, even as he takes a swipe at what he imagines to be the dominant form of the contemporary novel (2016: 64). According to him, elemental forces and off-scale events have no place in the hidebound genre of the realist novel, an absence especially noticeable in the "serious fiction" featured in *New York Times Book Review* and the *New York Review of Books*. Unchanged since Victorian times, these literary dinosaurs continue to assert the stabil-ity of the human world even when that stability is no longer tenable, ban-ning anything cataclysmic from their pages:

> To introduce such happenings into a novel is in fact to court eviction from the mansion in which serious fiction has long been in residence; it is to risk banishment to the humbler dwellings that surround the manor house – those generic outhouses that were once known by names such as the gothic, the romance or the melodrama, and have now come to be called fantasy, horror, and science fiction. (Ghosh, 2016: 24)

Like Bakhtin, Ghosh seems to be describing a phantom object, deliber-ately ossified for the sake of argument. This disaster-averse form of the novel hasn't been the dominant form for quite some time, as writers as different as Norman Mailer, Toni Morrison, and Don DeLillo could have attested. More recently, the novels of Margaret Atwood, Ian McEwan, and Cormac McCarthy show just how far catastrophes have been inte-grated into our experience of the everyday. Realism has been rendered epic by the Anthropocene, its nonhuman returning with a vengeance as the superhuman.

In a recent interview with David Wallace-Wells, author of *The Uninhabitable Earth*, Ghosh conceded that "the ground had shifted," that the hidebound novel is finally changing, citing Richard Powers's *The Overstory* (2018) as a "major turning point – not just because it is a great book, which it is, but because it was taken seriously by the literary main-stream" (Wallace-Wells, 2019). The house of fiction is a different house when a novel about trees can win the Pulitzer Prize. Lest we forget the bad old days, Ghosh offered Barbara Kingsolver as a cautionary tale, an

author whose reputation had suffered because her nonhuman subjects –
say, monarch butterflies in *Flight Behavior* – had always been dismissed as
a fringe concern.

*

Kingsolver herself, in her *New York Times* review of *The Overstory*, seems
to echo this point, but by turning it on its head, highlighting a flourishing
epic realism in the novel that Ghosh seems to have missed. Titled "The
Heroes of this Novel are Centuries Old and 300 Feet Tall," the review
begins with a taunt to the reader:

> Trees do most of the things you do, just more slowly. They compete for
> their livelihoods and take care of their families, sometimes making huge
> sacrifices for their children. They breathe, eat and have sex. They give gifts,
> communicate, learn, remember and record the important events of their
> lives. With relatives and non-kin alike they cooperate, forming neighbor-
> hood watch committees .... Some of this might take centuries, but for a
> creature with a life span of hundreds or thousands of years, time must surely
> have a different feel about it. (Kingsolver, 2018)

Trees are central to Powers because of their epic longevity, but there is a
danger. Novel-readers "will only read stories about people," Kingsolver
observes (2018). Knowing this all too well, Powers has come up with a
"delightfully choreographed, ultimately breathtaking hoodwink," fool-
ing us into thinking that the novel is about humans, when it is gradually revealed that these characters are just the "shrubby understory"
(Kingsolver, 2018). In time, these shrubby characters will become ecoter-
rorists, tree defenders, necessary to the fleshing out of the plot, but the
animating core of the novel belongs to the trees towering above them. It
is the trees that give the novel its experimental form, a web of connectiv-
ity initially unemphatic but eventually inexorable, making it possible for
Powers to tell an epic tale about a cast of mostly strangers.

Powers is the "winner of a genius grant," Kingsolver reminds us, known
for his brainy creations (2018). Given that he has "swept the literary-prize
Olympics, he should be a household name, but isn't quite. Critics have
sometimes blamed a certain bleakness of outlook, or a deficit of warmth
in his characters" (2018). It is an odd moment in the review, a sly jab at an
author she otherwise admires. Powers isn't quite a household name when
the standard is set by Kingsolver herself, each of whose books since 1993
has been a *New York Times* bestseller. And that 1993 novel that set her on
this path, *The Poisonwood Bible* – an Oprah's Book Club selection and a
finalist for the Pulitzer Prize – in fact has more than a little in common

with *The Overstory*. From the tree-centric title to the cast of characters revolving around it, this novel, written at the end of the last century, had already decided that business as usual wouldn't do, that a new literary form was needed to tell a different story about the world: who inhabits it, what disasters look like, and what it takes to keep going.

The poisonwood makes its appearance almost as soon as the novel begins. The year was 1959. Nathan Price, a Baptist missionary newly arrived in the Belgian Congo with his wife and four daughters, is alerted by Mama Tataba, his housekeeper: "'That one, brother, he bite,' she said, pointing her knuckly hand at a small tree he was wresting from his garden plot" (Kingsolver, 1999: 39). And sure enough, when Nathan wakes up the next morning, his arms and hands are covered with rashes: "Even his good right eye was swollen shut, from where he'd wiped his brow. Yellow pus ran like sap from his welted flesh" (40–41). As his daughter Leah observes, "Among all of Africa's mysteries, here were the few that revealed themselves in no time flat" (40).

Initiation into the mysteries of Africa begins with bodily mortification. On this continent, the nonhuman bites. It has no trouble fighting back when an intruder tries to impose his will on a native habitat. With pus running down his good right eye, Nathan has been taught a lesson in local knowledge, one that also teaches him something about himself. Shining a light on his preexisting condition (his left eye was injured in the war), it reveals just how invisible many disabilities are, how less than fully intact many functional humans prove to be. His appearance as well as his vision now compromised, Nathan looks not unlike Mama Tataba, who has a "blind eye. It looked like an egg whose yolk had been broken and stirred just once" (Kingsolver, 1999: 39).

The deformity is hard to miss, but nobody pays it any mind around here, for in this community, as in many others in Africa, "they've all got their own handicap children or a mama with no feet" (52–53). Another neighbor, Mama Mwanza, was even more seriously disfigured when her house burned down. Her "legs didn't burn all the way off but it looks like a pillow or just something down there wrapped up in a cloth sack. She has to scoot around on her hands" (51). Not having the use of her legs, however, is not necessarily disabling. She carries all her laundry in a big basket on her head, and "when she scoots down the road, not a one of them of them falls out. All the other ladies have big baskets on their heads too, so nobody stares at Mama Mwanza one way or another" (52).

Is "disability" even the right word here? Mama Mwanza is ablebodied, though not by a standard yardstick. Rosemarie Garland-Thomson refers to these nonstandard characters as "extraordinary bodies" (1997). Sami Schalk sees in them "bodyminds reimagined" (2018). In her fire-ravaged form as in her off-the-charts performance, Mama Mwanza is far outside the bounds of normalcy. She would have been stared at anywhere else but not here, a fact hugely gratifying to Adah, Leah's sister, no standard character herself:

> My right side drags. I was born with half my brain dried up like a prune, deprived of blood by an unfortunate fetal mishap. … [W]e were inside the womb together dum-de-dum when Leah suddenly turned and declared, Adah, you are just too slow. I am taking all the nourishment here and going on ahead. She grew strong and I grew weak. (Yes, Jesus loves me!) And so it came to pass, in the Eden of our mother's womb, I was cannibalized by my sister. (Kingsolver, 1999: 33–34)

Disability is not an African problem, symptomatic of a backward continent. It is everywhere, back home in Georgia, inside the Eden of the womb, shorthand for a kind of congenital imbalance plaguing the world, a root inequity with no obvious solution. Pieties such as "Jesus loves me!" can only be a sick joke here, for this Eden is Hobbesian rather than Christian, a state of nature in which life is "solitary, poore, nasty, brutish, and short" (Hobbes, 1968 [1651]: 186). Here humans will cannibalize one another, showing that we are matter after all, edible morsels that can be gobbled up. Bodily harm is simply something that happens, as it happens to other embodied creatures, a random and not infrequent fact of life. Our vulnerability speaks to our kinship with the nonhuman world.

That certainly seems to be the case with Adah. But it isn't the whole story. Adah's disabled right side has not stopped her from quoting poetry (Emily Dickinson and William Carlos Williams are her favorites) or learning the Kikongo tongue. It is she, knowing that tongue, who gives us an inside view of what happens to Christianity when, like Nathan, it too comes into contact with the poisonwood tree – in this case, linguistic contact: "'Tata Jesus is Bangala!' declares the Reverend every Sunday at the end of his sermon," Adah reports, and she adds: "*Bangala* means something precious and dear. But the way he pronounces it, it means the poisonwood tree. Praise the Lord, Hallelujah, my friends! For Jesus will make you itch like nobody's business" (Kingsolver, 1999: 276).

It is not for nothing that the novel is titled *The Poisonwood Bible*, for the scripture being disseminated here is indeed a pointedly local variant, touched by the Kikongo tongue and the vengeful tree that bears its signature. This is a scripture founded not on a special dispensation for humans, but on the impartial matter-of-factness of elemental forces, giving *Homo sapiens* no special status, treating our physical bodies as just that: physical bodies. What Kingsolver is offering here is the broad coordinates of a newly chastised realism, no longer insulated or human-centric, and not looking away from any future that might come. Such a realism will have tremendous consequences for how twenty-first-century disasters are imagined, represented, and responded to.

The power of this elemental realism is fully on display in the novel's climactic scene, featuring the African equivalent of "the Hand of God," the arrival of the flesh-eating *nsongonya*, the army ants (Kingsolver, 1999: 299). These ants feel like "burning liquid that had flooded our house … that had flooded the world," Leah says. "Every surface was covered and boiling," like "black flowing lava in the moonlight" (299). Adah, so often aligned with the nonhuman world, is trapped for once in her inadequate humanness. *Help me.* This cry of desperation sums her up and holds her prisoner. Endlessly playful and associative on other occasions, she is reduced to just these two words now, unadorned and involuntary. They come out of her mouth almost to spite her, for they will be in vain. Her mother, already carrying her younger sister, Ruth May, will ignore these words. "She studied me for a moment, weighing my life. Then nodded, shifted the load in her arms, turned away" (306).

Adah goes under almost instantly and is trampled upon, but regains her wits at just this moment, getting from anonymous strangers the help she fails to get from her own mother, a means of locomotion that propels her forward:

> I found my way to my elbows and raised myself up, grabbing with my strong left hand at legs that dragged me forward. Ants on my earlobes, my tongue, my eyelids. I heard myself crying out loud – such a strange noise, as if it came from my hair and fingernails, and again and again I came up. Once I looked for my mother and saw her, far ahead. I followed, bent on my own rhythm. Curved into the permanent song of my body: *left … behind.*
>
> I did not know who it was that lifted me over the crowd and set me down into the canoe with my mother. I had to turn quickly to see him as he retreated. It was Anatole. We crossed the river together, mother and daughter, facing each other, low in the boat's quiet center. She tried to hold my hands but could not. For the breath of a river we stared without speaking. (Kingsolver, 1999: 306)

In that unworded and unforgiving stare between mother and daughter, Kingsolver translates her epic realism into terms no one can fail to understand. Proud monuments of civilization – the human language, for instance, or the human family – can look very different when tested by catastrophes. They are less than what we think. Kingsolver is not waving any flags here, not even going out on a limb. Still, it is the case that one of the best-known topoi of the epic genre – Aeneas fleeing Troy with his father Anchises on his back and his son Ascanius by his side – is being turned upside down to yield a modern variant, a novel grappling with large-scale catastrophes, as does the epic, but doing so on a new terrain and yielding almost the opposite outcome.

In the *Aeneid*, it is the iconic trio of Aeneas, Anchises, and Ascanius that saves the day. This beacon of hope, shining through the convulsions of a sacked city, speaks to the power of filial piety and generational continuity. The only thing that mars it is Aeneas's inexplicable decision to have his wife, Creusa, follow at a distance. Not surprisingly, she soon gets separated and is never seen or heard from again:

> Creusa, taken away from us by grim fate, did she
> Linger, or stray, or sink in weariness?
> There is no telling. Never would she be
> Restored to us. Never did I look back
> Or think to look for her, lost as she was,
> Until we reached the funeral mound and shrine
> Of venerable Ceres. Here at last
> All came together, but she was not there;
> She alone failed her friends, her child, her husband.
>
> (Virgil, 1983: 2.960–968)

In Aeneas's telling, it is Creusa's fault that there is now this gaping hole within the family. Still, even he admits he never once looked back to make sure she is keeping up. Even more tellingly, when he goes down into the underworld, in Book VI of the *Aeneid*, the episode is dominated by his meeting with Anchises and the latter's prophesy about the future glories of Rome. There is no mention of Creusa, no attempt to find her and hear from her lips what happened that fateful night.

There is a flinty core to epic, unyielding and untender. As Lukacs (1974) suggests, the reference point here is the social totality, not the isolated individual. This is a pre-Christian genre, after all; individual salvation is not part of the script, not a legitimate hope with theological backing. Humans here are mortals and never more than mortals, finite through and through, distinct from nonhumans only for a brief spell of time. The unceremonious dispatch of Creusa, like the unforgiving slaying of Turnus at the end of the *Aeneid*, or the indiscriminate massacre of the suitors at the end of the *Odyssey*, is simply the intensified form of a social finitude that will sooner or later overtake all humans. The epic is without illusion from the first about who we are, how we die, and how we are forgotten. This realism Kingsolver takes to heart. For her, though, human finitude is not necessarily fatal, for it is above all a form of life, clear-eyed about what it can and cannot do, pivoted on and energized by limits, not a lack but a need-based perseverance, a form of life daily lived by the disabled.

Adah is exemplary for that reason. Her ordeal might not be a minority report after all, but a general portrait of humanity under epic realism. Being overwhelmed is nothing special in a century of floods and wildfires and pandemics. Cognitive disabilities unite us as calamities spiral beyond our knowledge and control. A planetwide need for help puts all of us on the same footing. But then again, needing help doesn't have to mean helplessness either. Adah is once again exemplary here: she might not be able to move fast on her own, but her quick-thinking brain and her "strong left hand" turn the heels of others into an effective means of locomotion. Disability here goes hand in hand with an ability to use help in whatever form it comes, an adaptability crucial to the survival of individual characters, and to the novel itself as it looks ahead to a future in which characters like Adah are probably closer to us than characters living unhandicapped and unimperiled lives. Epic realism offers no salvation, but it does grant a tenacious if precarious future, the birthright of the unfit.

*

Some such thought seems to have been percolating in the Richard Powers corpus for the past twenty-five years. From *Galatea 2.2* (1995) to *The Echo Maker* (2006), disabled characters have always had a nontrivial presence in his fiction. *The Overstory* outshines all of them. Best known as a novel about trees, it is more remarkable still in its cast of nonstandard characters, each disabled in a unique way. Patricia Westerford, eventually the celebrated author of *The Secret Forest*, was a "thing only borderline human" as a little girl, born with a "deformation of the inner ear" that makes her face "sloped and ursine," and her speech a "slurry hard for the uninitiated to comprehend" (Powers, 2018: 11). Douglas Pavlicek, ejected from an exploding plane, his tibia shattered by a misfiring sidearm, and saved from death only by a gigantic banyan, ends up with "one and a half good legs" (88). And Ray Brinkman, once an articulate property lawyer, can only speak "one syllable at a time," each syllable "mangled and worthless," after a stroke (497).

Among these characters, none is more striking than Neelay Mehta. Falling from an oak tree when he was eleven, Neelay will henceforth be "fused to his wheelchair," his legs "shriveled to thick twigs" (105). While remaining conscious for a minute after the fall, though, he has a chance to see the tree as it is rarely seen:

> stacks of spreading metropolis, networks of conjoined cells pulsing with energy and liquid sun, water rising through long thin reeds, rings of them banded together into pipes that draw dissolved minerals up through the narrowing tunnels of transparent twig and out through their waving tips, while sun-made sustenance drops down in tunes just inside them. A colossal, rising, reaching, stretching space elevator of a billion independent parts, shuttering the air into the sky and storing the sky deep underground, sorting possibility from out of nothing; the most perfect piece of self-writing code that his eyes could hope to see. Then his eyes close in shock and Neelay shuts down. (103)

Nothing can be further from the boiling lava of the *nsongonya*. This pulsing, swaying, photosynthesizing apparition – a miracle of sky, sun, and earth – is nature as we would like to imagine it. Yet the damage done to Neelay is tenfold greater than the damage done to Adah by the ants, even though the tree does not set out to cripple and maim. It is just an oak tree observing the law of gravity, enacting the consequences of its own height. From *The Poisonwood Bible* to *The Overstory*, the nonhuman world has evolved still further. It is on its own now, a primary dimension of reality, densely and superabundantly inhabited, and no more solicitous of humans than nonhumans. Epic realism here is the realism of elemental forces, impartial in their power to nourish and their power to destroy.

For Neelay, the run-in with these forces is life-changing, and not necessarily for the worse. Sure, he looks helpless, but his disability, like Adah's, has turned him into something almost like a force of nature, with not a little in common with the nonhuman world. At the novel's end, his mind is once again on fire, his "heart is beating too hard for what little meat is left on his skeleton, and his vision pulses" as he plans the next installment of the game that will send millions and millions of fans into a new frenzy (Powers, 2018: 496). An even more memorable scene, though, is probably an earlier one, the epic undertaking of lifting himself from his bed into his wheelchair. This requires, first, grabbing the overhead bar, "reaching out to one of the many hanging hooks filled with gear," snagging "the U-shaped canvas sling and, in a hundred small increments," spreading "it out in the bed around his body's upright stem" (194). Next,

> He stabs out again and spears the head of the winch, drags it across its horizontal brace beam until it's positioned directly above. All four sling loops go over the winch's latches, two per side. He pops the remote in his mouth

and, holding the straps in place, bites down on the power button until the winch lifts him upright. He affixes the remote to the sling and detaches the catheter's urine sack from the side of the bed. Holding the hose in his teeth to free both hands, he attaches the bag to the satchel he has wrapped himself in. Then he presses the winch button again, holds on, and goes airborne. (194)

Powers's description goes on for two pages. This spare-no-details account of Neelay and his wheelchair is not exactly fun to read. But it is a full-throated variant on Homer's full-throated account of Odysseus, "master shipwright," luxuriating in his craft in Book V of the *Odyssey* (Homer, 1998: 5.243–270). This lovingly built ship will take him to what he yearns for day and night: "my quiet Penelope," who, he tells Kalypso, "would seem a shade before your majesty, / death and old age being unknown to you / while she must die" (5.225–229). For Odysseus as for Neelay, mortality is the beginning of life rather than its terminus. And for both, that beginning can have a future only if the nonhuman world is on board as friend and foe, the testing ground for humans and a projectile into the unknown.

Survival is multiform and endlessly inventive. Darwin has already linked it to adaptability, the ability to coevolve and flourish with other life forms in an ecosystem. The twenty-first-century novel goes one step further. Honoring disabled characters as the most adaptable, it offers an epic realism that looks catastrophe in the eye, claiming it as a nonhuman future that remains a habitable home of the unfit.

PART III

Humanism after Darwin

CHAPTER II

Darwin's Human History

Ian Duncan

11.1 An Exceptional Animal

"How did humans come to be such an exceptional species?" asks evolutionary anthropologist Robert Boyd:

> Five million years ago our ancestors were just another, unremarkable ape. Today, our species dominates the world's biota. We occupy every part of the globe, we vastly outnumber every other terrestrial vertebrate, we process more energy than any other species, and we live in a wider range of social systems than any other creature. (2017: 10)

Boyd addresses the abiding question of the "natural history of man" since its foundation as a scientific genre in the late eighteenth century. Once human nature is embedded in terrestrial history and geography, severed from metaphysical causality, what makes the difference between ourselves and other creatures? His answer refreshes key tenets of Enlightenment anthropology. Humans have colonized the whole planet (Lamarck, 1914: 170); they are generalists, cognitively world-embracing (Herder, 2002: 78–79); their dominance arises from large-scale social cooperation, sustained through sympathetic imitation (Hume, 1985: 202–207) and traditional transmission (Burke, 2003: 29–30), rather than individual enterprise (Boyd, 2017: 42–52).[1] Above all, Boyd's invocation of "zoological criteria" (ecological range and biomass) poses the question in a historical rather than an ontological sense: not, "Are humans really exceptional?" but, "How did they become so?" (11).

The historicization of human difference follows Charles Darwin's extension of his evolutionary thesis to *Homo sapiens* in *The Descent of Man* (1871), which completed (at least notionally) the trajectory of naturalistic embedding, and located the crux of the difference at the developmental threshold of emergence from a prehuman state.[2] What changed, what did not, what was lost and what gained, when natural history became human history? Boyd proposes a temporal gear-shift, in which the accelerated

time of cultural evolution overtakes the slow time of biological evolution. Working according to the same organic principles, but faster, culture
outpaces and in certain instances may preempt biology. Whether or how
far such a shift might amount to a qualitative change, whereby human
history breaks free (if only partially) from a prior natural history (while
yet remaining "natural"), is the question that continues to haunt modern thought. Charged with metahistorical force, conditioning the histories of nations and civilizations, human natural history maintains its hold
on the popular imagination as well as on scientific inquiry, as is evident
in the succession of blockbuster universal histories in Darwin's wake,
from William Winwood Reade's *The Martyrdom of Man* (1872) and H.
G. Wells's *The Outline of History* (1919–1920) to global bestsellers of our
own time, such as Jared Diamond's *Guns, Germs and Steel* (1997), Noah
Yuval Harari's *Sapiens* (2011), and Rutger Bregman's *Humankind* (2019).
Strikingly, some of these anthropological histories recast the evolutionary transition between prehuman and human states as a *revolutionary*
transition: a "Great Leap Forward" (Diamond, 1997: 39), a "Cognitive
Revolution" – "the point when history declared its independence from
biology" (Harari, 2015: 21–37). Such formulations defy Darwin's gradualist principle, *Natura non facit saltum* ("nature does not jump"), more
brazenly than Boyd's insistence on an organic process common to the disparate temporal scales of biological and cultural development (Darwin,
2009 [1859]: 177).[3]

Given the authority of his evolutionary thesis, it is worth asking what
kind of human history – more precisely, what account of the transition from
a prehuman to a human condition – Darwin has to offer in *The Descent of
Man*. The operation of sexual selection according to aesthetic criteria (rather
than rational-choice reckonings of "fitness"), shared by humans with other
creatures, constitutes the book's original hypothesis of a human evolutionary
principle. Sexual selection becomes the main driver of (cosmetic) physical
diversity after humans have established ecological dominance, transformed
their material environment, and in effect domesticated themselves. It affords
a synchronic rather than a historical view of the continuity across human
and nonhuman animal life, as well as across human racial differences, which
is sustained rather than eroded by formal variation.[4]

There is a history of human emergence to be read in *The Descent of
Man*, but it is cryptic, legible in gaps and pieces rather than through a
continuous sequence. As in *The Origin of Species*, Darwin eschews a narrative organization of his argument, which had made earlier evolutionist
theses (by Herder, Lamarck, and others) vulnerable to dismissal as works

of conjectural history – more fiction than philosophy or science. The pressure points of Darwin's human history are the cognitive and ethical faculties, or rather the relation between them. Here, upon reason and morality, claims for human uniqueness keep being urged, in persistent attempts to reinstall an ontological difference between ourselves and other creatures. Here, too, Darwin stakes his account of a moral or cultural achievement of full humanity in the form of a universal extension of sympathy to all sentient beings. The achievement is at odds with the biopolitical imperative of human ascendancy according to the logic of natural selection, manifest in the worldwide march of European empire as it laid waste to local populations and ecologies. With their argument that the revolutionary rise of *Homo sapiens* entailed the mass extermination of other species, including collateral human species, Diamond and Harari revert to the faultline in Darwin's account. Harari identifies *fiction* – the imaginary construction of nonexistent states – as the secret weapon in our species' cognitive revolution. In so doing he echoes, if faintly, Darwin's conjectural history of the evolution of the moral sense through the work of the imagination: more richly nourished, in *The Descent of Man*, by the resources of the nineteenth-century novel.

11.2 A Moral Being

One of the main tasks Darwin sets himself in *The Descent of Man* is to dismantle the traditional barriers that separate humans from other animals – especially the cognitive barriers. "There is no fundamental difference between man and the higher mammals in their mental faculties," he declares; "the difference in mind between man and the higher animals, great as it is, certainly is one of degree and not of kind" (Darwin, 2004 [1871]: 86, 151).[5] The question persists as to whether, and at what point, a difference in degree might become great enough to constitute, functionally if not categorically, a difference in kind. Darwin's argument comes most strenuously to bear on reason and morality, the favored properties for dividing "man" from "the brutes."[6] Darwin efficiently demonstrates the evidence of a rational faculty in other animals, but when it comes to the moral sense, his argument grows more tortuous, until here we find the difference in degree widening into an apparent difference in kind.

"I fully subscribe to the judgment of those writers who maintain that of all the differences between man and the lower animals, the moral sense or conscience is by far the most important" (120), Darwin asserts, and later, more forcefully, "man ... alone can with certainty be ranked as a moral being" (135). It seems there is a threshold that must be crossed for humanity to come fully into its own. Darwin lays out a conjectural sequence of evolutionary steps through which the human forms of morality arose from prehuman "social instincts," which bond together all creatures that live together in swarms, shoals, or packs:

> *Firstly*, the social instincts lead an animal to take pleasure in the society of its fellows, to feel a certain amount of sympathy with them, and to perform various services for them. ... *Secondly*, as soon as the mental faculties had become highly developed, images of all past actions and motives would be incessantly passing through the brain of each individual: and that feeling of dissatisfaction, or even misery, which invariably results, as we shall hereafter see, from any unsatisfied instinct, would arise, as often as it was perceived that the enduring and always present social instinct had yielded to some other instinct, at the time stronger, but neither enduring in its nature, nor leaving behind it a very vivid impression. It is clear that many instinctive desires, such as that of hunger, are in their nature of short duration; and after being satisfied, are not readily or vividly recalled. (120–121)

The threshold stage is the second, in which a cognitive faculty – the ability to reflect upon past actions and motives – converts an instinctive sympathy into moral deliberation, which is (thirdly) codified in language and (fourthly) reinforced by heritable habit. At that second stage, instinct bifurcates along concurrent tracks, each of which affords a different subjective relation to time. Appetitive instincts, such as hunger, are bound to the body, and to the fleeting present moment, whereas the social instinct becomes morally efficacious through the mental capacity to inhabit past states and compare them with the present, an operation that dilates the present into an "enduring" state from which we can regulate the future. Darwin's language characterizes this as an imaginative operation ("images of all past actions and motives ... incessantly passing through the brain") before it becomes a rational one.

Humans alone, it seems, have evolved that imaginative ability to occupy different temporal states and combine past and present to form a durational continuum, which refines the social instinct into the moral sense or conscience:

> A moral being is one who is capable of comparing his past and future actions or motives, and of approving or disapproving of them. ... [In] the case of man, who alone can with certainty be ranked as a moral being, actions of a certain class are called moral, whether performed deliberately, after a struggle with opposing motives, or impulsively through instinct, or from the effects of slowly-gained habit. (135)

Moral actions performed impulsively through instinct are common to the lower animals as well as to humans. What distinguishes human conscience is the deliberation of the moral act through "a struggle with opposing motives." Internal conflict is the stigma of human nature. Its goal is a victory over bodily drives, bound to the sensuous, perishable present, achieved through a power of reflection rooted in the cognitive ability to access a transtemporal state by shuttling between present and past, and adjudicating their competing demands. With this constitution of the moral sense through an agonistic division between temporal states, in order to subsume them, Darwin reinstalls as a psychological condition the ancient figure of a dual human nature.

Darwin's conception, trailing a long literary, theological and moral-philosophical genealogy, has complex, nuanced play in nineteenth-century fiction.[7] George Eliot's *The Mill on the Floss* (the novel she was midway through writing when she read *On the Origin of Species*) may as well have provided Darwin with his model for the generation of the moral sense through a conflict between natural instincts keyed to different temporal states. Eliot's heroine, Maggie Tulliver, defends her sense of duty, imaginatively binding past, present, and future in an ethical continuum, against her lovers' arguments that it is "unnatural." "The feeling which draws us towards each other is too strong to be overcome," one suitor insists: "that natural law surmounts every other" (Eliot, 1981 [1860]: 475). "Love is natural," Maggie admits, "but surely pity and faithfulness and memory are natural too. And they would live in me still, and punish me if I did not obey them. I should be haunted by the suffering I had caused" (450). And later: "If the past is not to bind us, where can duty lie? We should have no law but the inclination of the moment" (475). Her responses articulate "that feeling of dissatisfaction, or even misery," in Darwin's formulation, that must follow the sacrifice of "the enduring and always present social instinct" to a momentary desire.

The cognitive capacity to inhabit different temporal states is key to an earlier classic of English realism, Jane Austen's *Emma*. (Darwin was an early, avid Janeite, as his letters to his sisters from H.M.S. *Beagle* bear witness [Darwin, 2008b: 54, 205].) Austen's heroines are famous for being able to reread and reassess their prior history, and through that reflection achieve a moral reformation that justifies their status as novelistic protagonists. Emma Woodhouse considers her relationship with Frank Churchill:

> Emma continued to entertain no doubt of her being in love. Her ideas only varied as to the how much. At first, she thought it was a good deal; and

afterwards, but little. ... She was very often thinking of [Frank], and quite impatient for a letter, that she might know how he was, how were his spirits, how was his aunt, and what was the chance of his coming to Randalls again this spring. But, on the other hand, she could not admit herself to be unhappy, nor, after the first morning, to be less disposed for employment than usual; she was still busy and cheerful; and, pleasing as he was, she could yet imagine him to have faults; and farther, though thinking of him so much, and, as she sat drawing or working, forming a thousand amusing schemes for the progress and close of their attachment, fancying interesting dialogues, and inventing elegant letters; the conclusion of every imaginary declaration on his side was that she refused him. (Austen, 2003 [1816]: 206)

As well as contemplating past and present, Emma entertains possible, hypothetical, and subjunctive states, in order to arrive at a moral deliberation and become (in effect) the author of her own story. Emma, in other words, is thinking like a novelist – like the novelist in whose novel she plays the leading role. In this case, her novelistic imagining is more authentically deliberative than her misguided attempts to plot the lives of her neighbors.

Emma's imaginative capacity, as it brings her close to the plane of narration, sets her apart from the minor or "flat" characters in Austen's novel. The hierarchical distinction in the character system (theorized by Alex Woloch as an economic division of labor [2003: 143–147]) corresponds to zoological and anthropological hierarchies of the human and less-than-human – beings who are incapable of reflection and hence incapable of joining the cognitive plane of the narration. In contrast to those privileged persons endowed with depth-simulating technical devices, such as free indirect discourse, the flat characters (Mr. Woodhouse, Miss Bates, Mrs. Elton, and the rest), however differently valued, are condemned never to develop – never to change. They are, so to speak, savages in Highbury.

11.3 The Great Leap Forward

To think like a novelist entails a capacity not only to reflect upon past states and compare them with the present, but also – amplifying Darwin's account of the moral imagination – to compare past and present with other possible, potential, and counterfactual states, in order to model alternative, unrealized pasts and presents as well as future outcomes. In his "brief history of humankind," Yuval Harari makes fiction-making the key technology of the "Cognitive Revolution" that produced *Homo sapiens* 70,000 years ago. Humans became human because they (we) alone could "imagine things that do not really exist" (Harari, 2015: 23).[8] The capacity to make up a fiction and, crucially, to persuade others to go along with it generates collective life on a large scale, beyond the face-to-face community of the band or tribe – an order of magnitude necessary to launch a civilization. A society of strangers needs a myth, an ideology, for it to cohere and act together. Harari's strictly instrumental view of fiction ("an imagined reality ... that everyone believes in" [2015: 32]) corresponds with what Wolfgang Iser (after Frank Kermode) calls "concord-fictions": inventions that command collective consent, endowing "reality with meaning that ... makes reality into what we think it is." This is in contrast to novels and poems, which exhibit their fictive status, doubling real and imagined worlds rather than subsuming one to the other, as a condition of their legibility (Iser, 1993: 89).

Harari argues that the cognitive revolution impelled a double wave of exterminations: of Pleistocene megafauna, following the human invasions of the Americas and Australasia, and also, more crucially, of the five other known hominin species that shared the planet with us in our early history (Harari, 2015: 13–18, 63–74). *Homo sapiens'* sudden "[jump] to the top of the food chain" produced an unamiable moral and political character. Unlike "majestic" top predators such as lions, who, coevolving with their prey species, inhabit a long (royal or aristocratic) genealogy of evolutionary slow time, humans are shifty arrivistes: "Having so recently been one of the underdogs of the savannah, we are full of fears and anxieties over our position, which makes us doubly cruel and dangerous" – "like a banana republic dictator" (Harari, 2015: 11–12). Harari follows Jared Diamond's correlation of the "Great Leap Forward" with human territorial expansion beyond Eurasia and the consequent "extinction spasm" of large animals in the New World (Diamond, 1997: 43). Diamond mentions only in passing the displacement of Neanderthals by *Homo sapiens* (1997: 40), which Harari amplifies into a full-scale genocide of our cousin species, boosted by the fiction-making superpower that gave us our overwhelming capacity for collective action. Extermination, in short, is the objective proof of human global ascendancy: our signature, or rather our bloody thumbprint, in the fossil record.

Or perhaps not, since the signature consists of an absence of evidence, a disappearance, for which paleoanthropologists have proposed other causes. Rutger Bregman challenges the hominin extermination thesis (Harari's "Replacement Theory") on the grounds that it lacks archaeological proof, and refutes a "Hobbesian" vision of human ascendancy in favor of what he calls his own "hopeful history." Humans prevailed because of our superior capacity to socialize, which evolved not through the weaponizing of fiction but through selection according to "friendliness," and a progressive acquisition of cute, childlike features – a Disneyfication of the human physiognomy (Bregman, 2020: 61–63). Bregman's nickname for our species, "*Homo puppy*" (2020: 65), makes for a cuddly riposte to Harari's cold-blooded killer ape – much as Desmond Morris's sexy "naked ape" was a hippie-era riposte to the Cold War–era angry ape of Robert Ardrey, in another widely read conjectural anthropology series. Natural man arrives, in Ardrey's account, as always already a settler-colonist, aggressively seizing and defending property, whereas in Morris's he comes into his own (both assume the masculine gender) with the liberation of sensuous skin from bestial pelt.[9]

The great leap forward thesis, with the extermination of other human relatives as its fatal correlative, was given full, popular articulation by H. G. Wells:

> The appearance of these truly human postglacial Palæolithic peoples [Cro-Magnons] was certainly an enormous leap forward in the history of mankind. ... They dispossessed *Homo Neanderthalensis* from his caverns and his stone quarries. And they agreed with modern ethnologists, it would seem, in regarding him as a different species. Unlike most savage conquerors, who take the women of the defeated side for their own and interbreed with them, it would seem that the true men would have nothing to do with the Neanderthal race, women or men. (1919–1920, 1: 54–55)[10]

Now, thanks to DNA analysis and paleoarchaeology, we know this was not the case. *Homo sapiens* interbred and enjoyed cultural exchanges with Denisovans as well as Neanderthals some 50,000 years ago, in a presumably amicable muddling of taxonomic borders (see Higham, 2021). Darwinian natural history softened the hard distinction between race and species, categories that, having "coevolved" (as Zakiyyah Iman Jackson argues), are "*mutually reinforcing*" – sustaining as well as blurring one other (Jackson, 2020: 12, italics original). If species difference relaxes into racial difference in current scenarios of prehistoric life, earlier human histories imagined the reverse: an antagonistic stiffening. Insisting (like Harari) on genocide as the signature of the "enormous leap forward," Wells finds it encoded psychologically, affectively, in an instinctively rooted aesthetic of racial hatred:

> We know nothing of the appearance of the Neanderthal man, but this absence of intermixture seems to suggest an extreme hairiness, an ugliness, or a repulsive strangeness in his appearance over and above his low forehead, his beetle brows, his ape neck, and his inferior stature. Or he – and she – may have been too fierce to tame. (1919–1920, 1: 55)

Species difference is guaranteed by an insurmountable aversion. After the Neanderthal extinction, Wells writes, "there is no great break, no further sweeping away of one kind of man and replacement by another kind between the appearance of the Neolithic way of living and our own time." Invasions, conquests, and mass-migrations follow, but the human species inhabits a continuous history: "There is no real break in culture from their time onward until we reach the age of coal, steam, and power-driven machinery that began in the eighteenth century" (1919–1920, 1: 62).

11.4   An Empire of Sympathy

Darwin has little to say about early human species. Only one, *Homo neanderthalensis*, had received a taxonomic description by the time *The Descent of Man* was published. Darwin's sole reference to "some skulls of very high antiquity, such as the famous one of Neanderthal" (75), follows T. H. Huxley's supposition that the remains were those of "a Man whose skull may be said to revert somewhat towards the pithecoid type," rather than "a human being intermediate between Men and Apes" (Huxley, 1863: 157; see also Tattersall, 2009: 28–34). Instead, Darwin looks forward in human history:

> At some future period, not very distant as measured by centuries, the civilised races of man will almost certainly exterminate, and replace, the savage races throughout the world. At the same time the anthropomorphous apes, as Professor Schaaffhausen has remarked, will no doubt be exterminated. The break between man and his nearest allies will then be wider, for it will intervene between man in a more civilised state, as we may hope, even than the Caucasian, and some ape as low as a baboon, instead of as now between the negro or Australian and the gorilla. (183–184)

Darwin's prognosis, the more chilling for its placid delivery, eradicates the distinction between human races and anthropoid species, along with the beings in question. Paving the way to "a more civilised state, as we may hope," these extinctions are its structural condition.

The condition seems starkly at odds with Darwin's vision of a more civilized state. If sympathy for fellow members of the pack or band constitutes the social instinct in prehuman animals, its human development takes place by a deliberative expansion beyond the local group:

> As man advances in civilisation, and small tribes are united into larger communities, the simplest reason would tell each individual that he ought to extend his social instincts and sympathies to all the members of the same nation. … This point being once reached, there is only an artificial barrier to prevent his sympathies extending to the men of all nations and races. …

Sympathy beyond the confines of man, that is, humanity to the lower animals, seems to be one of the latest moral acquisitions. … This virtue, one of
the noblest with which man is endowed, seems to arise incidentally from our
sympathies becoming more tender and more widely diffused, until they are
extended to all sentient beings. (146–147)

"Humanity," the plenitude of our species being, refers not to a biological condition but to a moral one, achieved by the imaginative capacity to
cross species boundaries and extend our sympathy to "all sentient beings."
Darwin reiterates this conjectural moral evolution:

As man gradually advanced in intellectual power … his sympathies became
more tender and widely diffused, extending to men of all races, to the imbecile, maimed, and other useless members of society, and finally to the lower
animals, – so would the standard of his morality rise higher and higher. (149)

The prescription carries rhetorical force. If sympathy with "the lower animals" is a token of moral advancement, then we should be able to accept
Darwin's argument that we are also kin to them. He rehearses this logic in
the book's conclusion:

For my own part I would as soon be descended from that heroic little monkey, who braved his dreaded enemy in order to save the life of his keeper, or
from that old baboon, who descending from the mountains, carried away
in triumph his young comrade from a crowd of astonished dogs – as from
a savage who delights to torture his enemies, offers up bloody sacrifices,
practices infanticide without remorse, treats his wives like slaves, knows no
decency, and is haunted by the grossest superstitions. (689)

Darwin weighs his admiration (rhetorically binding us to share it) of the
heroism of the monkey and baboon against the memory of his shocked
encounter, forty years earlier, with the inhabitants of Tierra del Fuego (see,
for example, Schmitt, 2009: 48–50; Richards, 2017: 424–426, 454–456).

   How may we reconcile Darwin's vision of this utopian summit of
morality – the deliberative expansion of sympathy to include "men of all
races" and, beyond that, "all sentient beings" – with the forecast of future
exterminations? Just before the forecast, Darwin writes:

The great break in the organic chain between man and his nearest allies,
which cannot be bridged over by any extinct or living species, has often
been advanced as a grave objection to the belief that man is descended from
some lower form; but this objection will not appear of much weight to
those who, from general reasons, believe in the general principle of evolution. Breaks often occur in all parts of the series, some being wide, sharp
and defined, others less so in various degrees … these breaks depend merely
on the number of related forms which have become extinct. (183)

Any distinction between species is a historical artifact, a phenomenological illusion, constituted by the extinction gap that divides us from our nearest kin. Darwin has explained the logic in *On the Origin of Species*:

> There will be a constant tendency in the improved descendants of any one species to supplant and exterminate in each stage of descent their predecessors and their original progenitor. For it should be remembered that the competition will generally be most severe between those forms which are most nearly related to each other in habits, constitution, and structure. Hence all the intermediate forms between the earlier and later states, that is between the less and more improved states of the same species, as well as the original parent-species itself, will generally tend to become extinct. So it probably will be with many whole collateral lines of descent, which will be conquered by later and improved lines. (2009 [1859]: 117)

Darwin is writing, of course, at the height of worldwide British colonial expansion. It may be the case that, with the establishment of civil society, "only an artificial barrier" prevents our sympathies from extending to men of all races; but, Darwin adds, "if such men are separated from [us] by great differences in appearance or habits, experience unfortunately shews us how long it is, before we look at them as our fellow-creatures" (146). It seems the pace of imperial progress, and genocidal struggle over territory and resources, will outrun the time needed to naturalize a sympathetic recognition of strange others – for instance, through our learning to relish (rather than be repulsed by) Darwin's catalogs of aesthetic variation among different races (see Duncan, 2020: 61–64). In a startling upset of the ratio of cultural evolution to biological evolution, instinctive hatred rides the revolutionary tempo of human history's "great leap forward," while the development of the moral sense crawls along in the slow time of a gradualist natural history. "Nevertheless the difference in mind between man and the higher animals, great as it is, certainly is one of degree and not of kind" (151): what appears to be a difference in kind is the product of an ongoing history of violence. This logic also governs the conflation of racial difference with difference between species – the product of that history of violence, retrojected as a moral cause. The extermination of hideous close relatives is the condition for that final dilation of fellow-feeling across the horizon of being which signifies our achievement of full, authentic "humanity": completing by literalizing the symbolic operation of "overrepresentation," in Sylvia Wynter's argument, that makes a particular "ethnoclass" – "the Caucasian" or his hyper-civilized descendant – identical with the human species (Wynter, 2003: 260, 314–326). Our visceral aversion to those close relatives encodes our recognition of them as ecological competitors, the more intransigently different from us for being almost but not quite the same as us – apparitions of the uncanny valley. Soliciting our appreciation of the relativity of aesthetic judgment across cultures and races, even as we may still find local differences grotesque or appalling, *The Descent of Man* inculcates in its readers the divided consciousness, split between tempo-rally conditioned affects, that brands human nature – and may yet forestall our ascension to full humanity.

11.5   The Exterminating Angel

The savage races, doomed to disappear into the extinction gap, play an anomalous role in Darwin's human history.[11] Their fate is prescribed in the place Darwin allots them in the evolutionary transition from prehu-man to fully human being. Standing on the near edge of that transition, the "lowest savages" instantiate an unsettling moral and cognitive blank-ness – a breach, or syncope, rather than a smooth progressive link, in the developmental process:

> If we look back to an extremely remote epoch, before man had arrived at the dignity of manhood, he would have been guided more by instinct and less by reason than are the lowest savages at the present time. Our early semi-human progenitors would not have practised infanticide or polyandry; for the instincts of the lower animals are never so perverted as to lead them regu-larly to destroy their own offspring, or to be quite devoid of jealousy. (66)

The advance from semihuman ancestor to the dignity of manhood requires a weakening – a failure – of instinct, in order for reason to be able to over-ride it: a gear-shift that takes the form of a horrible moral collapse. This is the dialectical negative of that imaginatively enriched enduring present through which reason can generate moral deliberation. And the creatures that exemplify this negative state – devoid of strong regulative instinct and reason alike – are the "lowest savages at the present time," an anachronis-tic, embarrassing, repellent remainder, lingering beyond the timeline of evolutionary succession, at least until their anticipated extinction.

In a footnote to the second edition of *The Descent of Man*, Darwin cites a comment by one of the book's reviewers:

> Mr. Darwin finds himself compelled to reintroduce a new doctrine of the fall of man. He shews that the instincts of the higher animals are far nobler than the habits of savage races of men, and he finds himself, therefore, com-pelled to re-introduce, – in a form of the substantial orthodoxy of which he appears to be quite unconscious, – and to introduce as a scientific hypoth-esis the doctrine that man's gain of knowledge was the cause of a temporary

but long-enduring moral deterioration as indicated by the many foul customs, especially as to marriage, of savage tribes. (66)

The theological theme was already made explicit, one year after the publication of Darwin's first edition, by Reade in *The Martyrdom of Man*. In Reade's polemically secular transposition of Christian providential history, humanity is crucified upon the dialectic between sympathy and extermination:

> At first the sympathy by which the herd is united is founded only on the pleasures of the breeding season and the duties of the nest .... But this sympathy is extended and intensified by the struggle for existence; herd contends against herd, community against community; that herd which best combines will undoubtedly survive; and that herd in which sympathy is most developed will most efficiently combine. Here, then, one herd destroys another, not only by means of teeth and claws, but also by means of sympathy and love. The affections, therefore, are weapons, and are developed according to the Darwinian Law. Love is as cruel as the shark's jaw, as terrible as the serpent's fang (1872: 445).

Reade's analysis generates a dismal forecast of perpetual war as the engine of human progress:

> Thus war will, for long years yet to come, be required to prepare the way for freedom and progress in the East; and in Europe itself, it is not probable that war will ever absolutely cease until science discovers some destroying force, so simple in its administration, so horrible in its effects, that all art, all gallantry, will be at an end, and battles will be massacres which the feelings of mankind will be unable to endure. (1872: 505)

As well as sketching a blueprint of contemporary British history – ostensibly at peace within Europe, while exporting war and famine across the earth – Reade's prognosis is eerily prophetic of twentieth-century specters of global, civilization-scale destruction.

H. G. Wells identified the moral and political impetus for his *Outline of History* in the carnage of the First World War:

> War becomes a universal disaster, blind and monstrously destructive; it bombs the baby in its cradle and sinks the food-ships that cater for the non-combatant and the neutral. There can be no peace now, we realize, but a common peace in all the world; no prosperity but a general prosperity. But *there can be no common peace and prosperity without common historical ideas.* Without such ideas to hold them together in harmonious co-operation, with nothing but narrow, selfish, and conflicting nationalist traditions, races and peoples are bound to drift towards conflict and destruction. ... A sense of history as the common adventure of all mankind is as necessary for peace within as it is for peace between the nations. (1919–1920, 1: 2)

A common human history will provide the script (Wells hopes) for the universal sympathy Darwin had imagined future humanity marching toward, across the killing fields of empire. Later, revelations of the Nazi death camps and Cold War scenarios of nuclear annihilation would give a fresh impulse to the writing of human natural history, and to ancillary new disciplines such as ethology, sociobiology, and evolutionary psychology. Now, in the shadow of biosphere-scale disaster – mass extinctions, and civilizational and ecological collapse – the genre flourishes again.

Notes

1 On Enlightenment human exceptionalism see Duncan, 2019: 9, 31–53, 202n27.
2 On *The Descent* as conjectural history see Palmeri, 2016: 165–178.
3 Boyd reaffirms the analogical method of comparative historicism that Darwin himself derived from novelistic refinements of Enlightenment conjectural history. See Griffiths, 2016: 216–237.
4 See Richards, 2017; Prum, 2017; Duncan, 2020: 51–73.
5 Further references given by page.
6 On affirmations of this division by Darwin's contemporaries (Charles Lyell, T. H. Huxley, and Alfred Russel Wallace), see Richards, 1987: 161–164.
7 For an analysis of critical treatments of Darwin and nineteenth-century fiction, see Griffiths, 2016: 230–237.
8 The cause is that magic bullet, "a change in DNA."
9 Robert Ardrey's *The Territorial Imperative: A Personal Inquiry into the Animal Origins of Property and Nations* (1966), the second of four books on "the animal origins and nature of man," was published in the same year as the English translation of Konrad Lorenz's ethological treatise *On Aggression* (1966). Desmond Morris's *The Naked Ape: A Zoologist's Study of the Human Animal* appeared the following year.
10 Arthur Conan Doyle's prehistoric romance *The Lost World* (1912) features a climactic genocide of "ape-men," identified as prehuman ancestors rather than a collateral human species. Wells (1921) resumes the theme in his tale "The Grisly Folk."
11 Patrick Brantlinger argues that Darwin and fellow evolutionists (Huxley and Herbert Spencer) reinforced a normative "extinction discourse" in nineteenth-century natural history. Brantlinger, 2003: 21–29, 164–182.

CHAPTER 12

Conscience after Darwin

Patrick Fessenbecker and Nikolaj Nottelmann

12.1 Introduction: Conscience Before Darwin

In one of the finer examples of the old saw that to explain a thing is to kill it, Charles Darwin destroyed the conscience by justifying it. By explaining how moral self-reflection could have appeared as an ordinary stage in the natural history of the human being, he stripped the conscience of its air of transcendence (something he did intend to do) and therefore of its authority (something he did not). Although the secularization of the conscience in Western thought did not begin or end with Darwin, his argument for the contingent historical origins of moral "intuitions" played a decisive role in undermining received religious and rationalistic moral systems. Authoritative appeals to moral intuitions would return, but they had lost their force. By 1903, G. E. Moore could only assert that the goodness moral intuitions tracked was a nonnatural property about which very little more might be said, thus revealing how the demonstration of the possibility of their evolution left such intuitions normatively denuded (Moore, 1993: 13). The absence of any attempt at a more substantive account of moral feeling paid a quiet tribute to Darwin: in the history of ideas as well as in politics, it is the silent concessions that matter most.

Destroying the conscience, however, was by no means something Darwin set out to do. Rather, he felt the need to explain human morality because it offered grounds for a potentially decisive objection to the developing theory of natural selection. As Robert Richards writes, "Darwin expended considerable effort on a theory of moral evolution, because he judged the moral sense, or conscience, to be by far the most important distinguishing feature of human nature" (1987: 207). A demonstration that humans had evolved via natural selection that could not explain their capacity for moral action was not, Darwin concluded, much of a demonstration at all. Grasping the bull by the horns, then, he set out to show how the faculty that many of his contemporaries viewed as the voice of God in man was simply the result of natural history.

"Conscience" is not a univocal term in historical or contemporary usage, a fact that has perhaps contributed to its durability.[1] Among the quite different elements of human moral life the concept has denoted are a personal set of core commitments, moral knowledge more generally, an emotional or affective force that motivates moral action, and most broadly the capacity to reflect on any or all of these. Positing a faculty that theoretically unifies these capacities, the conscience thus sits in a powerful position in psychic life, bringing the self new facts in an emotionally potent way. As Paul Strohm puts it, "conscience appears to speak from within as interior knowledge … but shows definite marks of a more expansive exterior knowledge as well" (2011: 10). In Victorian England, this doubleness made the conscience seem a vital source of evidence about the divinely governed nature of the universe. "In this special feeling," the prominent theologian John Henry Cardinal Newman explained, "lie the materials for the real apprehension of a Divine Sovereign and Judge" (1874: 82).

Alfred Russel Wallace, Darwin's close associate for much of his career, was certainly not a Christian in Newman's mold, yet in many ways he agreed with this analysis. In 1864, Wallace published an account of the evolution of human moral development similar to Darwin's. But by 1869 he had changed his mind, concluding that the moral faculties could not have been developed via natural selection and must have a spiritual source (Richards, 1987: 183–184). So, while natural selection might have produced the human body, something else had formed the human soul. The distinction did not go unnoticed: as *The Dublin Review* put it, "Had Alfred Wallace, instead of Charles Darwin, been the conspicuous author of the theory of organic evolution, it would never have given rise to an outcry on the part of theologians" (Anonymous, 1889). Grasping the power of accounts like Newman's – the moral sense as the last, best demonstration of the divine nature of humanity – is essential for understanding Darwin's turn to moral philosophy.

12.2   Darwin on Human Conscience

In Darwin's own words, he was "as ignorant as a pig" about moral philosophy before studying with James Mackintosh, the brother-in-law of his uncle Josiah Wedgwood II (Darwin, 1969: 66). This experience exercised a decisive influence on Darwin's moral-philosophical views, views that, as Richards explains, are in many ways a "biologizing of Mackintosh's ethical system" (1987: 116). In an 1839 manuscript on Mackintosh's *Dissertation on the Progress of Ethical Philosophy,* Darwin drafted the central ideas that, sometimes *verbatim*, were much later to form the backbone of chapter 3 of *Descent*. Against "sensationalists" like William Paley and Jeremy Bentham, who held that moral motivations were acquired by reinforced associations between pleasures and behaviors, Mackintosh and subsequently Darwin argued that altruistic instincts form the basis of moral behavior.[2] The characteristic feeling of repugnancy associated with particular vile acts and shared broadly across cultures, they argued, is best explained by an innate motivational-phenomenal mechanism.

Mackintosh, however, could not explain why human basic social instincts are universally shared, or why they would spontaneously deter us from action types that we would also deem inappropriate by rational reflection on their typical consequences. In an 1838 draft, Darwin proposed the following groundbreaking solution to the problem:

> Two classes of moralists: one says our rule of life is what *will* produce the greatest happiness, – The other says we have a moral sense. – But my view unites both & shows them to be almost identical & what *has* produced the greatest good or rather what was necessary for [the] good of all *is* the instinctive moral sense, ... In judging of the rule of happiness we must look *far forward* & to the *general* action – certainly because it is the result of what [has] *generally* been best for our good *far back*. (Gruber, 1974: 390)

In other words, a social instinct motivating us to do what is for the common good is a human universal, exactly because this is the kind of instinct we should inherit from our ancestors. On this model, altruistic instincts win out against opposing egoistic instincts in hereditary transmission because of use inheritance: "It is probable that becomes instinctive which is repeated under many generations" (Gruber, 1974: 402). In general, since our proximate ancestors were rational beings, they would have organized themselves to do what was for their collective best. Acting this way would have become habitual. Over many generations humans increasingly would have been born with an instinctive preference for their ancestors' habitual rational behavior, until such instincts were universally shared. This would explain the harmony between rational judgment and instinctive feeling.

Soon, however, Darwin saw why this model required significant modifications. The key challenges came from entomology. Henry Lord Brougham pointed out that some insects act on altruistic instincts that could not possibly seem rational from their perspective, for example, a female wasp's suicidal provisions for offspring hatched after her death (1839: I:18). Other entomologists alerted Darwin to the relevant fact that social insects display marvelous patterns of instinctive altruistic behavior, but could not possibly transmit their habits to offspring, since as neuters they have none

(Richards, 1987: 144). This underlines a general structural problem with Darwin's original account: why would individuals be motivated to engage in altruistic behavior to begin with, given they have no prior instincts for it? Without such instincts, it would be hard to explain how nonrational social animals acquired hereditary altruistic habits. And without such habits, there would be nothing to solidify into heritable instincts.

In response to these problems, Darwin came to maintain that human conscience is not *merely* an instinct shared with social animals, but also includes the more advanced capacity of *engaging* said instinct in response to intelligent reflections on planned or remembered behavior (2006b [1871], 818). Thus, when we humans manifest our natural proclivity for reflecting on our self-perceived antisocial behavior, we manifest our social instinct in the form of characteristic negative phenomenal experiences. Our aversion to such experiences not only deters antisocial behavior but also motivates our acceptance of rules against it:

> At the moment of action, man will no doubt be apt to follow the stronger impulse; and though may occasionally prompt him to the noblest deeds, it will far more commonly lead him to gratify his own desires at the expense of other men. But after their gratification, when past and weaker impressions are contrasted with the ever-enduring social instincts, retribution will surely come. Man will then feel dissatisfied with himself, and will resolve with more or less force to act differently for the future. This is conscience; for conscience looks backwards and judges past actions, inducing the kind of dissatisfaction, which if weak we call regret, and if severe remorse. (2006b [1871], 829)

Thus, our basic social instincts may have entered our evolutionary history long before we became capable of self-reflection or rational social behavior. Moreover, it is now explained how, once they began reflecting on their con- duct, our ancestors would be motivated to accept altruistic rule systems.[3] For Darwin, then, "conscience" primarily denotes the phenomenally mani- fested moral sense in the context of intelligent reflection. But for Darwin, a clear account of this phenomenal manifestation was intimately connected with the nature of altruistic motivation, a conjoining of faculties that ulti- mately made the conscience the basic source of moral knowledge.

Inspired by studies of neuter insects Darwin came to see group selec- tion as a key mechanism in the evolutionary history of our moral sense. Altruistic neuter insects are disposed only to sacrifice themselves for their colony. By doing so, they assist in the reproduction of their queen and bolster the fitness of their hive or colony in its competition with other communities within their species. Similarly, human or protohuman social groups with an internal dominance of strong altruistic traits could have outperformed – or even defeated and exterminated – groups of less altruistic humans, until only altruists remained alive (2006b [1871], 824).

Via this group selectionist element, Darwin's mature theory of the moral sense thus explained why enclaves of egoists or extreme kin chauvinists had not survived to the present day: they would have simply lost out to communities of altruists in the larger struggle for existence. Then, too, his appeal to the natural selection of communities addressed the objection that altruistic dispositions could hardly be favored by natural selection at the level of individual organisms, since by definition genuine altruism is not to the individual altruists' advantage.

This approach involved a fundamental change from Darwin's early approach to morality. As *The Origin of Species* has it:

> [C]an we doubt that … individuals having any advantage, however slight, over others, would have the best chance of surviving and reproducing their kind? On the other hand, we may feel sure that any variation in the least degree injurious would be rigidly destroyed. (2006a, 502)

This must also apply when the relevant units of selection are entire human collectives. Darwin's theory implies that the best social instincts manifest in a "good conscience" only when the actions they inspire improve a group's competitive edge. So, by the logic of natural group selection, this is the only stable universal configuration of the human moral sense. Now, since, by definition, the moral sense is directed toward the moral good, and moral verdicts require universality, Darwin was committed to identifying the moral good with the optimal fitness conditions of a human community:

> the term general good, may be defined as the means by which the greatest possible number of individuals can be reared in full vigor and health, with all their faculties perfect, under the conditions to which they are exposed. (2006b [1871], 833)

This move drastically breaks with Darwin's original idea in 1838–1839 of besting Mackintosh's theological explanation of the curious harmony between human moral instincts and moral reasoning. In his early manuscripts on conscience, Darwin followed Mackintosh in accepting a general hedonistic criterion of moral rightness ("the greatest happiness"). By the logic of Darwin's mature group selectionism this criterion must go. Societies prioritizing happiness over effective unhappy proliferation will not tend to dominate in the long run. Contrary to his original intentions, Darwin had not vindicated an intuitionistic normative ethics, but entirely replaced it with a naturalistic reductionism. The sense in which we *ought* to follow the lead of our social instincts is only the sense in which a pointer dog *ought* to point, since this is its nature. Similarly, we ought to do what our moral sense approves only in the sense that being disposed to do so is in our actual evolved psyche:

> The imperious word *ought* seems merely to imply the consciousness of a persistent instinct, either innate or partly acquired, serving him as a guide, though liable to be disobeyed. We hardly use the word *ought* in a metaphorical sense when we say hounds ought to hunt, pointers to point, and retrievers to retrieve their game. (2006b [1871], 829)[4]

This reductionism, as Darwin clearly recognizes, implies a curious relativism, since our universal instincts could very easily have been attuned very differently:

> If for instance, to take an extreme case, men were reared under precisely the same conditions as hive-bees, there can hardly be a doubt that our unmarried females would, like worker-bees, think it a sacred duty to kill their brothers, and mothers would strive to kill their fertile daughters, and no one would think of interfering. (2006b [1871], 819)

In this case, fratricide would be morally right, since it would be in a human hive community's best evolutionary interest.

This conclusion has troubling implications for the ways human communities ought to treat their "weaker" members. In the first case, a community should not tolerate members that contribute negatively to the group's overall fitness, whether it be by their neediness, their antisocial behavior, or their transmissions of inferior hereditary traits. In a notorious passage in chapter 5 of *Descent*, Darwin seems to admit as much:

> There is reason to believe that vaccination has preserved thousands, who from a weak constitution would formerly have succumbed to small-pox. Thus, the weak members of civilized societies propagate their kind. No one who has attended to the breeding of domestic animals will doubt that this must be highly injurious to the race of man. (2006b [1871], 873)

Also, it seems clear that any community ought uncompromisingly to prioritize its own proliferation over the welfare of outgroup organisms. The refusal to care for other groups, even outright genocide if need be, is simply nature's way. Even if Darwin does not (as he logically should) explicitly approve of the extermination of less competitive groups standing in harm's way, in *Descent* he often treats the topic with a callous matter-of-factness:

> as it has everywhere been observed that savages are much opposed to any change of habits .... decreasing numbers will sooner or later lead to extinction; the end, in most cases, being promptly determined by the inroads of increasing and conquering tribes. (2006b [1871], 913)

Curiously, however, such cynicism is purged from chapter 3 of *Descent*, where Darwin develops his moral theory. It seems quite plausible that Darwin's personal conscience could not stomach the obvious implications of his own central theses. Throughout the chapter, norms, cultures, habits, actions, and even instincts are compared on a normative scale completely alien to a naturalistic reductionism: social impulses are "higher" or "nobler," whereas egoistic impulses are "lower." Some rules of conduct are "higher" than others, predominantly those associated with Western societies closer to "the highest stage of moral culture" (2006b [1871]: 835). In a characteristic concluding passage, Darwin maintains:

> [Man's] sympathies became more tender and widely diffused, so as to extend to the men of all races, to the imbecile, the maimed, and other useless members of society, and finally to the lower animals, – so would the standard of his morality rise higher and higher. And it is admitted by moralists of the derivative school [the sensationalists] and by some intuitionists, that the standard of morality has risen since an early period in the history of man. (2006b [1871], 836)

Thus spake a tender-hearted humanist, an admirer of Mackintosh's universalist intuitionism. The highest moral culture, as Darwin portrays it here, is a culture completely oblivious to the moral good by Darwin's own naturalistic definition. Due to his own troubled conscience, Darwin left us a highly conflicted account of human conscience and its proper place in cultural and political practice.

12.3 Evolutionary Ethics after Darwin: Problems and Potentialities

12.3.1 *The Naturalistic Fallacy*

The contingency of moral norms Darwin hinted at in his discussion of insect fratricide became an explicit component of many reactions to evolutionary ethics, both approving and disapproving, in the next generation of thinkers. One of the most influential responses was G. E Moore's contention that evolutionary ethics depended upon a "naturalistic fallacy": any attempt to identify "the simple notion which we mean by 'good' with some other notion," he argued, is subject to the decisive objection that it is always open to a simple question: is the thing you say is equivalent to the good really good? (1903: 58). But since it must always be thus open, no attempt at such an identification can be conclusive. And certainly, Darwin seems guilty of this semantic offense, since he explicitly defines "the general good" in terms of group-level evolutionary fitness (2006b [1871]: 833).

Whether Moore's objection is decisive has been a matter of significant debate (see, e.g., Curry, 2006), but perhaps rather less remarked is Moore's own deeply impoverished account of moral knowledge. Moore offers an account of the conscience – "The idea of abstract rightness and the various degrees of the specific emotion excited by it are what constitute the specifically 'moral sentiment' or 'conscience'" (1903: 227) – but contends that it decomposes into cognition of intrinsic value combined with an appropriate emotion: "I am, in fact, unable to distinguish, in its main features, the moral sentiment excited by the idea of rightness and wrongness, wherever it is intense, from the total state constituted by a cognition of something intrinsically evil together with an emotion of hatred directed towards it" (1903: 266). Unfortunately and correspondingly, having eliminated the natural feelings of the conscience as moral authorities, Moore is left to assert his own cognitions of intrinsic goodness and evil as simply obvious:

> The answer to it, in its main outlines, appears to be so obvious, that it runs the risk of seeming to be a platitude. By far the most valuable things, which we can know or can imagine, are certain states of consciousness, which may be roughly described as the pleasures of human intercourse and the enjoyment of beautiful objects. (237)

One gets the sense that Moore knew things had gone awry. "It must be confessed," he concludes, "that some of the attributions of intrinsic value, which have seemed to me to be true, do not display that symmetry and system which is wont to be required of philosophers" 270). Like Darwin, Moore did not set out to reveal the emptiness of the moral sense: he too was trying to put it on a firmer ground. But what Moore's *Principia Ethica* reveals is that once one strips away the naturalistic elements of the conscience there is little left to work with.

12.3.2   Must Naturally Evolved Conscience Be Disenfranchised?

Indeed, the specter of evolution has continued to haunt intuitionist ethics. Peter Singer's more recent work sees exorcizing the ghost of evolved conscience as an essential part of recuperating the philosophical validity of real moral intuitions (2005). In what Scott James has aptly named an "Argument from Idiosyncrasy," Singer conducts an evolutionary debunking of evolved conscience's moral-epistemic authority (2011: 171–172): our evolved moral sense represents only an idiosyncratic response to the evolutionary needs of units of selection (whether those be genes, organisms, or groups). Had those needs been different, as they easily could have been, our moral sense would have offered us different directions. Hence, our moral sense cannot reveal anything about what morally *must* be the case. But, on a traditional conception, moral norms are absolute. So, evolved conscience cannot reveal moral truth. At this point, of course, typical sociobiologists are more than happy to let go of any absolutist conception of moral truth, but Singer sticks to his intuitionist guns. The uptake is that ethical action must be based on "intuitive propositions of real clearness and certainty" (2005: 351). Such intuitions could only be those for which we may safely reject an evolutionary genealogical account in favor of a genuine "rational basis" (351). Evolved conscience, as Darwin conceived of it, must be *ignored* in the moral life. Some modern philosophers have suggested that we ought even enhance this genuine moral reasoning system by using drugs and neurosurgery to repress our merely natural moral instincts (Persson and Savalescu, 2012).

One naturalistic response to the argument from idiosyncrasy is to deny the seemingly implicit assumption that basic conscientious judgments stand in need of justification, by intuition or otherwise. As submitted by Michael Ruse: "All one can offer is a causal argument to show why we hold ethical beliefs. But once this argument is offered, we can see that that is all that is needed" (1986: 102). If the calls of conscience require no justification, then Singer's argument does not undermine their authority. This response would seem problematic in more than one way, however. First, as noted by Paul Strohm, emphatic appeals to conscience may conflict (2011: 77). One drafted soldier may feel obliged to go to war, while another feels equally obliged to refuse military service. From the Darwinian supposition of the uniformity of genuinely authoritative conscience claims, Ruse could only deduce that at most one such conflicting claim is genuinely expressive of conscience, thus requiring no justification. But now we have no obvious way to decide which claim that is. Secondly, it is unclear that the argument from idiosyncrasy is ultimately about moral epistemology, as much as it is about the metaphysics of moral norms. If one insists that by their nature moral norms are eternal, the charge sticks that, whatever an accidentally shaped conscience authoritatively tracks, it cannot be moral truth.

12.3.3 The Rational Authority of Conscience

From a very different perspective, the neo-Hegelian philosopher Anthony O'Hear similarly disputes the rational status of the evolved conscience. "What self-consciousness looks for," he writes, "is an unforced recognition from the other, one which respects me for the qualities which make me what I am" (1997: 126). Such pointed discriminatory recognition, often of past actions, requires the ability to exchange reasons:

> Full self-consciousness then [including moral self-consciousness, a.k.a. conscience] presupposes that the self-conscious agent is a member of a community of other agents, who can judge each other, and as a condition of their judging, express and convey their judgments linguistically. (122)

At this point Darwin appears to be in big trouble. On his account, conscience's motivational force lies in the afflicted subject's basic aversion to the characteristic mental pain of remorse, not, in the first instance, in their quest for public recognition of their practical reasons. But why should other members of an agent's community endorse their aversion to certain pains (remorse and regret) as a sufficient reason for their conduct? After all, we often deem that an agent ought to do unpleasant things for the common good, such as undertake jury duty or take care of a colicky baby. And isn't a good conscience ultimately about giving oneself the green light as seen from the perspective of one's fellows?[5]

An orthodox naturalistic reductionist must reply that this theory puts the cart before the horse: we seek the recognition of our fellows because our conscience motivates us thus. And the reasons we exchange in mutual recognition are only approved via the reflective application of our social instincts. Those reasons happen to be universally recognized, because we share our basic social instincts as members of the same biological species. It is in our attendance to those deep instincts that we confront our shared humanity, not in the church or the public forum. The orthodox Darwinian W. K. Clifford waxed poetic on this point:

> From the dim dawn of history, and from the inmost depth of any soul, the face of our father Man looks out upon us with the fire of eternal youth in his eye, and says – "Before Jehovah was, I am!" (1999: 121)[6]

But why should we heed our conscience, then? Simply because its phenotypical pronouncements constitute the ultimate ledger in the field that we call the ethical. No further justification is called for. Even if formally the question is an open one, in practice it must be closed: we do not accept practices as ethically right, if our social instincts militate against them (for this response, see, e.g., Richards, 1987: Appendix 2; or Ruse, 1986).

12.3.4   Antisocial Conscience

Making our social instincts the highest court of appeal grants them a perhaps unwarranted degree of authority. What, after all, can Darwin say about conscientious objections to *social* behavior? Couldn't (and shouldn't) a perfectly functional human individual sometimes feel compunction about being *too* social, such as doing too much to fit in with their fellows? Indeed, doesn't moral progress often depend on just such dissent? "The desire for psychological security, which is manifested especially in a craving for respect from our fellow-men," Timothy Potts writes, "is almost certain … to come into conflict with conscience on one issue or another and, in nine cases out of ten, the conflict is eventually resolved in favor of respectability, conscience being changed to accord with it" (1980: 68). Darwin's view seems well-equipped to explain moments when immorality is antisocial, but much less well prepared to deal with the alternative.

Rejoinders are, however, possible. Perhaps a well-functioning conscience chastises the desire for social respectability when the relevant group (whose approval the subject seeks) acts contrary to the wider community's fitness, such as when an ex-cop feels remorse for some immoral act performed for the approval of his peers. And Darwin could argue that the unpleasantness of acting with the explicit disapproval of one's community is distinct, phenomenologically and motivationally, from the remorse and regret manifested by conscience proper. For example, here one could think of a Quaker who agrees to bear arms in a just war for the protection of their nation, but later regrets having violated their religion's pacifist code. Such theses could be assessed experimentally. Darwin's theory is not a complacent metaethics, or a merely retrospective just-so story. It is a naturalistic theory with clear prospective commitments regarding the outcome of future moral-psychological research.

12.3.5 Gene Selectionism

Many have objected to Darwin's view for offering too deflationary an account of human moral life, but sociobiology faults Darwin for not going far enough. Arguably the most important development in biology since Darwin's 1859 theory of evolution by natural selection was the discovery of DNA as the primary vehicle of the hereditary transmission of phenotypic traits. This discovery entirely side-railed use inheritance: since habits do not penetrate the molecular genetic code, they cannot affect the hereditary material transmitted to offspring. However, the geneticist "neo-Darwinian" paradigm also threatened to overthrow the most central element of Darwin's view of conscience: the group-level selection of altruistic instincts. If such instincts are encoded in the genome, by definition a carrier's transmission of their genes to their offspring would be disadvantaged relative to fertile organisms with genes coding for less altruistic behavior. In any in-group struggle between individuals, genes coding for genuine altruism would lose out.

A radical solution to this "problem of altruism" is the sociobiology of E. O. Wilson (1975) and Richard Dawkins (1976). Their proposal is simply to *eliminate* altruism as a biological explanandum. Their gene selectionism regards individual genes (or more precisely, gene-type representations in individual genomes) as the only significant units of natural selection. Traits of human persons are only selected for – or against – in the derivate sense that their manifestations affect the selection of the genes whose expressions they are. Obviously, in the relevant sense, genes are mere types of molecule parts. Thus, when sociobiologists make use of the so-called intentional stance and describe genes as ruthless egoists, this could only mean that any gene not involved in coding for effects, which promotes its chances of replication over competing alleles, will have perished.[7] Altruism and egoism at the organismic level are no longer traits of primary biological relevance.

Still, we would expect genes to "sacrifice" one organismic vehicle, if this promotes their replication across all such vehicles. This would explain parental self-sacrifice and would also go some way toward explaining general kin chauvinism. Also, we would expect them to code for reciprocal "tit-for-tat" exchanges, whereby a gene-carrier promotes the replicatory success of their genes by aiding other organisms in replicating *their* genes in the justified expectation of equal returns or better. But altruistic behavior toward genetic "strangers" and without justified hope of a profitable return makes no sense from a gene selectionist perspective. Darwin simply got phenotypic human psychology wrong. What he naively saw as the altruistic behavior of well-functioning organisms was mere kin chauvinism, reciprocal altruism, or pathological cases of dysfunctional genetic programming. Sociobiological versions of evolutionary ethics ultimately paint a bleak and alienating picture of human moral life.[8]

12.4   Conclusion: Gradualism vs. Saltationism, Darwin and the Will

One might sum up Darwin's approach to the conscience as the logical outcome of his stern gradualism applied to human moral life. As he stated in the first edition of *Origin*, "Natural selection can only act by the preservation and accumulation of infinitesimally small inherited modifications" (2006a [1859]: 511). Even distinguished naturalists stomached this claim with difficulty; the geologist Sir Charles Lyell, for instance, contended that the difference between human and animal altruism was of a radical and principled kind (1863). As with Newman and Wallace, to Lyell it seemed impossible for human altruism to appear via gradual natural selection alone. A saltatory mechanism, possibly supernatural, must have been at work.

Above all, *Descent's* countless anthropomorphic anecdotes of altruistic birds and baboons were meant to defeat this important objection. To the circumspect, unbiased etiologist, Darwin argues, the chasm is not anywhere as wide as his critics suppose. What sets the human animal apart is its high level of intelligence, not its basic motivational system or even its powers of reflection. And Darwin would probably have relished the great extent to which modern neurophysiology and cognitive science have corroborated this thesis. We share with nonhuman animals of our common evolutionary lineage the basic motivational structures in the subcortical brain responsible for social behavior such as the *nucleus accumbens* and the *ventral pallidum*. What distinguishes primates, humans not least, is the way our massive *cortices*, the layered structures near the brain's surface, are integrated with those ancient subcortical structures. And the *cortex* is where our intelligent reasoning is presumably supported (Churchland, 2019).

By way of conclusion, we might observe that this insight also fruitfully reframes the perennial philosophical problem of "the unity of the will" (Potts, 1980: 6). Does the human will strive toward one goal (the Good), but due to sin, sometimes get misled as to the proper routes toward that singular goal? Or is the will fundamentally split, such that by their nature, people always pursue two basic goals – the Good and Sin – and must learn to pursue the former goal with more diligence? If all cognitive processes affecting our motivations are filtered through one action-generating system, we have only one will. But if evolution has equipped us with two occasionally conflicting basic instinctive systems – one for our personal fitness and one for the fitness of our community – then our will is split at its root. In a twenty-first century in which action to preserve human communities from global climate change seems so utterly urgent at a social level and so impossible to motivate at the individual level, the Darwinian analysis finds new purchase.

Notes

1 See Guibilini (2016) for a clear explanation of the many different senses of the word.
2 Here and below, we use "altruism" and "altruistic" in the following senses: altruistic acts are acts objectively likely to diminish the agent's personal evolutionary fitness in favor of the fitness of affected others without a justified hope of compensatory reciprocation. In general, altruism names the tendency of a trait (e.g., an instinct) to dispose an agent to an altruistic pattern of behavior (Sober, 1998).

3 By the time he drafted chapter 3 of *Descent*, Darwin had become more cautious of appealing to use inheritance, now only regarded as a hypothesis with "not the least inherent improbability" (2006b [1871], 855).

4 This was a constant in Darwin's ethical thinking from the late 1830s onwards. See also Gruber (1974, 329–330).

5 An original etymological root of the term "conscience" is bearing witness to one's own deed (Potts, 1980: 2–3).

6 Regarding Clifford's Darwinism, see Fessenbecker and Nottelmann (2020).

7 For alternative senses of "gene," see e.g., Griffiths and Stotz (2013). For "the intentional stance," see Dennett (1987).

8 For an introduction to the heated debates over sociobiology, see Alcock (2001) and Driscoll (2018).

CHAPTER 13

Darwin, the Sublime, and the Chronology of Looking

Alexis Harley

In his "Recollections of the development of my mind and character," Charles Darwin complained of a lifelong "fatality" that led him "to put at first my statement & proposition in a wrong or awkward form" (1876–1882: 112). Many dozens of publications deep into his career, he still found himself suffering, he claimed, "as much difficulty as ever in expressing myself clearly and concisely," a professed weakness that he attempted to redress through laborious self-editing (112). The many erasures and additions penciled through his manuscripts, besides the many variations of wording in successive editions of Darwin's published works, confirm that he did worry at his writing. Darwin's struggle to say things, as Gillian Beer has established, was a crucial part of his struggle to think things (2000: xxv). But Darwin's struggle to say things was also in some vital sense a struggle to appeal to his reader, undoubtedly motivated in some part by an anxiety to bring readers to his hard-to-think – and, to many, heretical – ideas about species mutability.

Darwin marshaled a suite of rhetorical and aesthetic devices that helped commend his writing and thinking to a nineteenth-century readership (indeed his complaint about his faltering writing was perhaps one such device, calculated to endear the reader with its performance of humility). Besides acts of performative self-deprecation, Darwin deployed a range of formal strategies to beguile and persuade. Devin Griffiths has compared Darwin's and publisher John Murray's gorgeous, if not entirely success-ful, contrivances for the marketing of *Fertilisation of Orchids* (1862) with the orchid's own strategies to recruit pollinators: both Darwin's book and orchids themselves exhibit adaptations of form that will foster their propagation if they prove attractive to the right audience (2015: 440–445). In a similar vein, I want to suggest that Darwin's writing constitutes his effort to be read, understood, and propagated by his reader – to be selected. Though Darwin claimed late in life "that I have never turned one inch out of my course to gain fame" (1876–1882: 58), his manuscripts, scored through and relentlessly revised, show that he worked constantly at making his ideas intelligible and his writings eligible, for specific correspondents, general readers, reviewers, and publishers.

Eligibility, or "selectability," is one of the concepts on which Darwin's thinking through of sexual and artificial selection puts most pressure. Rather than inhering solely in the entity that is selected, as *Descent of Man* (1871a) shows it is produced in the coconstitutive relationship between selector and selected. Darwin's experience of observing and writing on the voyage of the *Beagle* immersed him in a selective dynamics that complicate the object/agent binary, dynamics that he would come to theorize in his account of evolutionary processes that hinge on aesthetic phenomenology (attraction, taste, erotic feeling). These are sketched out in most detail in *Descent*, the key idea of which, as Ian Duncan puts it, being that "the aesthetic sense is the medium of a specifically human evolution" (Duncan, 2020). But they are everywhere in Darwin's writing: in the *Origin*, where the breeder's capacity to "give elegant carriage and beauty to his bantams, according to his standard of beauty" (1859: 89) provides the reader with a way into understanding how rapidly the back and forth between form and vision (the form of a bird's body, the desiring vision of the breeder) can reshape life; in the coevolution of orchid and moth, nectary and proboscis; and, I show, in a pretheoretical form, in Darwin's early notebooks and his *Beagle* diary.[1]

This chapter turns to Darwin's earliest writing, the *Beagle* diary, in order to illuminate the ways that his phenomenal and aesthetic experience of the natural world was entangled with the processes of both reading and writing about it – and impacted by the anticipation and reality of being read. It argues that this early work anticipates his later conclusions about both variation and about the place of anticipation itself in evolutionary processes that operate through aesthetic phenomenology.[2] I have suggested above that Darwin the writer was the would-be object of his readers' selection. But that also made him a selecting agent, choosing words and modes of expression in anticipation of his readers' responses. In Section 13.1, I turn to Darwin's account in the *Beagle* diary of observing tropical nature. Here the notion of the "selecting agent," or of aesthetic choice-making, is disrupted by the sublime's spectatorial dynamics, which draw agency away from the viewer. In eighteenth-century aesthetic theory, the sublime is roughly parsed as the quality of greatness, a quality that robs the viewer of their capacity to fathom or represent what they see. Darwin attributes his experience of sublimity here to botanical variety. Although variety, as I show in Section 13.2, is more commonly associated in eighteenth-century aesthetic theory with the beautiful, by complicating this association Darwin brings the subject-object confusion of Burkean aesthetics to his thinking of variation. Variation, as Darwin will later show, is simultaneously a cause and an effect of evolutionary relationships. Finally, Section 13.3 traces this baffling of subject and object, of cause and effect, in Darwin's later writing of aesthetically mediated evolutionary relationships (between pigeon-fancier and pigeons in the first chapter of the *Origin* and between songsters, bird and human, and their audiences in *Descent*). This is not to suggest that the evolutionary ideas published from 1859 and beyond were apprehended on the pages of the 1830s; rather, that in writing his aestheticized experience, Darwin apprehended the form or grammar of those ideas.

Such inferences are of course drawn with the benefit of hindsight, which makes easy a reading of young Darwin as always *en route* to his eventual theoretical position. Far from condemning this methodology as a biographical fallacy, I want to build a case for such readings via Darwin's own retrospective analyses of modifications that seem to be developing toward a future – Darwin's present – in which they have become meaningful adaptations. Darwin's writing is thick with seemingly teleological phrasing: the "various contrivances" by which orchids are fertilized; natural selection, which "works solely by and for the good of each" (1859: 201). If his thinking was not exactly teleological, a question much disputed by Darwin's exegetes,[3] his writing nonetheless shows just how much evolutionary relationships disturb narrative sequences: "natural selection works by and for the good of each" assumes a continuous present tense, but of course natural selection has only worked "for the good of each" once selective pressures have whittled into extinction all the maladapted organisms that do not count as "each" because they are no longer extant. Likewise, evolution makes trouble for our demarcation of beginnings (the much-remarked irony of "the origin of species" is that there are no originating coordinates for species, which themselves become mutating categories). It disturbs our plotting of causal sequences. Coevolutionary relationships make particularly obvious trouble for chronologies: a change in one party is retroactively made a purposive contrivance by the other.

This relational temporality is present throughout Darwin's nature, but it is produced perhaps most obviously in Darwin's theorizing of those evolutionary relationships that are mediated by aesthetic phenomenology, where desire is generated by and generates its own object in a temporal loop resistant to tidy sequencing or plotting. Such relationships suggest that life has the properties of language (Darwin certainly pointed out often enough in philological analogies for the genealogy of species that life is *like* language). Its constituents read and write each other, are implicated in relations that could be described as grammatological. In the final phase of this chapter, I will bring the temporality of coevolution to how Darwin reads, writes, and is read. This is, ultimately, to be a defense of reading Darwin in light of present theory that hopes to borrow its arguments from Darwin himself.

13.1   The *Beagle* Diary and the Chronology of Looking

None of these arguments had yet come into being when Darwin wrote the *Beagle* diary, but it is still perhaps the most useful place to locate Darwin's phenomenal experience of writing. He wrote it in the present tense, in the thick of his travels, in close proximity to environments that his reading had prepared him to apprehend with heightened wonder. And he wrote the diary, in significant part, to be read. The young Darwin was, as he recollected in his autobiography, "ambitious to take a fair place among scientific men" (1876–1882: 56), and simultaneously to target a nonexpert readership (the diary would travel through the hands of his sisters and transform into the bestselling *Journal of Researches*). The diary – which was not just an account of his observations, but also a depiction of how Darwin observes – was to recommend both him and his writing to a disparate array of potential readers. The roles of discriminating natural historian and person of aesthetic sensibility, roles that in the 1830s were just beginning to diverge,[4] are conflated in Darwin's writing through the observer's response to teeming variety. This response rehearses the dynamics of the sublime, confounding object and subject, and destabilizing the chronology of looking.

In April 1832, a twenty-three-year-old Charles Darwin left the *Beagle* to collect insects and reptiles in the tropical rainforests of Brazil. Writing up this venture back on board, in a present tense that collapses the experiencing, the remembering, and the writing, Darwin seems to be moved to raptures over the variety of species he has encountered in the forest:

> If the eye is turned from the world of foliage above, to the ground, it is attracted by the extreme elegance of the leaves of numberless species of Ferns & Mimosas – Thus it is easy to specify individual objects of admiration; but it is nearly impossible to give an adequate idea of the higher feelings which are excited; wonder, astonishment & sublime devotion fill & elevate the mind. (2001: 59)

These remarks display a recurring motif in the *Beagle* diary, a destabilization of the temporality of the subject's and object's relating. The *eye* (notably not *my eye* or *I*) is *turned* and *attracted*, somehow summoned by what it will see before it has seen it. The mind's inability to calculate the number of plant species is ascribed, in another act of subject-object confusion, to the numberlessness of the plants themselves. Passively, and as if from without, this mind is "filled with wonder, astonishment and sublime devotion," though those might seem to be modes of its own manufacture. This passage rehearses a similar scene of bewildering variety recorded in the diary a few weeks earlier: " – if the eye attempts to follow the flight of a gaudy butter-fly, it is arrested by some strange tree or fruit; if watching an insect one forgets it in the stranger flower it is crawling over. – if turning to admire the splendour of the scenery, the individual character of the foreground fixes the attention" (2001: 42).

Here again the eye surrenders its agency to what it sees. In the last of the three conditionals, the viewer disappears all together: "the individual character of the foreground" both does the work of fixing attention, and, in Darwin's rapturous syntax, seems to be the subject of the participle, turning to admire the splendor of – itself. As Darwin works out on the page this experience of his own sensory and cognitive subordination to variety, he substitutes the same pronoun for both the eye and the butterfly, so that it becomes unclear which is arrested by the strange tree or fruit. Watching an insect, the eye loses itself in the flower as if Darwin were the insect rifling for nectar, in turn an image that foreshadows Darwin's theorization of the pollinator–flower relationship some thirty years hence. Perhaps anticipating that he is foreshadowing something, Darwin concludes this passage: "The mind is a chaos of delight, out of which a world of future & more quiet pleasure will arise. – I am at present fit only to read Humboldt; he like another Sun illumines everything I behold" (2001: 42).

While Alexander von Humboldt's *Personal Narrative of Travels to the Equinoctial Regions of the New Continent* (1819–1829) is the acknowledged influence in this passage (indeed, Darwin half implies that he is reading Humboldt and writing in his diary in the same moment), there is more than a hint of William Wordsworth in his anticipation of the tranquil recollection of present emotion. Wordsworth's model of cognition, where recollection becomes revelation in the writing, may illuminate some of what is happening here. These passages depend on the recall of sensory experience. In rendering that recollected experience on the page, Darwin begins to instantiate the grammar of coevolutionary relationships, where the coconstitutive chatter between subject and object becomes a vehicle for the generation of variation. In Darwin's future writing, variation constitutes the material on which natural selection operates. It is the already differentiated ground on which differentiating pressures work, simultaneously the cause and effect of evolutionary relationships. Natural selection both works on variation and, through that work, produces "endless diversity of structure" (Darwin, 1862: 349), "endless forms most beautiful" (Darwin, 1859: 490). The sentences in Darwin's diary about his apprehension of variety blur subject and object, prefiguring the way he comes to blur cause and effect in his thinking about variation. His theorization of both the temporality of evolutionary relationships, and the role of the aesthetic in evolutionary processes, emerges from a writing experience that mediates between sensorium and world.

As Darwin's overt allusion to Humboldt and his tacit invocation of Wordsworth imply, tracking the relationship between sensory experience, the experience of writing, and Darwin's theorization of the aesthetic reveals the concomitant importance of his reading to how he encounters and interprets the world. Darwin's representation of himself reading Humboldt in the very moment that he writes in his diary suggests the dynamism of his relationship to the page. He is, simultaneously, reader and writer – reading and writing are, perhaps, facets of the same relational process. What Darwin reads does not exert a unidirectional influence on his thinking or feeling; rather, he transforms the text's significance as he reads – even if the unfolding effect of this transformation only begins to become apparent as Darwin is in turn read.

13.2   Variety and Variation

In the passages quoted above, Darwin treats the variety of life-forms in the Brazilian forest as a trigger for apprehension of the sublime, and in this he draws on and revises the treatment of variety as a category taken up by eighteenth-century aesthetic theory. In later life, Darwin claimed Milton's *Paradise Lost* to have been his "chief favourite" and the book he chose to take on excursions from the *Beagle* (1876–1882: 61). Milton's poem deploys variety formally, in contrasting ideas, images and syntactical structures, and thematically. The angel Raphael compares the various beauties of Paradise to that of Heaven: "God hath here Varied his bounty so with new delights, / As may compare with Heaven" (Milton, 1667: 5, ll.430–432). The sublime allure of the rebel angel-turned-serpent is captured by the poem's narrator in his baffling variety, the "surging maze" of his unfathomable coils and colors. A lengthy simile describing the serpent's veering, shifting progress toward Eve concludes: "So vary'd he, and of his tortuous train / Curl'd many a wanton wreath, in sight of Eve, / To lure her eye." (9, ll.516–518).

These lines are printed above the word "Variety" on the title page of William Hogarth's *Analysis of Beauty* (1753), where they supplement

Hogarth's sketch of a serpentine line with a tiny snake's head (the Hogarthian "line of beauty") imprisoned within a transparent pyramid. Between his inscription in the 1660s and Darwin's reading in the 1830s, Milton's serpent becomes simultaneously the type of beauty and of variety. In the creation-and-fall story of Genesis that *Paradise Lost* revises, Satan brings death to the organic realm; with that in mind, Hogarth's treatment of variety as serpent figures variety as an agent of death. Darwin's aestheticization of variety as he recalls wandering, *Paradise Lost* in pocket, through the forests of Brazil potentially preempts both his own treatment of variation as a cause and effect of aesthetic phenomenology, as well as variation as intimately bound up with death – or, in the geological scale of his later theory, extinction.

Scale will do vital work in Darwin's theorization of the mutability of life. Changes of scale allow him to imply or conceal qualitative differences (as in the differences between individual death and extinction) as he moves between quantitative categories (individual, variety, species). As Darwin will later show in the *Origin*, the species-making meaning of minute individual variation becomes realized along a scalar axis. From the mid-eighteenth-century, scale entered aesthetic experience through the discourse of the sublime. Darwin's depiction of a mind elevated and bewildered by tropical variety deploys a vocabulary proper to the eighteenth-century philosophers of the sublime that he had read in the late 1820s at Cambridge – Joshua Reynolds and Edmund Burke. But in using their vocabulary to work out his own experience, he transforms their schemata and revises the meaning of scale.

When Darwin remarks in his diary that the forests of Chiloé Island "were incomparably more beautiful" than those of cold climate Tierra del Fuego, he conflates variety with *both* beauty and sublimity: "instead of the dusky uniformity of that country we have the variety of Tropical scenery … such an abundance of elegant forms … the teeming luxuriance of the forests …. This walk called to mind all the delights of the sublime scenery of Brazil" (2001; 245). Burke would surely not have allowed that numberless, "abundant elegant forms" – a proliferation of variation – could excite feelings of the sublime. Reynolds, who claimed that "many little things will not make a great one," seems unlikely, too, to have considered a proliferation of ferns and mimosas sublime. Indeed, Darwin could hardly have mentioned plants less conventionally associated with the sublime: in his grandfather's *The Botanic Garden*, "ferny foliage nestles" (Darwin, 1793; 57), and the mimosa folds "her thin foliage, close[s] her timid flowers" (150).

Barbara Larson argues that what Darwin would make useful in Burke's aesthetic theory was a materialist account of aesthetic emotion that emphasized innate rather than learned responses, and, perhaps more importantly (since Darwin could and did find that materialism elsewhere), "a program dividing the individual under threat, which could be applied to the struggle for life within and without species, countered by a theory of the need for and pleasure found in society" (Larson, 2013: 3). In his aestheticized accounts of botanical variety, though, the young Darwin seems to have disrupted the canonical dichotomy between the sublime and the beautiful. Darwin combines potential sources of distress with potential sources of pleasure: the strange teeming forest is full of elegance, and tropical scenery is as readily described as "beautiful" as it is "sublime." Variety, which Burke (1757) considered beautiful when it is gradual and only sublime when it is sudden or "angular," for Darwin seemed to be indiscriminately both beautiful and sublime. In this, it prefigures Darwin's theorization of variation in the *Origin*. There, variation is both infinitesimal in detail and infinite in potential. Darwin has both to train his readers in apprehending the significance of small differences and to magnify our sense of what variation can produce, collapsing the polarities of the sublime.

Apprehension of the sublime was supposed by Burke and Reynolds to be induced by the greater volume or speed or heft or generality of phenomena relative to the viewer, not just with respect to variety. Reynolds imagines how a great artist with an eye for the sublime should see and represent nature: "He will permit the lower painter, like the florist or collector of shells, to exhibit the minute discriminations, which distinguish one object of the same species from another; while he, like the philosopher, will consider nature in the abstract, and represent in every one of his figures the character of its species" (Reynolds, 1997: 55). Darwin would produce a totalizing theory of nature that *is predicated* on minute discriminations. Under sufficient differentiating environmental pressures, slight differences between flowers or mollusks could retroactively become the ground for the extinction or proliferation of entire genera. Tiny variations could be remade by the future as origin points for species or their abrupt termination.

Ian Duncan finds the evidence for Darwin's Lyellian-gradualist reworking of the sublime in his 1845 *Journal of Researches* and the *Beagle* journal on which the *Journal of Researches* is largely based. Darwin, Duncan writes, "rationalizes and domesticates the sublime by calibrating it to the gradualist scale of everyday life: removing, in so doing, its catastrophic threat" (Duncan, 2013). No surprise that Darwin goes on to do exactly this in *Origin of Species*, writing, for instance: "so profound is our ignorance, and so high our presumption, that we marvel when we hear of the extinction of an organic being; and as we do not see the cause, we invent cataclysms to desolate the world, or invent laws on the duration of the forms of life!" (Darwin, 1859: 73). Darwin's sanguinity in the face of species extinction, an idea that had been seriously credited for only a few decades, seems owing to his refusal to travel the emotional meaning of death along the quantitative axis that is so important to realizations of the sublime. In other words, he does not allow the scale of extinction to make extinction qualitatively different from individual death. A couple of lines in his Red Notebook read "There is no more wonder in extinction of species than of individual" (Darwin, 1980: 67), and, as if to underscore the equivalence between an individual's death and a species' extinction – the insistence that neither species nor individual is prior to the other – in his Notebook B the formulation is reversed, "There is no more wonder in extinction of individuals than of species" (Darwin, 1837–1838: 153e). As several commentators have remarked, Darwin regularly inverts too-ready distinctions between death and life, pleasure and pain, competition and sociability. Beer, for one, offers an account of Darwin's redemptive treatment of extinction as an essentially benign process and "as a corollary of evolution" (Beer, 2009a: 329).[5]

It is a common belief that Darwin's theory of natural selection was still half a decade away from crystallizing when he extolled the sublimity of mimosas and ferns in his *Beagle* diary. But Darwin's writing here in the diary, as he describes the "sublime" tangle of mimosas and ferns, deconstructs the Burkean association of the sublime (with death and extinction) and the beautiful (with sociality and interdependence) in a way that *foreshadows* or even makes the conditions through which he can think of variation (as a differential rate of survival and reproduction) as simultaneously sublime and beautiful, death-dealing and mutualistic. In all this, the temporality of action is superbly wobbly. When do "wonder, astonishment & sublime devotion fill & elevate the mind"? In the moment that Darwin stands in the forest; in the moment, sometime later on board the *Beagle*, that he puts his pen to the page; in the moment that the words are read, and, if so, will his sisters' reading suffice, or does the reading need to be done by the wider public that devours his *Journal of Researches* from 1845 on? When does aesthetic experience inform the theory of natural selection? Or is it the theory of natural selection that informs aesthetic experience?

The *Beagle* diary enacts a conversation between what Darwin has read and what he will write, his theory-to-be. It is of course possible to locate in the *Beagle* diary locutions that (in retrospect) suggest that Darwin's theory was already fermenting: there are two passages in 1832 where Darwin describes animals that "mark the passage" between one species and another

(Darwin, 2001: 85, 109), and a claim in 1834 that nature has "fitted" a people "to the climate & productions of his country" (Darwin, 2001: 224). These could be construed to suggest the transmutationist Darwin already exists. But in the diary's writing and rendering of aesthetic experience there is an even more radical idea than transmutation writ with a clarity largely lost in later published works. This is the idea that Darwin is not personally outside the processes of nature, but thoroughly implicated in them, and implicated in them by virtue of phenomenal, aesthetic experiences.

13.3   The Distributed Agency of Selection

The *Beagle* diary is peppered with reasonably tame, if mildly embarrassing, performances of the young Darwin's erotic disposition – another indication that he is living inside the natural processes that he will come to theorize. In *Descent of Man*, Darwin will venture a generalization about men's sexual aesthetics that shows pronounced parallels with the attitudes of his younger self toward both the comb-wearing, shawl-draped women of Buenos Aires and the tropical picturesque. "The men of each race," he writes, "prefer what they are accustomed to behold; they cannot endure any great change; but they like variety, and admire each characteristic point carried to a moderate extreme" (Darwin, 1871: 2.354). In the unfolding argument of *Descent of Man*, this erotic hesitation between custom and variety will be made to account for the production of (radically de-essentialized) categories of race among humans.

A similar set of tastes supposedly structure the activities of the pigeon-fancier (Darwin is, by all accounts, one of these, writing about pigeon diversification and inheritance in the *Origin*, *Descent of Man*, *Variation Under Domestication*, and *Expression of the Emotions in Man and Animals*). The first chapter of the *Origin* eases Darwin's reader into the logic of natural selection by describing "selection by man," with an emphasis on pigeons. On the one hand pigeon-breeding provides a homely analogy for natural selection; on the other, as we will see, this chapter foreshadows the weirding of causal sequences to which Darwin's theory will return, more explicitly, in *Descent*.

Darwin begins the *Origin* by referring to "domesticated animals" and "cultivated plants" (1859: 4), as if the agent and object of domestication or cultivation are clearly distinguishable. He allows that "our domestic races show adaptation in their structure or in their habits to man's wants or fancies" (1859: 38). But before the reader can get too comfortable with the view that the breeder chooses the shape of the domesticated animal, Darwin clarifies that the human breeder "can never act by selection, excepting on

variations which are first given to him in some slight degree by nature"
(1859: 39). Further dismantling the fantasy of humanity's exceptional
intentionality, Darwin does not allow humans' wants or fancies to arise
through their own spontaneous imaginative agency:

> No man would ever try to make a fantail, till he saw a pigeon with a tail
> developed in some slight degree in an unusual manner, or a pouter till he
> saw a pigeon with a crop of somewhat unusual size; and the more abnor-
> mal or unusual any character was when it first appeared, the more likely it
> would be to catch his attention. (1859: 39)

The variation *catches* the fancier's eye, and like the myriad variations in
the forest that turned and attracted young Darwin's eye, they render the
pigeon-breeding observer – this stand-in for the agency of natural selection – a passive object. And if the pigeon's deviation of structure is given
to it, through no action or effort of its own, so is the breeder's enthusiasm
for variety: "it is human nature", Darwin writes, "to value any novelty,
however slight, in one's own possession" (1859: 39).

Individual pigeons and pigeon-breeders are both constrained by innate
characteristics. The desire for variety and the variation itself can be equally
innate. As if that were not enough to secure the ontological commonality
of putatively mental aesthetic feeling ("wants or fancies") and putatively
material variations in pigeon structure, Darwin moves swiftly to a comparison between animal breeds and languages: "we know nothing about
the origin or history of any of our domestic breeds. But, in fact, a breed,
like a dialect of a language, can hardly be said to have had a definite origin"
(1859: 40). This comparison does not just suggest that both (nonhuman,
material) animals and (human, mental) language have unfathomable genealogies, it also reminds us that they have a *shared* unfathomable genealogy.
Language (like our domesticated breeds) "can hardly be said to have had
a definite origin." That is, there is no abrupt rupture between the prelin-
guistic and the linguistic.

In the absence of such a break, the fanned tail and the unusually sized
crop exist in ontological continuity with the literary flourishes deployed in
Darwin's own writing. A chapter in *Descent of Man* on "the mental powers
of man and the lower animals" sees Darwin bounce back and forth between
considerations of human language development and birds' cultivation of
song repertoires. The structure of his discussion produces an equivalence
between these two development stories, neither one the ground against
which the other is figured. The parataxis within and between these paragraphs functions as an invitation to readers to make their own connections

between adjacent claims about birds and humans. Darwin writes that the "first essays" of young male birds showed "hardly a rudiment of the future song; but as they grow older we can perceive what they are aiming at" (1871: 1. 55). "Essay" is a synonym for "attempt," its obvious meaning here, but it is also the medium via which a young male natural philosopher communicates the rudiments of his future song (or theory). This is perhaps an unlikely pun, but whether Darwin's sentence alludes to Darwin's own early writing as a tentative courtship song to the reader (a variation that is honed and drawn into being by his readership's selective acumen, then amplified and propagated by the attraction it exerts for those readers), this sentence nonetheless mounts a case for the collaboration of the songster and his listener in realizing the song – a song that exists in the listener's clairvoyant desire to hear it before it is even sung.

Comparing the development of birds' courtship songs with the development of human speech, Darwin offers a theory of language as a modification or deviation that is drawn out by the aesthetic preference of its auditors, itself a modification or deviation. Speech begins, he suggests, with "musical cadences" – a variation that Darwin conjectures helped "primeval man" court sexual partners (1871; 1.56). Observations like these explicitly bring language within the fold of Darwinian analysis and underscore the importance for Darwin of the formal, material, aesthetic, and erotic aspects of language as a mechanism of organic change. In turn, by reading for the formal, material, aesthetic variations of his language, by looking at form in detail, we are perhaps better able to happen upon these intimations that Darwin's writing can be understood as inhabiting the same ontological plane as birdsong, where desire makes and is made by the thing it anticipates.

Darwin's comparisons of the genealogy of languages with the genealogy of species are enriched by the revelation that the development of language, or something language-like, both ensues from and mediates the development of species. Darwin makes language both the object and subject of selection, as his language makes *him* both the object and subject of selection. And so too his writings become the simultaneous objects and agents of the struggle for existence – or participants in something like its more generous variant, sexual selection – desiring and in turn reaching to be desired through the formal discriminations of writing and reading.

As others (notably Morton, 2010) have remarked, both languages and Darwin's world, teeming with life, are relational ecologies (indeed, as Morton, understands it, language and the world are the same relational ecology – a point to which I think Darwin's philological analogies get him very close). As Donna Haraway has it: "beings do not preexist their relat-ings" (Haraway, 2002: 6). Her gerunds convey the weird temporality of the coconstitutive relationships that Darwin sketches, in which the signifi-cance of a variation is only realized in its future, in the form that its relat-ings take. If this is the case both for language and other material deviations of structure, then it is also true for Darwin's own writing: its significance is made by the differential pressures to which it is subject, pressures that, in changing over time, change the significance of Darwin's writing. This amounts, I think, to an argument from within Darwin's own writing for reading it in light of the present.

Notes

1 For more on Darwin's studies of domestication, see Chapter 8 by Kathleen Frederickson. For a further discussion of Darwin and human evolution, see Chapter 11 by Ian Duncan.
2 Miranda Butler similarly discusses Darwin's aesthetics and "acoustemology" in the *Beagle* notebooks and the *Voyage* in Chapter 4.
3 See John Lennox's synthesis of over 150 years of debate on this subject (2013).
4 In 1834, "an ingenious gentleman" (William Whewell, according to Sydney Ross) suggested to the newly formed British Association for the Advancement of Science the general adoption of the word "scientist" – "by analogy with *art-ist*" (Whewell [?] quoted in Ross, 1962: 72). This "scientist"-"artist" analogy would coincide with, and ultimately amplify, a new divergence between the discursive practices of the (Romantic) artist and the (rational) natural philoso-pher. Peter Galison has suggested that after about 1830, the ideal natural phi-losopher became no longer "a transcendental Genius improving or idealizing nature" but instead was someone who would practice "self-abnegation" and thereby let nature "'speak for itself' through a set of instrumentalities that min-imised intervention, hamstrung interpretation, and blocked artistic license" (1998: 328). This trajectory away from an explicitly subjective, emotive, aes-thetic empiricism was by no means unidirectional. John Herschel's *Preliminary Discourse* (1830), read enthusiastically by Darwin and widely recognized as *the* nineteenth-century primer on inductive reasoning, is, as George Levine notes, "thick with a Romantic passion for knowledge, a sense of the divine signifi-cance and richness of the natural world" (2006: 25).
5 For more on Darwin's attitude toward extinction, see Chapter 2 by Jesse Oak Taylor and Chapter 5 by Allen MacDuffie.

CHAPTER 14

Instinctive Moral Actions
Darwin and the Ethics of Biology

Angelique Richardson

In 1837, newly returned from the five-year voyage of *HMS Beagle*, Darwin opened Notebook B and began to write against elements of the Enlightenment: "But who with the face of the earth covered with the most beautiful savannahs and forests dare to say that intellectuality is only aim in this world" (Darwin, 1987: 252). Instinct, emotion, and morality would come to sit alongside reason as its vital counterparts. A few weeks after the publication of *The Descent of Man, and Selection in Relation to Sex* (1871), Darwin wrote to the philologist Hensleigh Wedgwood, "We seem to agree about what may be called instinctive moral actions" (Darwin, 1871b). The phrase acts as commentary on Darwin's understanding of biology: a convergence of instincts (associated with the body) and ethics (associated with the mind), which replaced any clear distinction between the life of the body and the mind with a relationship that was one of continuity and exchange. It also demonstrates the challenge that Darwinian biology posed to Cartesian dualism – the separation of mind and body – and its colonial implications in configuring bodies to varying degrees according to a hierarchy that was both racial and sexed as unruly, and in need of subjection to a scientific control that was masculine and European.

By contrast, Darwin plunged humanity into a world of instincts, impulses to action that were products not of reason but of habit, sympathy, fear, anger, or memory; one in which "enduring social instincts," unless impeded by a selfish disregard of others, might be a guide to ethical conduct (Darwin, 1871b). The sensate world was prioritized and the body became the seat of morality, housing a fundamental, instinctive urge toward sympathy:

> the sight of another person enduring hunger, cold, fatigue, revives in us some recollection of these states, which are painful even in idea. We are thus impelled to relieve the sufferings of another, in order that our own painful feelings may be at the same time relieved. In like manner we are led to participate in the pleasures of others. (Darwin, 1871a: 81)

In his next book, *The Expression of the Emotions in Man and Animals*, out the following year (and only a separate book because *The Descent* had grown so big), he set out to understand and explain human–animal kinship, the physiological basis of morality, and the development of social instincts. Contrary to mid-Victorian expectations, the intellect and reason were no longer invariably at the top, with emotion and instinct below.

In this chapter, which offers a counterpoint to readings of Darwin that foreground the expression in his work of sexist or chauvinistic attitudes, I will outline ways in which, as a child of the eighteenth century, he introduced an evolutionary framework which both drew on Enlightenment writers for moral theory and in relationship to sympathy and sensibility, from Edmund Burke, Adam Smith, and David Hume to Jane Austen (see White, 2013), and also called into question elements of Enlightenment thought and concomitant colonial hierarchies of race and sex. Darwin would regularly remind himself not to use the terms higher or lower (although he did not always succeed), first in Notebook B (1837), or in the margins of his 1844 edition of Robert Chambers' *Vestiges of The Natural History of Creation*— "Never use the words higher or lower"—and in a letter to his friend the botanist and explorer J. D. Hooker ten years later (see Darwin, 1854).

Situating Darwin in relation to contemporary political debates over race, slavery, and sex brings into focus the challenge he presented to the notion of racial difference, which held white European men to be biologically superior, and to ideas of biologically determined social roles and behaviors. Darwinian biology allows us to examine behaviors; it doesn't enforce them on us as biologism. Darwin's is the ethical response; biologism is ideologically driven (and generally self-interested). Evolution presented a forceful argument against innatism, and in this it shared significant and often overlooked common ground with the philosophy of John Stuart Mill (see Richardson, 2011).

14.1   Historical Contexts

Darwin envisaged science at its best as impartial, writing of a "pure & disinterested love of Science" (Darwin, 1862b). While history suggests that science is not itself detached from the social and political structures and currents of the world it describes, his assertion was made in good faith. For Darwin, the acute observation on which he set so much store was not separate from the emotions (on which he came increasingly to focus); objectivity does not necessitate detachment. Indeed, seeking to see what was there required some attachment, respect, sympathy, and empathy, the ability for imaginative fellow-feeling. In 1853, Thomas Henry Huxley (who for Thomas Hardy "united a fearless mind with the warmest of hearts and the most modest of manners"; Hardy, June 1878, in Millgate, 1985: 125) had emphasized the need in biology for "a careful combination of the deductive method with the inductive" and for "bringing the powerful aid of the imagination, kept, of course, in due and rigid subordination, to assist the faculties of observation and reasoning" (Millgate, 1985: 125; Huxley, 1853: 248–249).[1]

Attached, emotionally engaged science – bearing the imprint of his passionate relation to his work – went hand-in-hand for Darwin with objective science. His abhorrence at slavery meant he departed from many of his compatriots; the reciprocity of his ethical and scientific commitments allowed him to see the baselessness – and baseness – of contemporary, racist ideas of physical anthropology and polygeny. Even Robert FitzRoy, captain of the *Beagle*, had observed in 1839, "the immense extent and increase of the slave population is an evil long foreseen and now severely felt" (*Narrative of the Surveying Voyages of His Majesty's Ships*, II, 62), writing in 1846 of Maori, "in nearly all the affrays,—the origin of which I have been able to ascertain—the white man appears to have been the aggressor, not always unintentionally" (1969, 6; see Paul et al., 2013: 221). But Darwin's abolitionism was a driving force in his research, as in his politics (see Moore and Desmond, 2009; Brown, 2010). It animated the conversations at home, and the letters of the Darwin siblings. In the early decades of the century, the family were desperate for abolition in the colonies. Recording scenes of abject cruelty toward enslaved people, Darwin's diary entry for August 19, 1836 (later published in the *Voyage of the Beagle*) read: "we finally left the shores of Brazil. I thank God, I shall never again visit a slave-country. ... I will not even allude to the many heart-sickening atrocities which I authentically heard of" (Darwin, 1845: 499). He added that he would not have mentioned such "revolting details" had he not "met with several people" so blinded "as to speak of slavery as a tolerable evil." He wrote to his sister Catherine reiterating his abhorrence at enslavement, and of how this had intensified now that he had witnessed it first hand, and of "almost wishing for Brazil to follow the example of Hayti." He could find some consolation watching from afar "how steadily the general feeling, as shown at elections, has been rising against Slavery" (Darwin, 1833a). Susan, the youngest of his three older sisters, wrote to share her relief when slavery was abolished but lamented that enslaved people would be left for another year "at the mercy of the Planters," who were the ones who would receive compensation. In the same letter she wrote with a sense of respectful wonder, rather than appropriation, of the vegetation of

Sri Lanka, described "in a kind of novel called 'Cinnamon & Pearls'" (Darwin, 1833b) by the early feminist sociologist Harriet Martineau.

The debate that raged in Parliament through the summer of 1833, until the Abolition Bill passed into law on August 28, indicates the extent to which the Darwin family stood against contemporary racist thought. One Tory Lord, Wynford, argued that to abandon "property in the slave" would bring about "an end of all property" (House of Lords, 1832; see also, for example, House of Lords, 1833). Darwin wrote to express his hope that "honest Whigs … will soon attack that monstrous stain on our boasted liberty, Colonial Slavery." Some three decades later, in the first weeks of the American civil war, Darwin remarked to his botanist friend Asa Gray, "Some few, & I am one, even wish to God" that "the North would proclaim a crusade against Slavery"; "Great God how I sh^d like to see that greatest curse on Earth Slavery abolished" (Darwin 1833). He wrote subsequently, "It is a cruel evil to the whole world" (Darwin, 1861; 1863).

Personally and politically committed to abolition, Darwin had embarked on research that made the fictions on which slavery was based philosophically and scientifically untenable. By contrast, the hold of these fictions on sections of the social and scientific population intensified, as the establishment in 1863 of James Hunt's Anthropological Society and Galton's first articles on eugenics in *Macmillan's Magazine* in 1865 demonstrate. Also in the year that Galton began his dissemination of eugenics, the British Governor of Jamaica, Edward John Eyre, authorized the killing of 439 Jamaicans following the Morant Bay Rebellion. For over two years John Stuart Mill chaired the Jamaica Committee, aimed at prosecuting Eyre for murder and abuse of power, and spoke out in the House of Commons against British "military violence" (see Chutkan, 1996).[2] He received hate mail for doing so. Darwin joined Mill in supporting Eyre's prosecution, while Charles Dickens and Anthony Trollope rallied on the side of Eyre and Thomas Carlyle led the Eyre Defense and Aid Fund Committee (Richardson, 2020).[3]

Darwin's wariness of hierarchy and fixed social forms informed, and was informed by, the political world he inhabited from childhood. On July 5, 1832, en route to Montevideo and unaware that the Reform Bill had already received royal assent, he wrote to his sister Catherine, "We are all very anxious about reform; the last news brought intelligence that Lord Grey would perhaps re-continue in" (Darwin, 1832b). Later (shortly after Darwin had seen Mount Osorno erupt in the Chilean Andes) she informed him, in a joint letter with their sister Caroline Darwin:

Shropshire has actually returned 12 Tory Members who are called Lord Powis's Twelve Apostles. Toryism rages in Shropshire more than ever, and there certainly has been a slight reaction in favor of the Tories over the Country; in general though, the Reformers are much stronger, and will, I trust soon rout out Sir Robert Peel, and his odious Ministry. (Darwin and Darwin, 1835)

With America divided over slavery, Hooker (who described himself as a Whig and elsewhere as "a philosophic Conservative"; "a strong Unionist, but not a Tory"; Miscellaneous Notes, 1918: 350) wrote to tell Darwin that there was value in the aristocracy. He tried to use natural selection as justification, conflating nature and nurture to say the aristocracy consisted of "the best trained, bred and ablest," allowing those who have "intellect enough to rise to their own level" (Hooker, 1862). Darwin pointed out that aristocratic privilege did not sit well with evolution – "primogeniture is dreadfully opposed to selection" – but was amused by the interpretation: "The 'Origin' having made you, in fact, a jolly old Tory, made us all laugh heartily" (Darwin, 1862).

There was, though, a risk that the establishment would attempt to coopt Darwin, as Charles Kingsley, Chartist supporter and one of the earliest advocates of Christian Socialism, remarked, observing that so-called progressives didn't allow themselves to see how progressive Darwin was:

> I have found actually a Darwinian Marchioness!!!!! So even the Swells of the World are beginning to believe in you. The extreme Radical press is staying off from you, because you may be made a Tory & an Aristocrat of. So goes the foolish ignorant world – It will go, believing & disbelieving not according to facts, but to *convenience*. (Kingsley, 1867; emphasis in original)[4]

Kingsley himself was in thrall to paternalism and imperialism, but on reading *Uncle Tom's Cabin* (1852) he had written to Harriet Beecher Stowe, telling her that his Barbados-born mother had been struck by the way Stowe brought out the "common humanity" of the enslaved characters, and that "an excellent critic" had found it "the greatest novel ever written" "in that marvellous clearness of insight and outsight, which makes it seemingly impossible for her to see any one of her characters without shewing him or her at once as a distinct individual man or woman, different from all others" (quoted in Stowe, 1889: xxv). Fiction seems to have allowed Kingsley to grapple with some of his own limitations; in his novel *Two Years Ago* (1857) he again embraced biological unity, in opposition to the racist polygenism that was receiving new impetus from Robert Knox's *The Races of Men* (1850).

For Marx, Darwin's theory put paid to the inevitability, or naturalness, of working-class famine, since it held that humans were able to act for others. As Darwin elaborated in *The Descent*, "Nor could we check our sympathy, even at the urging of hard reason, without deterioration in the noblest part of our nature" (1874: 134). From this it followed that human hunger was in part the result of failings in social organization.

Darwin had observed in the *Origin*: "the Struggle for Existence amongst all organic beings throughout the world, which inevitably follows from their high geometrical powers of increase … is the doctrine of Malthus, applied to the whole animal and vegetable kingdoms" (Darwin, 1859: 4–5). Marx remarked to Engels that "Malthus's theory is based on the fact that he set Wallace's geometrical progression of man against the chimerical 'arithmetical' progression of animals and plants," and pointed out to him that Darwin's work contains "a detailed refutation, based on natural history, of the Malthusian theory": Darwin had applied "the 'Malthusian' theory also to plants and animals, as if the joke in Herr Malthus did not consist of the fact that he did not apply it to plants and animals but only to human beings – in geometrical progression – in contrast to plants and animals" (Marx, 1921: 1:S.315; Marx, 1972: 172). If both plants and animals, being largely edible, expand geometrically, then subsistence would increase commensurate with population. When Marx sent Darwin a copy of *Das Kapital* (1867), Darwin thanked him for his "great work," noting, "I believe that we both earnestly desire the extension of knowledge, & that this in the long run is sure to add to the happiness of mankind."

14.2   Darwin and Mill on Biologism

While Darwin and Mill are often assumed to have occupied separate and opposing camps (one that foregrounded biology, the other society and ethics), seeing beyond this constructed binary allows new understanding of the interconnections between, and often inseparability of, the two. This is key to understanding Darwin's evolutionary ethics and has not been fully acknowledged. Mill posited in *Utilitarianism* (1863: 61) a distinction between intellectual and animal, writing "we might have intellectual instincts, leading us to judge in a particular way, as well as animal instincts that prompt us to act in a particular way," with neither infallible. But he also wrote feeling firmly into the narrative of morality, with "the good of others" becoming a thing "naturally and necessarily to be attended to, like any of the physical conditions of our existence": hence "the smallest germs of the feeling are laid hold of and nourished by the contagion of sympathy and the influences of education" (47). In the *Descent*, Darwin acknowledged that "Mr. J.S. Mill speaks, in his celebrated work, 'Utilitarianism,' of the social feelings as a 'powerful natural sentiment,' and as 'the natural basis of sentiment for utilitarian morality'; but on the previous page he says, 'if, as is my own belief, the moral feelings are not *innate*, but acquired, they are not for that reason less natural'" (Darwin, 1871a: 7; emphasis in original). Darwin's "but" might well have been "and," though.

For both Mill and Darwin there was a clear continuity between their theory and practice. Both attributed much to the environment: biology was a way towards acknowledging its place. Both believed not in fixed and immutable hierarchies but in close, fluid, and intimate relations between nature and nurture that allowed change and social progress and redress for past error. Mill was fiercely opposed to innatism, seeing it as an obstacle to progress. This meant he was an opponent of biologism, not biology, and, like Darwin, he was opposed to racism. If biology denotes the "branch of science that deals with living organisms as objects of study," or "the biological characteristics of an organism" (*OED*), then "scientistic" or "biologistic" denotes the reductive viewpoint which excludes all else. Biologism, denoting "the interpretation of behaviour from a (purely) biological point of view" was recorded in 1912 (Wright, 1912: 315), and appeared in its adjectival form in August 1920 when *Scientific Monthly* referred to "a biologic or, since there is a difference, biologistic theory of the universe" (Lloyd, 1920).[5]

In the *Descent*, Darwin would show that the races "graduate into each other" – race, and racial fixity, had no basis in biology: "it is hardly possible to discover clear distinctive characters between them" (1871a: 226). Descent carried with it this sense of the held in common. Darwin's understanding of biology allowed him to make a pronouncement on race that was the very opposite of biologistic. In this way, he differed from such men of science as the hereditarian biologists Patrick Geddes and J. Arthur Thomson, who in *The Evolution of Sex* (1889) sought to extend their own power as well as the reach of a past that had served patriarchy (and them) well, and which they increasingly conceived as deterministic (a bulwark against the changes that modernity was bringing in train). Such changes included the emancipation of women, as women sought to defend themselves precisely from that past, acknowledging commonalities with other women, in the decades that would see the growth of unionization, with the Bryant & May matchgirls striking in 1888. Darwinian biology revealed that there was no fixed aspect to race, as current research also makes clear. Linnaeus and Blumenbach's systems of classification, based on physical traits including the adaptive trait skin color, rested on false premises, while genetic ancestry draws on complex clusters of environmental, historical, and demographic factors (see Sirugo et al., 2021), and points not to intrinsic racial but environmental and geographical differences, even in the case of Tay-Sachs disease (see e.g. Brower, 2002).

Darwinian biology, as the evolutionary feminist Mona Caird articulated so clearly in her novels and writing for the periodical press, came to the aid of women who sought to *limit*, not *eliminate*, biology.[6] It is in an apprehension of biological difference, conjoined with a lust for power, that misogyny is rooted. Acknowledging both the reality of biology and its historical and relational aspects provided feminism with the impetus and knowledge to understand that misogyny was endemic but not inevitable. The women and men who took up this position were anti-essentialists, embattled against the oppressions of innatism.

John Stuart Mill had lamented in his *Autobiography* "the prevailing tendency to regard all the marked distinctions of human character as innate, and in the main indelible." Essentialism, the idea that a thing possesses an essence consisting of a defining set of properties, when used of humans, can move rapidly and without basis into a reification of particular properties (or an "essence"), to the exclusion of their historical determinants and relations (see Richardson, 2011). The acknowledgement of biological phenomena, far from constituting essentialism, can work to ensure that complex relations and determinants form part of the focus of natural history and biological science.

Darwinian anti-essentialism did not erase sex; rather, it spoke to increasing numbers of women who sought neither to be defined solely by biology, nor reduced to, or by, it. Some, such as Sarah Grand, saw the theory of sexual selection as having the potential to provide them with agency and choice; by foregrounding change, it took them of necessity out of stasis. Sexual oppression (which takes such forms as sexism and sex discrimination) was as real to the Victorians as it is in the twenty-first century. To deny sex would not make that oppression go away, but it would banish the means by which to address it. More than a century later, sex-selective abortion, female genital mutilation (FGM), menstrual huts, and the child marriage of girls to adult men, for example, are experienced by females (see Adhikari, 2020; Kmietowicz, 2019: Mackenzie, 2019; Masukume and Mapanga, 2020; Sax, 2002; National Institutes of Health, n.d.). Male circumcision is also a global concern, but it does not originate in hostility to or fear of males, whereas FGM begins both in misogyny and biology. By contrast, unlike sex, there is no biological basis for race, but a historical and legal definition of the term is necessary for redress and to guard against discrimination. On sex, evolution provided not a denial of its existence as a biological reality, but a limit to its apprehension as social construct, ideal, or stereotype. While in practice biologists would use biological science to seek to entrench sexed roles, philosophically evolution allowed a new biological framework for critiquing biologistic arguments for social roles based on sex, or innatism.

While Mill was concerned that setting too much store by biology could slip into innatist or biologistic ways of thinking, Darwin acknowledged the limits of hereditarian explanation, not as a denial or disavowal of biology but as an acceptance of its boundaries, and resisted viewing biology as an all-sufficient justification or alibi for social action/inaction, as if these were inevitable. Indeed, it was a concern over the slippage between biology and the biologistic that lay behind Mill's and Darwin's shared hesitancies. This is a fundamental distinction that gets lost, then as now, and it is one that might play a formative role in considerations of Darwin today. In a time of climate emergency and accelerating global poverty, as we think about humanity's place in nature and the relation between natural and social systems, it might illuminate ways toward an ethics of nature and a Darwinian ethics of biology.

In 1845, when Darwin wrote to tell the geologist Charles Lyell (who had not supported the abolitionist movement) that he had been delighted to receive from him a letter "in which you touch on slavery," he also took him to task:

> I wish the same feelings had been apparent in your published discussion. – But I will not write on this subject; I sh^d. perhaps annoy you & most certainly myself. – I have exhaled myself with a paragraph or two in my Journal on the sin of Brazilian slavery: you perhaps will think that it is in answer to you; but such is not the case, I have remarked on nothing, which I did not hear on the coast of S. America. (1845)

What struck Darwin most was Lyell's failure of sympathy and imagination: "How could you relate so placidly that atrocious sentiment about separating children from their parents; & in the next page, speak of being distressed at the Whites not having prospered; I assure you the contrast made me exclaim out. – " Darwin had marked the passage with an exclamation mark and pencil underlining, and was prompted to add two paragraphs to the second edition of his journal, detailing the human rights abuses of enslaved peoples he had witnessed in a Spanish colony in Brazil (Darwin, 1845). Crucially, his letter indicates the place of feeling in his research. It would infuse his work and thought, evidencing the power of undetached observation: "My few sentences, however, are merely an explosion of feeling. But I have broken my intention, & so no more on this odious deadly subject. – "

Emma Darwin would articulate a sense of the Darwins being out of kilter with public opinion, referring Hooker on Boxing Day, 1863, to the work of Frederick Law Olmsted, whose works challenging slavery in the US were regularly praised by the Darwins: "About America I think the slaves are gradually getting freed & that is what I chiefly care for. The Times evidently thinks that is to be deplored, but I think all England has to read up Olmsted's works again & get up its Uncle Tom again" (1863).

Such acts of resistance, however small, would be found not in policy or statute books but in newspapers, novels, and poetry, in letters between scientists, philosophers, writers, and ordinary people, and, undoubtedly, in anonymous and untraceable actions. But Darwin had a more far-reaching contribution to make.

14.3   Darwin and the Biology of Sex

While Darwin's language and social commentary were freighted with the conventional and hierarchical ideas of his time, his theory of evolution called fixity and stasis, and resultant stereotypes, into question and opened doors for others to make similar challenges. The progressive implications of evolution for women and other groups whose subordination was both enabled and defended by misuses of biology were immediately seen by one of the most rigorous and committed feminists of the day, Mona Caird, for whom Mill and Darwin were pivotal influences (Richardson, 2003, 2011). Likewise, Antoinette Brown Blackwell, the New York women's rights campaigner, saw the impetus in evolution for social change, writing in *The Sexes Throughout Nature*:

> Evolution has given and is still giving to woman an increasing complexity of development which cannot find a legitimate field for the exercise of all its powers within the household. There is a broader, not a higher, life outside, which she is compelled to enter, taking some share also in its responsibilities. (1875: 135)[7]

Darwin corresponded with some hundred women, many of whom provided him with scientific observations; others evaluated his work (see www.darwinproject.ac.uk/letters/correspondence-women). In 1877, writing to Eleanor Mary Dicey, who had been involved in the foundation in 1871 of the Cambridge women's college, Newnham, and was a supporter of science education for women, he expressed concern regarding women being discouraged from the study of physiology (Darwin, 1877). His relations with the women in his family are likewise commensurate with the intellectual and philosophical implications of his evolutionary theory. Soon after the *Descent* was out, he wrote to his daughter Henrietta (who had read it and suggested corrections), addressing her as his "coadjutor & fellow-labourer" and remarking, "Several reviewers speak of the lucid vigorous style etc. – Now I know how much I owe to you in this respect, which includes arrangement, not to mention still more important aids in the reasoning."[8] In acknowledging Henrietta's prowess in both arrangement and reason, labeled female and male respectively by Victorian separate sphere ideology —as evidenced, for example, in John Ruskin in *Of Queen's Gardens* (1865)—Darwin pushed against stereotypes. In 1877, Darwin wrote to Dicey, "I should regret that any girl who wished to learn physiology sh^d. be checked, because it seems to me that this science is the best or sole one for giving to any person an intelligent view of living beings, & thus to check that credulity on various points which is so common with ordinary men & women" (1877).

Darwin set in train an epistemological revolution with the potential to release women from fixed social roles. Similarly, his work made it impossible to think of race as a fixed ontological category, underpinned by biology. The assumption that stereotypes were consistently and invariably reinforced by Darwin's work (or practices) is symptomatic of wider biologistic, and uninterrogated, assumptions around sex: while sex-based stereotypes and biases are present in his work, most notably the *Descent*, Victorian feminists and more recent evolutionary biologists and humanities scholars use biology to resist rather than to buttress deterministic and essentialist ideas.[9] As for a biology of sex, and dimorphism, that is, physical differentiation along lines of sex, which has been alleged to be a colonial European imposition, Darwin's remarks to the naturalist Fritz Müller suggest its prevalence in the animal and plant kingdoms came as a surprise to him: "It is curious how dimorphism prevails by groups throughout the world, shewing as I suppose that it is an ancient character" (Lugones, 2007). To Gray, when denouncing slavery as a cruel evil to the world, he had remarked upon the complexities of sexual dimorphism: "I know that there are many cases of dimorphic plants; but are not the two forms always borne on same plant?" (1861a). The following year, he wrote, "thanks for your new cases of Dimorphism: new cases are tumbling in almost daily" (1862a).[10]

It was not sex, and the physical forms in which it found expression, but rather ideals, stereotypes, and coercions of sex that were inculcated and policed wherever patriarchal structures obtained. These were often in place before colonisation, though also reinforced by it. Nonetheless, in Europe the developing idea of companionate marriages, based on romantic love and personal choice (see Stone, 1977), served at some level to challenge these coercive forms (see Behrend-Martínez, 2021: 66). But in both the middle and working classes economic factors impacted the ideal of the companionate marriage, in the one case because marriage was seen as the main vehicle for the transmission of property, in the other because poverty, or the threat of it, enforced the need for both partners to work separately and for long hours, usually outside the home. Even then it was overshadowed by property interest and, in the working class, by destitution and its concomitant abuses (see Macfarlane, 1986; Ferraro, 2021).

Moving beyond humans to questions of sex in the wider world, Darwin was able to see the *variety* of physical forms through which dimorphism found expression. The Darwin household would have brought his attention early on to its complex relations and organizations of sex in the plant world. Erasmus Darwin used analogies between flora and human families to propose a tripartite analysis, translating Linnaeus's twenty-four taxonomic classes to characterize the various arrangements of male and female forms, so that, for example, in the "one house" class, which described plants which had both male and female flowers, "husbands live with their wives in the same house, but have different beds." In the "two house" class male and female flowers were on different plants, while the class of "polygamies" was characterized by hermaphrodite flowers as well as male or female ones.[11] Flora and fauna teemed with multiple forms and behavioral strategies in striving to unite the small and large gametes of the male and female sex, respectively, which characterize almost all complex life. Male and female reproductive structures were often found in the same plant, with anthers producing pollen grains (containing male gametes) and the ovary producing ovules (containing female gametes). Darwin observed that at a species level male and female gametes are found in hermaphroditic forms in the majority of individual plants; many out-cross with other plants but also self-fertilize under particular conditions; others are unisexual, always requiring cross-pollination. Such arrangements overturned conventional sexual hierarchies and uniform difference.

Darwin readily acknowledged the predominance of female choice in sexual selection in the animal kingdom:

> From the ardour of the male throughout the animal kingdom, he is generally willing to accept any female; and it is the female which usually exerts a choice. Hence if sexual selection has here acted, the male, when the sexes differ, ought to be the most brilliantly coloured; and this undoubtedly is the ordinary rule. (Darwin, 1871a: 1: 403)

Female agency had been, almost exceptionally, reduced in humans: "There are, however, exceptional cases in which the males, instead of having been the selected, have been the selector" (Darwin, 1871a: 2: 371). Darwin saw that female agency was a separate strain in reproductive behavior from male–male competition, and that, when it prevailed, "very ugly, though rich men, have been known to fail in getting wives." A number of Victorian feminists took interest (Beer, 2021).

Attending to orchids and barnacles, Darwin wrote of sex characteristics: "it occurred to me that, although no instance of the separation of the two sexes was known in Orchids, yet that Acropera might be a male plant" (Darwin, 1827), detailing that the orchid Catasetum turned out to have three forms – male, female, and hermaphrodite – which had previously been thought to be different genera of flowers. In his barnacle research, he found some males with multiple or extraordinarily long penises, and others that had previously been dismissed as parasites, but which were in fact complemental males, attached to wifely hosts and consisting of little more than a penis. Unbeholden to the strictures of sex stereotypes, he observed, "P.S. Mr Blyth tells me that according to Jerdon, the natives say the male Turnix alone incubates & attends to young" (March 4, 1867); drawing on Jerdon's *The Birds of India*, he wrote in the *Descent*: "the natives assert that the females after laying their eggs associate in flocks, and leave the males to sit on them" (Darwin, 1871a: 2: 201–202, see Jerdon, 1864).

While finding continuity with other animals was part of Darwin's move from fixity (and the stereotypes it enshrined) to evolution, when it came to sex-based expectations and stereotypes his remarks on mental differences between men and women bore the imprint of Victorian separate sphere ideology. However, he also couched his observations in hesitancy, conceding that some writers "doubt whether there is any inherent difference" and explaining social differences between the sexes as historically contingent rather than fixed (Darwin, 1871a: 2:326). Echoing Mary Wollstonecraft's argument for the education of girls along the same lines as boys in *A Vindication of the Rights of Woman* (1792), Darwin had remarked in the *Descent*: "in order that woman should reach the same standard as man, she ought, when nearly an adult, to be trained to energy and perseverance, and to have her reason and imagination exercised to the highest point; and then she would probably transmit these qualities chiefly to her adult daughters" (Darwin, 1871a: 2: 328). He would later remark to American feminist Caroline Kennard that there was reason to believe that, while women were morally superior to men but intellectually inferior, they had initially been intellectually equal "& this w^d. greatly favour their recovering this equality." To do this, though, they would need to become "as regular 'bread-winners' as are men" and he expressed concern as to what the social effects might be, as he had as to the effects of contraception (Darwin, 1882; 1877).

Kennard, like Caird, used the logic of Darwinian evolution in her response, urging the importance of environment and stating that women were indeed "breadwinners" with the same capabilities as men but lacking their education (Darwin, 1882). In his early transmutation notebooks Darwin had written, "Educate all classes – avoid the contamination of castes. improve the women. (double influence) and mankind must improve – " (Darwin, 2009: 309). While class is a social category, caste is a grouping which shares characteristics held to be biological. By double influence Darwin appears to allude to the social change that education brings within a single generation, and to the biological transmission of environmental effects – incremental change between generations along Lamarckian lines. In the decades that followed, eugenicists worked to write the environment out of the picture, valuing and asserting heredity over education. By contrast, while Darwin did not escape many of the social biases of his time, he increasingly opposed eugenics and used a nonbiologistic understanding of the relations of biology and society to do so (Richardson, 2014).

14.4   Darwin and Mill on the Relational Self

Recognition of the commonalities between Mill and Darwin, their differences notwithstanding, allows a more accurate apprehension of both, and challenges the idea that they were more narrowly focused on, respectively, the environment and the organism: "As for my meditations, they are most often devoted to questions of biology," Mill had remarked to Comte in 1846 (Haac, 1995: 366).[12] He told the philosopher and educationalist Alexander Bain that the *Origin* "far surpasses my expectation" (Mill 1860).

Acknowledgment of their common ground remains crucial for understanding the interplay of biology and society. Both Mill and Darwin understood the self as primarily relational and used the term "social" both in its widest sense, to mean characterized by living in and interacting with other members of a community, and in the more specific senses of gregariousness, mutuality, and empathy. Darwin defined organisms through their relations within and to other species, and his conception of environment (a term he first used in 1875) included the presence of other species and embraced a web of ecological relations that were often conceptualized as social. Comte developed the term "*milieu*" (1838) as an abstract singular term to replace plural terms such as "circumstances" or "conditions of existence," with Lewes translating the term as "medium" (Lewes, 1887: 1) and Harriet Martineau translating it as "environment" (Martineau, 1853). Darwin brought together Lamarck's idea of circumstances as contingent and Cuvier's narrower idea of conditions essential to life. The term "environment" was popularized by Spencer in the second half of the nineteenth century (Spencer, 1855), foregrounding the idea of interaction between organism and environment. Writing at a time when the idea of the environment was receiving unprecedented attention in imaginative, scientific, and philosophical writing, Darwin would lend new priority to social relations as part of a wider sense of reciprocal relations between environment and organism.

The ethical was interwoven into the world view and framework of imaginative empathy and dialogue, foregrounding relations both with individuals and the wider social environment (Fawcett, 1861).[13] Mill and Darwin's reciprocity of respect indicates the meeting points between ideas of community and responsible individualism. In 1861 Henry Fawcett, scholar economist and, from 1865 to 1884, a Liberal MP, remarked to Darwin that Mill "considers that your reasoning throughout is in the most exact accordance with the strict principles of Logic. He also says, the Method of investigation you have followed is the only one proper to such a subject" (Darwin, 1861). "Considering how high an authority he is, this pleases me much, & I think you will be pleased," Darwin wrote to Lyell a few days later, quoting Mill's words. The following year, Darwin observed to Asa Gray (Darwin, 1862) that the essay Gray had sent him, Mill's "The Contest in America," which was underpinned by abolitionist commitment, was "very good," and in the 1862 (fifth) edition of the Logic, Mill would describe Darwin's theory as an "unimpeachable example of a legitimate hypothesis" and "a wonderful feat of scientific knowledge and ingenuity," a passage George Darwin sent to his father a decade or so later (G. H. Darwin, 1874; Robson et al. 1974: 7:498–499).[14] Darwin argued that individual variation was the motor of evolution, while Mill argued that individual difference, dissent, and eccentricity were crucial to humanity. Mill published his views in On Liberty in the same year that the Origin appeared, but stressed two years later that the individual is always fundamentally social and defined through the relations it entertained with others: "The social state is at once so natural, so necessary, and so habitual to man, that, except in some unusual circumstances or by an effort of voluntary abstraction, he never conceives himself otherwise than as a member of a body" (Mill, 1863). On the sociality and interdependencies that individuality, accurately appraised, entails, Kwame Anthony Appiah remarks in the Ethics of Identity on "the myriad ways in which our individual well-being depends on others" (Appiah 2004).

This would have resonated with Darwin's subsequent exposition of the development of the social instinct. The temporalities of the biologistic and of biology are in opposition; a biologistic viewpoint invites the hereditarian, a determining by the past. By contrast, biology is immediate and present. We have much more to learn from it, from its embodied emotions and its joyful aspect toward the future.

When Kant had referred to moral feelings he had argued that the supreme principle of morality was a standard of rationality, referring to this in his *Groundwork of the Metaphysic of Morals* (1785) as the "categorical imperative." In his discussion of the transcendental aesthetic and in the transcendental deduction sections of the *Critique of Pure Reason* (1781) he had argued that it was the mind, with its receptive, synthetic, and conceptualizing capacities, that makes human experience possible. By this reasoning, all immoral actions were irrational. But Darwin pulled at this reason-unreason dualism, which mapped loosely onto mind-body dualism, and instead centered the body and the environment in the development of the social instincts and moral sense. Sympathy was informed by a nexus of bodily responses, and the moral sense emerged in humans and animals from instincts and emotions which developed from life in the social medium.

John Morley wrote to Darwin soon after the *Descent* was out to say "I don't think Mr. Mill's expressions ... point to any fundamental difference between him and yourself. He admits the moral faculty is capable of springing up 'spontaneously' in 'a certain small degree' ... and this is as much as you want, is it not?" (Morley, 1871). Morley, an anti-imperialist who would oppose both the Boer War and the First World War, and supported Home Rule for Ireland, was returned to Parliament as a liberal MP in 1883. His probing question was a good one, and it goes some way toward revealing an overlap between Mill and Darwin that was not only political but also philosophical. He added, "I don't know whether you are indignant or amused at writers who call you reckless for broaching new doctrines as to the moral sense, at a time when Paris is aflame" (Morley, 1871). The Paris Commune had seized power in March, governing Paris until they were suppressed by the national French government late in May; Darwin's situating of the moral sense at the heart of biology and social existence seemed one more revolutionary disruption.

As the *Descent* describes the moral instincts developing from the social, in *Expression of the Emotions* (1872) Darwin conceives of expression as predicated on, and also a record of, social relations, lending a new priority to an organism's relation to others and to the environment as he indicated the centrality of social relations for the development and expression of emotion. While the stimuli for reflex mechanisms are often internal – hunger, for example – and expression is largely a by-product of physiology, Darwin showed emotions to be caused by states of affairs outside the body—as opposed to sensations such as hunger, pleasure, and pain—but experienced in the body and constituted by bodily actions,[15] and noted: "Mr. Herbert Spencer ('Essays,' Second Series, 1863, p. 138) has drawn a clear distinction between emotions and sensations, the latter being 'generated in our corporeal framework'. He classes as Feelings both emotions and sensations" (Darwin, 1873, p. 27). Darwin drew on Gaskell, Dickens, and other contemporary novelists for material on the expression of the emotions. In turn, George Eliot would take detailed notes from Darwin's *Expression of the Emotions* as she prepared material for her final novel, *Daniel Deronda* (1876). Three years later she gratefully received and annotated a copy of Spencer's *Data of Ethics* (1879) which (like much of her own fiction) examined cooperation and the growth of conscious altruism. Her copy was inscribed "Mrs Lewes with the kindest regards of the author."

As early as 1848, as revolution raged across Europe, Darwin can be seen to have been challenging the new hereditarian ideas that he is more usually credited with intensifying, as this early letter to Emma reveals if we pay attention to the tone and register of irony: "I daresay not a word of this note is really mine; it is all hereditary, except my love for you, which I sh[d] think could not be so, but who knows?" (Darwin, 1848). In Notebook M, "Metaphysics on morals and speculations on," he recorded that Hensleigh had insisted that to say that "the brain thinks is nonsense" (Darwin, 1838: 61e). But, Darwin observed, "seeing a puppy playing cannot doubt that they have free-will" (Darwin, 1838: 72) and hence consciousness (Darwin, 1837–1840: 25). Later in Notebook M (Darwin, 1838: 101e) he had argued for "the brain bringing thought," for biology constituting a significant aspect of mind: "the mind is function of body. — we must bring some stable foundation to argue from." Even Darwin's theory of pangenesis, developed in *The Variation of Animals and Plants under Domestication* (1868a), can be seen as an extended reformulation of the organism-environment dichotomy that, in opposition to Galton and other hereditarians, lent new priority to the environment. This theory was much more deeply debated than has been acknowledged and its influence has only recently begun to be understood (see Richardson, 2014; Müller-Wille, and Rheinberger, 2012).

A dominant strand was soon to emerge from this early reception of Darwin that took the adjective "Darwinian" to be synonymous with ruthless, competitive, and selfish (first used in this sense in the *Eclectic Magazine*,

1867). Throughout the twentieth century, evolution came increasingly to be seen as a deterministic process reducible to competition among individuals, even when explaining the evolution of altruistic behavior (see, e.g., Fisher, 1930; Hamilton, 1963; Courtiol, et al., 2012). Opposing such views, a number of biologists, primatologists, philosophers, historians, and literary critics argue that Darwin did not subscribe to a competitive, individualist ethos (see, e.g., Richardson, 2014; Bekoff, 2013; De Waal, 2009; Desmond, and Moore, 2009; Dixon, 2008; Maienschein and Ruse, 2009; Ruse, 1986b). Still, considerable debate continues among biologists and philosophers as to whether Darwinian evolution operates exclusively at the level of the individual, or at the level of populations exhibiting various degrees of integration and social cooperation (see, e.g., Sapp, 1994; Borello, 2010; Deen, et al., 2013). Thinking with Darwin's ethics of biology today provides ways toward collaboration and cooperation. Given the increasing shift to the right in governments at a time of rising global poverty and climate emergency, Darwin's own strong sense of interdependence and interrelation stands at odds with the return of racial thought and renewed hostility to migrants. His understanding that race was unfixed, his ambivalence about how much was known about heredity, his awareness of the evolutionary value of variation and complexity and the influence of environment countered callous and authoritarian disregard for the vulnerable and disadvantaged, and he increasingly took issue with Galton's hard hereditarianism.

In 1871, Hensleigh Wedgwood had written to Darwin about the *Descent*'s talking dog, a dog which, if able to reflect on past conduct, would say to himself, "I ought (as indeed we say for him) to have pointed to that hare and not have yielded to the passing temptation of hunting it," and resolve to behave differently in future (Wedgwood, 1871). Wedgwood begged to differ. Why would the gratification of giving chase (an animal instinct) weigh any less than gratification from his apprehension (a social instinct which put another before oneself) of his owner's pleasure at his obedience? Darwin annotated the words, "you suppose indeed that he would have to compare the memory of our kind of gratification with the dissatisfaction actually felt in disobedience to the other instinct. But the disobedience to the pointing instinct is no more present than the obedience to the running one," adding in pencil, "but this is not only innate or inherited & has been constantly practised," rejecting the notion that the dog's instinct to point (to indicate prey to its owner) was strong by virtue (simply) of its being innate or inherited; rather, it was also because it was habitual, part of the dog's daily experience. Bringing in the environment and the social realm this way, he rejected a simplistic account of heredity. Next to Wedgwood's statement that shame was the essence of conscience, rather than, as Darwin believed, resolution as to future conduct which involved a mind-embodied combination of feeling (remorse), and temporal cognition, he penciled, "but would you not call it moral sense" (Wedgwood, 1871).

Replying to Wedgwood, Darwin shifted the debate from dogs to a man saving a drowning man, or a beaver trying to save his fellow beavers from a rill of water (Darwin's animals, like those of his century, default to the masculine). He concluded: "But as yet I nail my colours to the mast" (Darwin, 1871e). These colors were the centrality of the social instincts to the conduct of both human and animals (a semantic distinction Darwin upheld, while asserting continuity), and a conception of the moral sense as emerging from the conflict between social feelings and more transient desires.

The geneticist Jonathan Howard's regularly reprinted *Oxford Very Short Introduction to Darwin* claims that the theory of evolution has little if anything to do with ethical prescriptions (Howard, 2001). It doesn't necessarily follow that Darwin's own sense of what was ethical formed a constituent part of his theory of evolution, but the two should not be considered entirely in isolation. If we understand that Darwin's philosophy – perhaps most clearly evidenced in *The Expression of the Emotions* – was the product of his deeply imaginative sympathy then it becomes even more important that we acknowledge that Darwin worked all his life toward developing an evolutionary ethics. In the words of fellow writer Thomas Hardy, a keen observer of nature, writing in 1910 to the Humanitarian League:

> Few people seem to perceive fully as yet that the most far-reaching consequence of the establishment of the common origin of all species, is ethical; that it logically involved a readjustment of altruistic morals by enlarging as a *necessity of rightness* the application of what has been called "The Golden Rule" beyond the area of mere mankind to that of the whole animal kingdom. Possibly Darwin himself did not wholly perceive it, though he alluded to it. (April 10, 1910, cited in Millgate, 1984: II: 377; emphasis in original)

Darwin's understanding of ecological balance, of the interdependencies of the entangled bank, offers a vital point of resistance and sense of an interconnected world in a state of vulnerable imbalance. Discourses of science continue to be mobilized against those who have least, the transnational poor, and biologistic points of view currently underpin and further entrench discourse around poverty and migration, reworking Malthusian ideas in arguing for the limiting of the working class and of low-income country populations. Such authoritarian discourse sidesteps the assumption of inevitable competition and the effects of unregulated capitalism in a world of scarcity, and makes no acknowledgment of Darwin's intimation of abundance in nature, which has significant implication for a world of equity. Instead, in a reinscription of Victorian eugenic discourse, it castigates the working classes of all nations, appealing to a language of environment and climate emergency, but without any real accommodation of the held in common. The rhetoric reveals an annexation of biologistic and environmental ideas for an economic and nationalist argument, while in reality the threat to the environment is not the global poor who, instead, are the first and most vulnerable victims of climate breakdown. Darwin saw the importance of place and cooperation in ways that were informed not by the ravages of capitalism but by an appreciation of the collaborations of nature.

Perhaps what is most significant about Darwin's dialogue with Wedgwood is his acknowledgment of, and ability to work with (rather than flaunt), complexity. "What an awfully complex subject it is. I suppose no two persons would even quite agree; & I expect hardly any one will even partially agree with me," he observed (Darwin, 1871e). Darwin worked all his life with a wide range of people with views different from his own, resistant to what Mill referred to as "the tyranny of public opinion" (which is now mediated, relentlessly, via bifurcating social media platforms). He knew the value of uncertainty and the importance of dialogue, of being exposed to people not like him and who didn't think like him, in developing his ideas. The social environment that was vital to his concept of biology was as key to its dialectic formation as a discipline, bringing with it new possibilities for the golden rule that lies at the heart of most religions and ethical traditions. "'As ye would that men should do to you, do ye to them likewise;' and this lies at the foundation of morality," Darwin had written to his daughter Henrietta. "I fear parts are too like a Sermon: who w^d ever have thought that I sh^d. turn parson?" (Darwin, 1870).

Unlike many of his contemporaries, Darwin rejected slavery, challenged racial hierarchies, undid any supposedly scientific basis for race, and gave scientific limit to the expression of sex in the form of stereotypes that oppressed both women and men. Henrietta's response to Darwin points to his awareness that the mind was enworlded and embodied and that it was in such reciprocity, and in humility, that ethics begins: "Certainly to have you turned Parson will be a change – I expect I shall want it enlarging not contracting – cos I think you think an apology is wanting for writing abt any thing so unimportant as the mind of man!" (Darwin, n.d.).

Acknowledgment

I would like to thank the Leverhulme Trust for supporting my research on the cultural history of biologisms through a Research Fellowship.

Notes

1 A number of the letters Darwin wrote and received evidence the love and passion that science could excite; see as a further example, Weir, 1868. On objectivity in relation to scientific study, see Daston and Galison, 2007.
2 See Sheller (2019), which explores multiracial, cross-class alliances.
3 On the invitation to join Mills, see Spencer, 1866. Darwin recorded a payment of £10 under the heading "Jamaica" for November 19, 1866 in his Account books–cash account (Down House MS).
4 From May to August that year, Kingsley had been running the progressive *Fraser's Magazine*.
5 The *Oxford English Dictionary* notes that "Scientism" was in use before biologism, appearing in *New Englander* in 1870.
6 For discussion of the evolutionary feminist Mona Caird, see Richardson, 2003. See also Richardson, "Mona Caird" in Felluga, et al. (2015).
7 For further discussion of Caird and Blackwell, see Richardson, 2011.
8 H. E. Darwin, March 20, 1871. Henrietta was paid for her work by her father, though "as a memorial or souvenir rather than as wages," 143.
9 On challenges to determinism posed by current understanding of biology, see Rose, 2003; Dupré, 1995; Richardson, 2011b, 2010; Bloomfield, et al., 2015. See also Rose, 2006.
10 Darwin published the results of his study on dimorphism in Primula in Darwin, 1977 [1862]: II:45–63.
11 Erasmus Darwin's translation of a synopsis of Linnaeus's classification scheme for plants, as given in *The Families of Plants* (Botanical Society, 1787): lxxviii–lxixix. I am grateful to the Syndics of Cambridge University Library for permission to quote from this.
12 Darwin's work shows familiarity with Mill's *A System of Logic* (1843), *Utilitarianism* (1863), and *The Subjection of Women* (1869).
13 See also Darwin's letter to Lyell and Gray noting Mill's approval.
14 Darwin refers to this in an exchange with George Bentham April 21 and June 19, 1862, thanking him for drawing his attention to this.
15 See Richardson (2013). See also Griffiths (2002); Dixon (2013). While Charles Bell conceived of emotion as a movement of the mind, he was the first to give a constitutive role to bodily moments.

CHAPTER 15

Darwinian Analogies in Thinking about Art and Culture

Haun Saussy

> So careful of the type she seems,
> So careless of the single life.
> — Tennyson (1850: 78)

The proper name "Darwin" stands for an author and, thereby, for a body of knowledge and a theoretical position. But Charles Darwin did not sit down to write as someone who already knows. He discovered what he thought in the act of making it transmissible to others:

> There seems to be a sort of fatality in my mind leading me to put at first my statement & proposition in a wrong or awkward form. Formerly I used to think about my sentences before writing them down; but for several years I have found that it saves time to scribble in a vile hand whole pages as quickly as I possibly can, contracting half the words; & then correct deliberately. Sentences thus scribbled down are often better ones than I could have written deliberately. (Darwin, 2008a: 421).

What kind of composition process is this? A seemingly profligate, directionless one: a hasty "scribble in a vile hand" that produces many "wrong or awkward" statements, followed by a phase of "deliberate" pruning and organization. It is as if the author of *The Origin of Species* had adopted random variation and selection for fitness as laws of his personal literary ecology. The directionlessness of Darwin's writing process resembles the indirectness of biological evolution: living things, like prose paragraphs, are subject to chance, environment, and the linked weighting of what is transmitted and what is discarded. (On Darwinian style, see also Chapter 13 by Alexis Harley.)

Can *The Origin of Species* account for its own emergence? The book is about nature, to be sure, but like any book it belongs to the sphere of culture. It is a representation in language of thousands of observations and inferences about finches, pheasants, ants, fruit trees, and so forth. The fact of its being *about* – that is, intentionally directed toward – nature might seem to mark a difference from brute nature.[1] Yet intention is not a simple thing, according to Darwin's recollection. His writings were not created by unwavering pursuit of a fixed aim; Darwin let himself go, we might say, and like an empiricist of introspection gave free rein to the unconscious or automatic production of sentences by his brain and hand before reasserting control at a later stage. If the composition process that created the book bears similarities to the evolutionary processes it describes, it implies that the distinction between nature and culture may not be a profound one. At the very least, the existence of the book raises the question of whether culture is continuous with biology or in some way independent from it – whether a claim to have explained the one entails an explanation of the other. Darwin would opt for continuity, however discreetly. The two chapters on "Comparison of the Mental Powers of Man and the Lower Animals" in *The Descent of Man* show him testing the limits of material causation in matters of culture and society, so as to sketch a bridge between the animal kingdom and such purportedly human attainments as language, morals, and the sense of beauty.

Just as Darwin did not restrict himself to having opinions on plants and animals, so too philosophers, poets, musicians, historians, lawyers and the like had opinions on Darwin. The broad outlines of the cultural diffusion of Darwinian ideas are well known (see Irvine, 1955 and Richards, 1987). The task of this chapter is to examine some instances of cultural theories that draw on the conjectures of Lamarck, Darwin, and others in their discursive tradition. We will see analogy as an indispensable operator in forming those conjectures, working as it so often does to leverage knowledge of a more familiar domain in support of claims about a less familiar domain: it works in both directions, as cultural knowledge informs hypotheses about biology and as observations drawn from biology are used to frame theories of cultural development. (For a sustained exploration of this territory, see Griffiths, 2016.) The overall story to be told is how Lamarck, Darwin, and their successors opened a space for the naturalistic understanding of cultural facts. There is not room here to offer an inclusive survey – only to bring forth some examples that show how such questions have tended to be posed and the sorts of answers they have elicited.

Jean-Baptiste de Lamarck (1744–1829), inventor of the term "biology," contended that animal species were not fixed but in a constant state of transformation owing to the needs imposed on them by the conditions of their environments. Among the central tasks of biology as he conceived it was explaining "the *progression* manifested in the composition of the organization [of lower and higher animals], as well as the successive acquisition of various special organs, and consequently of new capabilities corresponding to these new organs" and "how actions, having become habitual and energetic, gave rise to the development of the organs that perform them" and thus are passed on to future generations (Lamarck, 1994 [1809]: 68; translation mine). Given the state of natural history in his time, it would be unrealistic to expect Lamarck to have offered a mechanism of heredity: he simply argued that "if the circumstances [affecting a species] persist, the internal organization [of those animals] is modified in the course of time, and generation among the individuals under consideration retains the acquired modifications, in the end producing a distinct race" of animals (210).

Lamarck's account of speciation can be faulted for exactly the features that make it persuasive. It telescopes the individual into the species, as in the unduly famous fable of the giraffe whose neck grows longer generation by generation (Lamarck, 1994: 230), and it focuses on the protagonists who adapt and survive, forgetting entirely about those who fail to leave behind progeny. Further, the rhetorical vividness of anecdote and narrative that enhances Lamarck's persuasiveness hinges on an analogy to human experiences. Through an individual adapting to its environment, a species *learns*, in a way that transcends the individual lifespan. The immediacy of the analogy sidesteps the question of whether such transmission is not more proper to culture, the reservoir of human techniques for preserving acquired behaviors. For culture is nothing if not a mechanism for "the inheritance of acquired characteristics." An innovation (say end rhyme, polyphony, or woodblock printing) arises in some place on the basis of earlier inventions; those who study the process imitate it, acquire it and pass it down to others, the cultural "muscle" in question being strengthened by more frequent use; refinements in the technique likewise find or fail to find imitators, and for the community of users it is not absurd to speak of a tendency toward "perfection." Imitation, and secondarily instruction, are the organs of transmission; it is rare indeed for cultural historians to be much concerned with discovering any physical means for the characteristics of a literary genre or a painting style to pass from generation to generation. Counting on this tacit knowledge of what learning is, Lamarck could afford to be economical with the details.

"The inheritance of acquired characteristics" is a later shorthand expression credited to August Weismann (1834–1914) and intended to show Lamarck's theory as absurd. Darwin, who first absorbed Lamarck by way of Lyell's *Principles of Geology* (Young, 1971), saw nothing unreasonable in linking circumstance, habitual action, bodily form, and species in a causal chain. Whenever Darwin examines behavior, Lamarckian vocabulary comes quickly to the fore. The chapter on "Instinct" in *The Origin of Species* argues that habit shades into instinct and instinct into corporeal adaptations: "As modifications of corporeal structure arise from, and are increased by, use or habit, and are diminished or lost by disuse, so I do not doubt it has been with instincts" (Darwin, 1859: 207–244). Writing a dozen years later, he adds:

> It is notorious how powerful is the force of habit .... This applies to the nerves of motion and sensation, as well as to those connected with the act of thinking. That some physical change is produced in the nerve-cells or nerves which are habitually used can hardly be doubted, for otherwise it is impossible to understand how the tendency to certain acquired movements is inherited. (Darwin, 1916: 29)

Learning, then, occurs in individuals and is somehow passed down to their progeny as habit or instinct. Just as we saw with Lamarck, such acquisition is scarcely to be differentiated from what in humans we call culture. Neurologists and psychologists in Darwin's circle sought to capture the "physical change ... produced in the nerve-cells" that might connect experience with somatic inscription and thence pass down memory traces to future generations, and thus leave the door open to what would later be called epigenetics (Darwin, 1916: 29). Automatic behavior seemed to testify to an inscription of memory in the body, whence it might reemerge as programmed action (Maudsley, 1878: 512–538; Janet, 1889). Indeed, as Thomas Huxley put it in his lecture "On the Hypothesis that Animals are Automata, and its History," if "all states of consciousness in us, as in them, are immediately caused by molecular changes of the brain-substance," then "we are conscious automata" (Huxley, 1888 [1874]: 240). The outcry that followed Huxley's lecture was hardly less than that provoked by Darwin's ancestral apes.

Not every critic, creator, or theorist of culture shared the increasingly exigent demands in which Lamarck and Darwin participated for a style of explanation founded on observables and dissatisfied with spiritualist terminology (on these epistemic conditions, see Goldsmith and Laks, 2019). Carpenter (1875), for example, was quick to assert, against Huxley's automatism, that an ego commanded the body by means of the moral sense. (On the "conflicting allegiances" of Victorian psychologists, see Daston, 1978, and Dixon, 2003: 135–171.) But the ambition of extending an explanatory style already tested in physics and biology to the domain of culture is seen in many nineteenth-century thinkers. In England, these were often people of Dissenting background, and thus excluded from the two ancient universities. In France and Germany, they were products of the secular university, and presumably less constrained by established hierarchies of value held by churchly, monarchical, or aesthetic institutions. The immensely popular English writer Herbert Spencer, who coined the Darwinian-sounding phrase "survival of the fittest," contended in the 1857 essay "Progress: Its Law and Cause," that "from the earliest traceable cosmical changes down to the latest results of civilization, we shall find that the transformation of the homogeneous into the heterogeneous, is that in which progress essentially consists" (1904: 9–10). The increasing differentiation and complexity that defined progress for Spencer were originally derived from reading in the embryology of Karl Ernst von Baer. He found confirmation of that pattern in musicology, linguistics, literary history, psychology, sociology, and a great many other special sciences, durably imprinting on them a linear and hierarchical model of change. More recent scholarship emphasizes Spencer's differences from Darwin, who was careful to dissociate his thinking from teleology (Bowler, 2013: 221–229, 243–247).

Darwin's originality, in a biology suffused with Lamarckian thinking, lies in great measure in his awareness that a species is a class of individuals moving through time, and also in his attention to failure (chiefly, death without issue, but all sorts of sports, deviations, and vestiges as well) as shaping, no less than progenitive success, the properties that will characterize the species. Neither of these insights lends itself to a protagonist-centered narrative, which was exactly the sort of story that Spencer, working on a Lamarckian basis, could deliver.

During Darwin's lifetime, there was no need to differentiate Darwinian and Lamarckian understandings of adaptation and transformation among plants and animals; indeed, Darwin often used Lamarck's terminology. Selection, however, had the last word in Darwin's account of descent and change. Although Lamarck pronounced it a law that "whatever has been acquired, encompassed or changed in the organization of individuals during their lifetime is conserved by generation and transmitted to the new individuals who stem from those who have undergone these changes" (Lamarck, 1815–1822: 1:181–182), his suggestions about the mechanism whereby characteristics were transmitted to future generations were indefinite. Darwin suggested that a special type of cell, which he called "gemmules," were collected from all the organs of the body and served to represent the characteristics of the parent in the process of sexual reproduction. Observing that "the cells or units of the body increase by self-division or proliferation, retaining the same nature, and that they ultimately become converted into the various tissues and substances of the body," Darwin hypothesized:

> [T]he units throw off minute granules which are dispersed throughout the
> whole system ... These granules may be called gemmules. They are col-
> lected from all parts of the system to constitute the sexual elements, and
> their development in the next generation forms a new being; but they are
> likewise capable of transmission in a dormant state to future generations
> and may then be developed .... Gemmules are supposed to be thrown off
> by every unit, not only during the adult state, but during each stage of
> development of every organism. (1874: 2: 457)

Those characteristics might include habits, experiences, or injuries. Clearly
the purpose of Darwin's "panspermia" hypothesis was to make room for
every kind of variation. But this model of generation, open to Lamarckian
adaptation to the milieu, was controverted when August Weismann's
experiments led him to segregate the germ cells, which were responsible
for the transmission of inherited characteristics, from the somatic cells
(Weismann, 1883; see also Churchill, 2015: 313–321). Germ cells, we might
say, carried information, whereas somatic cells merely provided matter: with this distinction Weismann came suspiciously close to reprising
Aristotle's ontology of reproduction, in which one parent, the male, contributed the form, and the other parent, the female, contributed the matter of the developing fetus (Aristotle, 1984: 1184).

The Russian anarchist thinker Pyotr Kropotkin rose up against
"Weismann's barrier" in a series of articles (Kropotkin, 1910, 1912; discussion in Garcia, 2015; further materials in Confino and Rubinstein,
1992). By separating the germ cells from the somatic cells, Weismann had
excluded the action on the animal of the milieu, from which any acquired
characteristics would derive. Kropotkin staked future human progress
on advancing the understanding of the influence of environments, both
natural and social, on living things. Demonstrations of mutually benefi-
cial actions among animals would encourage the development of similar
social reflexes among people, by showing that possessive individualism and
competition for the means of existence were by no means inscribed in
our nature. Kropotkin marshaled anecdote and experiment to maintain
that "mutual aid" between the animal and its fellows had played a role in
evolution, rather than attributing all adaptive variation to the "struggle for
life." Learning and plasticity would thus be restored to the history of life.

Likewise, the separation of germ cells from somatic cells seemed a peculiar and arbitrary move to the neo-Lamarckian naturalist Félix Le Dantec
(1869–1917), a student of Alfred Giard who followed his mentor in occupy-
ing the first chair of biology at the Sorbonne and published some thirty
books on evolutionary theory, scientific method, atheism, and ethics.

Le Dantec makes Weismann's "erroneous but convenient" language a symptom of the "crisis of transformism" (Le Dantec, 1909: 27) and offers a conjecture to replace it. Was there a good reason for making reproduction such a specialized business that it could be carried out only by a small number of cells set aside for the purpose? After all, the maintenance of individual existence is indispensable to the maintenance of species-existence, and from a philosophical point of view hardly less mysterious. Let us grant that all living things are constantly undergoing change and being affected by countless external impulses. How then do they produce progeny that are reasonably stable variations on, but not identical copies of, the parents?

> Life is not characterized by a pure and simple assimilation in which a living body, once it has been established, maintains its initial properties for as long as it lives. Were that the case, no evolution would arise; the transmission of a living thing's initial properties to all its descendants would take place with perfect rigor in the descent group, whatever circumstances might have been encountered. That would be *absolute heredity;* education would no longer play a role in the history of living things, or rather, its role would be reduced to one of mere feeding. (Le Dantec, 1908: 167)

Relying on the likelihood of his readership's familiarity with pianos and piano tuners, Le Dantec advanced an analogy with the propagation of sound waves. The soundboard of a piano vibrates at the same rate (and thus the same pitch) as the struck wire, whichever wire it be, and that is how a note can be amplified and transmitted over longer distances. The soundboard is designed to be an "indifferent resonator," whereas a tuning fork, a "specific resonator," will vibrate only in response to another vibrating body moving at a single designated frequency. Resonance, Le Dantec suggests, is the key to understanding heredity in living things:

> Under certain rare circumstances, a body that has imitated a sound or a shade of light, in a milieu where sounds or lights were perceptible, carries with it, for a more or less extended time, the sound or light which it previously imitated, and by which it has become in its turn, for the new milieu in which it is introduced, a model to be imitated. The quantity of energy accumulated, by resonance, in a body is generally too small to be communicated to a new milieu that must be energized without fading away quickly. Most of the time, a body that has received light will grow dark as soon as it enters a dark environment. But there are some bodies that, having been exposed to light, carry a durable glow with them into a dark environment. These bodies are of colloid structure. (Le Dantec, 1907: 162–163)

Let us pause a moment and consider the new technologies that Le Dantec is obliquely hinting at in his analogy. The phonograph, thirty years old

at the time that he is writing; photography, seventy years old; color photography, much more recent; the cinema, only fifteen years old – all these
nineteenth-century technologies had in common the ability to capture and
repeat some kind of vibration, whether sonorous or luminous, by inscribing
it durably on a surface that could be made to reproduce, through mechanical or chemical agency, the original vibration. A wax cylinder inscribed
with the voice of Enrico Caruso did not look anything like Caruso. But in
a way it was the "child" of his voice and of Edison's machine.

A recording is in Le Dantec's terms an "imitation with translation" of
the voice (the sound vibrations are translated into incised channels, the
temporal sequence is translated into spatial positions, and so forth). A
child must then be an "imitation with translation" of its parents. To better
focus the analogy, Le Dantec invites us to consider

> the recent attempt by the dancer Isadora Duncan to *mime* the music of
> Beethoven …. Many people have mocked this example of expressive chore-
> ography; others have found it admirable; I find it philosophically interest-
> ing …. The term "imitation" is usually reserved for the act whereby a living
> being reproduces a phenomenon which, *for an outside observer*, greatly
> resembles the phenomenon that provided its model. In this sense, Isadora
> Duncan did not *imitate*, did not *mime* the sounds produced by the orches-
> tra, for it is in her mind alone that the imitation really existed. (Le Dantec,
> 1908: 184–188)

Duncan chose for her dances examples of music that had not been composed for dancing ("absolute music" in the terminology of the time), and
gave them a visual correlate through gesture and movement – not a perfect
reproduction of the thing imitated but a transformation of some of its
properties into a different order (d'Udine, 1910: 64). Le Dantec's use of
this example, evidently still resonating in the minds of the Parisian public
of 1908, is meant to clarify the nature of heredity as a creation of similarities out of differences.

In 1910, the musical critic Albert Cozanet published, under his usual
penname of Jean d'Udine, a theory of artistic behavior called *Art and
Gesture*. It includes a psychology of art effects, an account of the identities
and differences across art media, and a means of translating the effects of,
for example, architecture into those of music or poetry. Gesture, the movement of the human body in space and time, is made the common denominator of all the arts (and indeed, for d'Udine, of learning, memory, and
action in general; on memory and social transmission, see Ian Duncan's
chapter in this volume). Long before, Aristotle in his *Poetics* (1448, b 5) had
stated that humans have a "natural propensity, from childhood onwards,

to engage in mimetic activity"; humans are "thoroughly mimetic and through mimesis take [their] first steps in understanding" (Halliwell, 1987: 34). In d'Udine's thinking, this insight becomes: "Every artistic genius is a specialized mime" (d'Udine, 1910: vii). What he means by genius is just an intensification of the motor capacities of sensation and action common to all of us. A mimetic faculty based on experiences of duration – space and time – assures the possibility of translation among the arts.

D'Udine is mainly interested in arts grounded on rhythm, symmetry or shape, not in narrative content: "The totality of lines formed by a monument, the spatial rhythm of a colonnade, cause an aesthetic emotion in us through their translation into musical rhythm in our perceiving brains" (d'Udine, 1910: 54). Dance is for him the central art, the one through which our ability to sense the weight and movement of the shapes in a painting or of the phases of a melody is translated: "To every auditory sensation, of whatever kind, there corresponds a movement which … is the translation, the equivalent of this audible formula" (d'Udine, 1910: 67). The perception or reception of works of art is not different in kind from their production, only in intensity: "When Isadora Duncan imitates [through dance] the music of Chopin or Beethoven, hundreds of people participate in this imitation, no doubt because they feel themselves capable of conceiving a similar imitation" (d'Udine, 1910: 65). Through the example of Isadora Duncan, d'Udine reaches toward Le Dantec and tries to ground his intersubjective, mimetic aesthetics in transformationist biology.

Thus, a biologist trying to solve the question of heredity and an aesthetic theorist trying to hit on the formula of Symbolisme both find themselves using analogy to pursue their unknowns. And as Le Dantec and d'Udine quote from the same sources, quote each other, and elaborate on each other's ideas of imitation, a common language emerges, though of course the speakers of that language approach it differently and bring different resources to bear on it. In some respects, of course, this is an analogy: the way imitation of reality operates in art and the way imitation of ancestral traits operates in heredity have a tangential relationship that might, if explored, suggest new aspects of either field. But the place where the dialogue becomes most intense is where the relation between art and science aspires to be no longer one of analogy, imitation, or translation, but one of extension. That is made possible by the physics of colloids.

Colloids, organized compounds in which insoluble molecules of one substance are suspended in another substance, were the leading area of research on the frontier between biology and chemistry around 1910 (Ghesquier-Pourcin, 2010). That frontier was becoming porous, as all through the nineteenth century chemistry successively accounted for more and more of the properties of life, starting with Liebig's proof that the conservation of energy applied equally to living beings as to any department of physical matter. Chromosomes had recently been identified as the site of hereditary transmission, but their exact role was still undetermined and Mendel's (1866) experiments on heredity were sometimes understood to support random mutation rather than predictable inheritance. As a neo-Lamarckian, Le Dantec was persuaded that acquired characteristics could be imprinted on the genetic material and transmitted to future generations, but he sought a physical basis for the inscription and transmission of these acquisitions. He outlined three levels at which living things could be represented scientifically: the atomic, the colloidal, and the mechanical. He saw the colloidal state as an intermediary stage between the chemical state and the mechanical state (Le Dantec, 1909: 58). It is a layer where constraints apply, both from above (the direct effects of the environment on the animal, which we can perceive) and from below (the chemical constitution of the animal's body, which in Le Dantec's view we cannot observe directly but can calculate from our knowledge of elements and physical law). In the colloid, experiences, imprinted on the individual animal, would become acquired characteristics and then be transmitted to the next generation of animals (Le Dantec, 1909: 59). Now colloids have the property of being "perfect resonators":

> Every particle of these bodies is in balance with the next and with all the other particles, such that if any cause perturbs it yet does not break its linkages, it must oscillate around its original position ... Thus, there can occur [among colloids] what happens in a confined mass of air, that is, the bonds of the colloid with its exterior walls facilitate or hinder its resonance with certain frequencies. (Le Dantec, 1907: 163–164)

This description enlarges Darwin's already expansive "panspermia" hypothesis beyond biology to the more general domain of chemistry. Colloids allow for the conservation, selection, transmission, and transformation of energies, which is why they could appear to be the solution of problems of individual memory, genetic heritability, the nexus of mind and body, and even the artistic instinct or Aristotelian mimesis at the root of culture.

For Jean d'Udine, the resonant vibration of colloids serves to ground the existence of culture in nature – in biology and chemistry:

> Let us come back to the imitation of rhythms by colloids, those imitators, and resonators *par excellence*. A series of observations that we cannot enter into here shows that the colloids constituting our nervous centers are not

specific resonators, but indifferent resonators. But these nervous centers have the particularity of being able to store the results of their imitations [now quoting Le Dantec] "in the form of what psychology calls memories." ... "[A] protoplasm that has once imitated a certain rhythm will conserve, for a longer or shorter time, a specific acquired characteristic related to this rhythm." (d'Udine, 1910: 115–116, paraphrasing and citing Le Dantec, 1907: 170)

D'Udine makes the coy gesture of skipping over the tedious scientific discussion, but it is clear what is going on here. The artistic practice of human beings is presented as continuous with their properties as biological entities having a transmission of genetic inheritance. (On the scientific and cultural traffic among Lamarckian biologists and members of the artistic avant-garde, see Loison, 2010, and Brain, 2015.) Learning as psychologists understand it is, thanks to the resonating colloids, not similar to but the same thing as transmission of an acquired characteristic. This is Lamarckianism redoubled.

This particular dialogue of art and science is now somewhat inaccessible to us, because the discovery of DNA in the 1950s finally unlocked a different chemical interpretation of the chromosome, rendering useless the previously attractive physics of vibrating colloid suspensions (as well as several other hypotheses about the physical form of the gene; see Saussy, 2021). But it points to an unusual way of conceiving the relation between Darwinian evolution and human cultural activity: not as if they were not analogous, nor as if one could be reduced to the other, but as if they were consubstantial. The vibrating colloid, existing under the particular conditions of Paris in 1910, was the "boundary-object" (Star and Griesemer, 1989) that enabled the confluence of two intellectual fields, performing "imitation with translation" between them.[2]

Though unfounded in any experimental results, this shifting of the locus of heredity to the resonance of vibrating colloids is a brilliant rhetorical move. It recovers the unspecialized, wandering omnipresence of Darwin's "panspermia"; it suggests a physical basis for the most controversial aspects of Lamarckian inheritance; with its subdivision of "specific" and "general" resonators, it allows for both spontaneity and memory; it couples the organism and the environment in a moment-by-moment interchange, making learning possible; and it permits us to conceive of natural and cultural variability, the sea-squirt, Isadora Duncan, malaria-resistance, landscape painting, and emotions as analogous entries in a vast inventory of mimetic behaviors. Le Dantec seems not to have known of Kropotkin's critique, but the purport of his "resonance" is the same. Kropotkin would have found it a suitably large response to the Weismannian restrictions

that confined generation to a specialized set of cells and walled off ancestry from the workings of the milieu. The isolated germ-plasm isolates the
animal's essence, its species-being, from its daily existence. That essence is
held apart from the traffic with the world that teaches – obliges – living
creatures to adapt. If there is to be a Darwinian–Lamarckian account of
society and culture, it can only grow out of that traffic.

Notes

1 However, Millikan (1984) offers an account of meaning that makes intention
   the basis of a homology between biology and language.
2 The colloid had a further outing in the anti-essentialist linguistic philosophy of
   general semantics (Korzybski, 1933: 111–122). Like "resonance," the colloid as a
   figure of thought often has a programmatic role in analogical inquiries.

Afterword

George Levine

When I began my studies of Darwin in scholarly innocence some forty years ago, I had a few conventionally inadequate ideas of what I would find in his famous books and absolutely no idea what was to come – or that *anything* would come. I had no idea that I was working my way into so abundantly fertile a literature. Forty years later, I find myself being asked to write a kind of postscript to a volume devoted to considering what Darwin can "tell us about the problems that haunt us now." That's not what I bargained for forty years ago.

Darwin, insofar as he was on the right track (obviously not always right) and insofar as he opened huge fields of knowledge that future generations might develop has always been telling us about the problems that haunt us now. But I take as justification of this postscript the possibility that the track of my long Darwinian career might make an interesting footnote to a volume that, in other respects, is not looking back, which was my original direction, but toward the future. It might suggest both continuities and differences, though it comes from a critic who has, in a very unscholarly way, become an unabashed and unembarrassed Darwin fan – with several sweatshirts, t-shirts, and hats marked with Darwiniana. I love in particular the shirt that reproduces Darwin's first evolution diagram from his notebooks, with the words "I think" hovering over that crude, astonishingly fertile, branching image. "I think" marks the beginning of an ever-expanding world with ever-extending ramifications, through space and time. The Darwinian "I think" empowers the kind of probing of future possibilities to which this book is dedicated.

Back in the early 1980s, I began by looking at Darwin as, distinctly, a Victorian, to be seen through the eyes of the Victorians. Gillian Beer's idea that the intellectual traffic went both ways, not only from science to literature, but from literature to science, hadn't yet significantly arrived on the scholarly scene. Although I had, despite my own profound incompetence in science, thought a lot about the relations between science and literature, my reading had been pretty much confined (the formulas and the graphs just kill me) to cultural commentary on science: history of science, philosophy of science, sociology of science. I had barely dipped into Darwin, and took him to have said what was generally assumed by lay readers. And of course, I hadn't thought for a second about *how* he wrote.

I took the plunge with some trepidation – and I haven't yet come up for air. Darwin, it turned out, wasn't "background" at all. He was the thing itself, and, among other things, literature. In the early 1980s, the only edition of his letters was an edition edited by his son, Francis Darwin, published in 1887. Those volumes still sit on my shelves, a monument to the Victorian moment when the "life and letters" of famous, recently deceased Victorians were obligatory, and usually edited by friends or family safely protecting the fallen hero from slander – or the truth – in three volumes (F. Darwin, 1887). I did not at first know of the astonishing Darwin archives, and the extraordinary, indeed epic work of the Cambridge Correspondence Project. My shelves now contain twenty-one of the thirty volumes in the set, to be finally completed in 2022 and containing 15,000 letters. And as those volumes have been appearing, so too have volume upon volume of Darwinian research, scientific, historical, and cultural, emerged, most of them meticulously edited. The Darwin industry has become perhaps the most voluminous (aside, I would guess, from the Shakespeare industry) in the history of English letters. Had I started out in the face of that abundance of material (which includes not only a preliminary calendar of Darwin's correspondence, but an invaluable edition of *Charles Darwin's Notebooks: 1836–1844*), in all likelihood I would have been overwhelmed.

There was enough out there already to make me think that I was only catching up with what any good Victorianist, any good historian, and probably most sophisticated thinkers anywhere would already know. About that time, the concordance to the *Origin* (1981) appeared, and that, until the digital age transformed everything, was an indispensable tool. Although, like most people, I thought I knew what Darwin had said, I wanted to find out what the writers with whom I was most concerned had seen in him. Which is to say that from the first, I approached Darwin as context for literature. Although that entailed a wide cultural view well beyond literature, I had little thought at the moment that Darwin would end up dragging me into engagement with the kinds of cultural problems that are, as the introduction to this volume shows, the motivation for this enterprise.

I felt all the more in catch-up mode because the literary modernist culture in which I grew up knew, I thought, all about Darwin: it understood his "theory" (which, as the editors here point out, ought not to be thought of as singular). He was in some circles even denigrated as not being original at all – after all, there were Erasmus Darwin and Lamarck before him, as well as several others, some of whom finally got (inadequate) mention in the foreword to a later edition, while he got most of the glory. I remember reading Gertrude Himmelfarb's very conservative biography, *Darwin and the Darwinian Revolution* (1859), in which that distinguished historian more or less trashed the idea of natural selection and Darwin's competence and originality in science.

It became clear then that one couldn't embark on Darwin studies without getting embroiled in cultural and even political controversy. Not being a scientist, and with no scientific instincts, I didn't expect to be tramping around in evolutionary biology for the next forty years; I certainly didn't then or even now want to be making assertions, like those that the very unscientific Himmelfarb was making, as though I were qualified to enter into scientific debate (the Sokal affair of 1996, in which a physicist at NYU wrote a parodic post-structuralist paper on Einstein that was accepted as serious by the journal *Social Text*, confirmed my decision on that score). I should even have been neutral on the validity of the idea of natural selection, but of course, I was entirely sold by the consensus of modern biology. In fact, in a very unscientific way, I was thrilled, as T. H. Huxley was when he first encountered it. But I knew I had to be careful, as Himmelfarb hadn't been, not to make claims on scientific issues that I knew very little about. That's always a danger in the cultural study of science.

Still, I wanted to be hip, and to be so, I realized, I would have to read much more about Darwin in culture. I needed, in particular, to read Stanley Edgar Hyman's *Tangled Bank: Darwin, Marx, Frazer and Freud* (1974), a book that already and importantly treated Darwin as a writer, a tragedian. I would have to look again at a quite remarkable essay that I myself had had published with Bill Madden in *The Art of Victorian Prose* (1968), A. Dwight Culler's "The Darwinian Revolution and Literary Form," which should have alerted me to the complexity and richness of Darwin's writing long before. Culler, as opposed to Hyman, saw Darwin's writing as comic in import and form, an insight that still needs emphasis and whose accuracy can be traced in the writings of many writers who were influenced by him.

In any case, when I set out on my Darwinian adventures, it was hot to know about Freud, and Freud was influenced by Darwin, ergo .... And there was before all this Jacques Barzun's influential, *Darwin, Marx, Wagner: Critique of a Heritage* (1941), which also builds a strong case against Darwin's theory because it seemed to drain mind out of nature. I later discovered that this kind of critique had already been powerfully developed by Samuel Butler and George Bernard Shaw, whom I went on delightedly and skeptically to read. I knew about associations of Darwinism with Hitler and Fascism, justified or not. (In *Was Hitler a Darwinian?* [2013], Robert Richards definitively answered in the negative.) More parochially for us English professors, I had yet to read Lionel Stevenson's still important *Darwin Among the Poets* (1932) (whose title, when I finished my first book on Darwin, I tried to circumvent), and the somewhat less influential, *Darwinism and the English Novel*, by Leo Henkin (1940). But reading Darwin himself was decisive: he went from context and background to literary (and philosophical) foreground. Hyman had come closest to capturing something of the singularity and richness of Darwin's writing. I am not talking about the more narrowly focused and therefore more technical works, like his tracts on barnacles. The canon became *Voyage of the Beagle* (1839), *On the Origin of Species* (1959), *The Descent of Man* (1872), *The Expression of Emotions in Man and Animals* (1872). Later literary scholars, particularly Jonathan Smith, have widely extended the Darwinian canon for cultural consumption, not least the final work (which in its day outsold the *Origin*), with the wonderfully unlikely title, *The Formation of Vegetable Mould Through the Action of Worms, With Observations on Their Habits* (1881).

This latter, I came to believe, was the ideal Darwinian fadeout, for it enacts, in tracing the habits of earthworms, the enormous significance in his writing of minutiae, the centrality of gradualism to his arguments, and, without making a fuss (another characteristic of Darwin's prose) demonstrating in a quiet extreme the continuity and entanglements of all forms of life. For the most part, earlier works on Darwin in culture focused on the "ideas." The miracle for me, as I settled into Darwin was – as Hyman and Culler had demonstrated – that the writing demanded attention, the form of the books and the arguments, the intricacy of the cultural inweavings. The center of the arguments that Gillian Beer and I were making was that Darwin's way of looking at the world was remarkably consonant with the dominant realistic mode of Victorian fiction (an idea that has been importantly modified by Amy King's *Divine in the Commonplace* (2020), with emphasis on religious elements in natural history before Darwin).

But my incentive for the work was primarily that it was hard to escape Darwin in Victorian literature, most particularly in the novel: then as now, Darwin's thought impinged on almost every major cultural concern. It was time to catch up. Thus, as a Victorianist with his heart in George Eliot, Dickens, and Hardy, I wandered naively into science, seduced by the surprising pleasure of Darwin's prose. Darwin struggled hard at it; he professed to find writing very difficult. And yet the *Origin* is a book thoroughly, meticulously *written*. Darwin was a "gentleman of science," not strictly a professional scientist at all: he wrote like a gentleman, without the professional jargon essential now to genuine scientific discourse. Janet Browne led me to notice that contemporary portraits and pictures of Darwin never show him at work.

As I immersed myself in this canon, I didn't think at all about the possibility that what I was doing in reading Darwin with attention to the rhetoric, the metaphors, the style, the similarities to fictional modes of representation, was unusual. My coeditor at *Victorian Studies*, Philip Appleman, had long been working on Darwin. His *Norton Critical Edition of Darwin* (1970) has been invaluable in making Darwin available popularly and to undergraduates for fifty years. But slow to learn, I only discovered that what I was doing might be regarded as unusual when Gillian Beer invited me for a year to Cambridge, during which she produced her absolutely fundamental, *Darwin's Plots* (1983) and, may I say, blew me away. Reading that book made me shift gears and to my joy and embarrassment, I am usually cited with her as having initiated the kinds of Darwin studies that point directly to this volume.

As a Darwinist literary man, I was delighted and surprised along the way to find that he knew his Milton and his Wordsworth (good heavens, he seems to have read *The Excursion* twice!) and that the traffic flowed both ways. But the literature inevitably forced me to attempt to locate Darwin in the battles of his moment, Darwin as an historical figure. And those battles have brought me here to write this perhaps self-indulgent postscript to a volume that recognizes how Darwin's work, digging deep into the foundations of life and of cultural myth with an empirical abundance and precision that made it inescapable, continues to matter, to expand, to exfoliate. While his ideas will be constantly modified, many of them ultimately rejected, his vision and his methods, even his mistakes, will continue to be invaluable resources in confronting the problems that haunt us now. Inevitably, as his work engages something of everything, there is no escaping consideration of the moral and cultural significance of his ideas. Darwin seems always to be relevant, and there is nothing more "Darwinian" than looking toward future developments.

Reading Darwin can be, and certainly was for a nonscientist like me, an entire reeducation. Taking me through the adventure of nineteenth century geology, as deep time opened up and uniformitarian principles of understanding took firmer hold, into the burgeoning of biological resources coming from collectors all over the world, through the chaos of species identification and the enormous diversity of life forms, it helped break down sharp distinction between science and culture, although with this there is always the danger of substituting ideology for science. The discoveries making possible the new science, voyages like Darwin's – a survey mission for the navy – were implicated in the politics and technology of his moment. And for this fresh reader, crossing the science-culture divide, what could have been more crucial than coming to recognize the nature of the language necessary to describe the new discoveries, and the new efforts to come to terms with the decentering of the human, with the challenges to essentialism, with the abundance and multiplicity of all forms of life?

For me, as I suspect for many Victorians, that language set the world in motion; all of its details, when I had presence of mind enough to observe my own garden and the birds I have for a long time tried to identify, became significant in new ways, forcing recognition of relations in time, and space, revealing the present to be comprehensible only as an embodiment of history, and history a source of meaning and a model for the future. Even the mysteries of bird identification, with its constant renaming and reclassifying of species – designed I had thought primarily to drive birders mad – began to make sense. My Darwinian enterprise took me through controversies and detailed technical analysis of speciation, through exploration of cultural battles that extended way beyond battles over whether evolution was "true," into the critiques of Himmelfarb and Barzun, through alternative interpretations and offshoots of Darwin's theories, to, at last, modern applications – evolutionary biology, evolutionary psychology, sociobiology. Darwin, it turned out was large; he contained multitudes.

On the Origin of Species was – despite its rhetoric of modesty, despite its dogged accumulation of facts and examples (or rather, in great part, because of them) – not merely a speculative scientific work, but a reimagination of the world, of humanity's relation to nature, to history, to all other forms of life, to the future. Astonishingly also a book with a voice, a recognizable narrator whose sensibility and cleverness lead us, with affect, through the complications of a world endlessly entangled and complex, it makes a powerful, careful, delicately argued scientific case that along the way revises some of the essential myths of our culture.

Obviously, its effect on lay Victorian readers had far more to do with culture than with science, yet the persuasiveness of the science, of the facts accumulated so scrupulously and with so firm a logical framework, made it increasingly necessary to come to terms with its implications here and now. Reading it with that kind of affect, I found myself dragged into engagement with the Butler-Shaw-Himmelfarb-Barzun argument that Darwin's world was bereft of meaning. That view of Darwin had been (and remains) the dominant one. I was struck early on by Shaw's passionate condemnation, not of Darwin, he insisted, but of the Weismannian followers of the idea of natural selection. If that view of natural selection, he says,

> be no blasphemy, but a truth of science, then the stars of heaven, the showers and dew, the winter and summer, the fire and heat, the mountains and hills, may no longer be called to exalt the Lord with us by praise; their work is to modify all things by blindly starving and murdering everything that is not lucky enough to survive in the universal struggle for hogwash. (Shaw, 1921)

Alternative evolutionary theories, those popular and yet determinedly "scientific" ones of Teilhard du Chardin, or Henri Bergson, all tried to save traditional moral and spiritual meaning by including a telos – which Darwin conspicuously didn't think to do – sort of.

It would be disingenuous not to take seriously this persistent effort to reconcile science with traditional "meaning." All the more so because I began to realize that the "affect" of Darwin's prose, and the history of his own relation to his theory, were themselves engaged in this effort. (It is striking that Shaw actually excuses Darwin, but blames it all on Weismannian mechanistic followers). Darwin himself, after all, persistently noted, as he described "chance" movements and developments, that he did not himself believe in "chance." Robert Richards has shown how intimations of teleology and divine presence was built into Darwin's initial work toward the development of his theory (Richards, 2002).

It is perhaps presumptuous to insert my own reading and response to Darwin into the almost two-century argument, but such a radically dispirited reading of Darwinian naturalism seemed to me from the very start inadequate to Darwin's language. My "literary" approach to Darwin entailed an attention to verbal nuance and to affect that would usually be absent from a reading that sought only Darwinian "ideas." For despite complaints about meaninglessness and mindlessness, in the world under Darwinian scrutiny, scrutiny itself requires attention. With it, every natural phenomenon becomes a complex narrative, and nature becomes almost infinitely interesting. In retrospect, I began to find paradoxical that pervasive reaction to Darwin's theory. Paradoxical because it assumes that natural processes cannot be merely natural, but paradoxical also because the theory, far from chasing meaning from the universe, finally made sense of what John Herschel and other contemporary scientists had called "the mystery of mysteries, the replacement

of extinct species by others" (Lyell, 1881: 5). Paradoxical, because it made
sense of things that hitherto had required the invocation of nonnatural
forces to explain.

Meaning in Darwin virtually oozes from the branches, from the peacock's feathers, from bee geometry, from ants' division of labor. How
many times did Darwin claim that the phenomena he was attempting to
explain were wonderful? Well, at least forty times in the first edition. And
those expressions of wonder are not throwaways; they come usually in
response to the remarkable and *explicable* ways natural phenomena work.
Darwin's usual rhetorical strategy is to note how "struck" he is by some
apparently strange phenomenon, a phenomenon he wants to understand.
He proceeds with very careful and detailed investigation of that phenomenon, and with all explained he concludes with expressions of awe once
again, but this time at what nature has achieved by such simple, gradual
means. Mere wonder at inexplicable forces in effect cuts off inquiry; but
wonder after inquiry becomes the proper emotional response to the power
of the natural world itself.

Darwin's rhetorical modesty is a provocation to ask questions and to do
double-takes, to move into "open fields" beyond those already revealed in
his most rigorous and sometimes quite loving observations, and to discover
connections, processes, histories. The frightening thing to many readers
who continued to resist Darwin's vision was just that his way of looking
at the world threatened to make it understandable, to make its meanings available. This is what Max Weber was talking about in his famous
discussion of the increasing intellectualization and rationalization of the
world. The problem is, as he put it, that science creates the belief that "if
one wished one could learn" whatever had seemed to be mysterious. The
paradox of negative responses to Darwin is that the results of his investigations are so positive, that he explained the "mystery of mysteries" in an
intellectually satisfying way. As Weber argues, mystery banished, the sense
of the world as enchanted is also banished (Weber, 1946: 141). But reading Darwin's language one finds the world reenchanted: fertile, mutable,
abundant, intricate. It is not so much "meaning" that is lost (since that
had always been enshrouded in mystery) but the comforts that came from
inexplicable meanings buried in the mystery of mysteries.

I know that this argument ignores the affective meaning of "meaning,"
But Darwin's language supplies us with affective meaning anyway: learning to understand how something works, how it is naturally, historically,
socially related to other things, is itself thrilling. Darwin's meanings are so
remarkable that he doesn't lament the loss of mystery but fills his pages

with "wonder." His language does not leave us with "hogwash" but explanations, injunctions to inquire yet further, meanings.

Dogged attention to detail; intent listening, observing; resistance to cultural assumptions or ideological imposition: these Darwinian strategies help disenchant the current mysteries of issues such as the ones this book engages: issues of gender, diversity, race, disability, morality, aesthetic preferences. It is more than meaningful that Darwinian disenchantment works to help us understand and maneuver through this world in more fully humane ways. The connectedness about which the editors of this volume write in their introduction entails dependencies, responsibilities, and significances that a work more intent on explaining nature as "mindfully" developed, more conforming to human desire, could entirely miss, or, more likely, distort.

There are virtually no boundaries to its implications for us humans. Certainly, it rewrites our myths of origin, a *Paradise Lost* for our times. And it is no accident that two of the major commentators on things Darwinian, Robert Richards and Gillian Beer, attend carefully to the fact that *Paradise Lost* was literally, physically, with Darwin through the entire *Beagle* voyage, and that the language of the *Origin* reverberates with Miltonic qualities. One didn't have to be a scientist to recognize immediately that Darwin's scientific pursuit of the fundamental question of species and speciation entailed fundamental questions about life in general and human life in particular. Reading Darwin offers not only an argument for connectedness and interdependence; it enacts the experience of it, for page after page, it juxtaposes paradoxically apparently unrelated things. And so one finds oneself forced to think about the breeding of pigeons and Platonic essentialism at the same time, about the question of why there are woodpeckers surviving happily in zones where there are no trees and about the transitory nature of time and the radical changeableness of things, about the plumage on a peacock and the question of racial difference, about the awful breeding habits of the ichneumon fly and the question of nature "red in tooth and claw," about the increase of the missel-thrush in parts of Scotland and the question of the intricate interrelation and interdependence of all living things: "here cattle absolutely determine the existence of the Scotch fir; but in several parts of the world insects determine the existence of cattle" (Darwin, 1964: 72). Bit by tiny bit, Darwin builds an enormous imaginative structure that touches upon just about everything, and he does it with a strategically brilliant rhetoric of modesty.

Darwin was intent on convincing the scientific community, which he knew would be resistant, but of course, he knew there was a broader public out there overhearing, who would be resistant in other ways. They all had to be convinced, and so he made his book doggedly reasonable and factual. That was the road to persuasion. He stakes out the imagination in the name of reason. Forcing upon us another almost incredible fact, he pauses to plead that the readers' "reason ought to conquer his imagination" (188). What Darwin demonstrates as "reasonable," however, was in literary terms barely imaginable. Could "a structure as perfect as the eye of an eagle" really have been developed by natural selection? Be reasonable, Darwin enjoins us: don't let your "imagination" (of an external designer outside the norms of nature) dominate. Put aside your conventional sense of how mechanisms are created. Drop that Paleyan metaphor. Take the imaginative leap into a new way of looking at the world. This was not a novel by George Eliot but a scientific treatise aspiring to convince a skeptical world, with an abundance of evidence and complex inferences from the facts, of an entirely new way to see and understand. The book that became the foundation of all modern biology invites the endless and often radical kinds of exploration that great literature has always demanded. And here, 165 years later, we are asking, with quite reasonable expectations, that it tell us something about now. How could it not?

It is, then, altogether appropriate, altogether Darwinian, that with this book, the editors propose, to "explore the profound and continuing influence of Darwin's theories well beyond the biological sciences, from his contributions to critical understandings of human difference, including race, sex, and gender; to aesthetic theory and philosophy; and, above all, to the complex interrelations of people, their societies, and nonhuman nature."

In their introduction, the editors make another claim with which I must disagree: that, with their very various interests in Darwin's relation to current cultural concerns, the original essays gathered here are outside the "Darwinian tradition." On the contrary, nothing could be more central to the "Darwinian tradition" than the focus on contemporary cultural problems. Near the end of the *Origin*, Darwin claims "to look with confidence to the future" (Darwin, 1964: 482), to the work of younger generations not influenced by older ways of seeing and explaining, and with the younger generation will come "a considerable revolution in natural history" (484). That revolution has been going on since then, beyond natural history, into science and psychology, race theory and gender studies, social theory and anthropology, and literary experiments; this book, in its further investigation of future possibilities, simply honors Darwin's vision.

When first I set out on my Darwin adventures, I thought that one of the most interesting books that might be written (I didn't write it, alas) would be a consideration of how Darwin had been used. Was there a field of knowledge or of cultural controversy, even almost immediately after the publication of the *Origin*, that didn't find some aspect of his arguments to support their positions? *The* Darwinian tradition, if we mistakenly think that there was only one, was always at work thinking about Darwin in ways that make him relevant to virtually any important cultural cause – in race, in gender, in art, not to mention biology. Darwin's ideas always reverberated well beyond their literal subjects.

Once the authority and importance of his theory were recognized, Darwin was immediately enlisted in contemporary squabbles, in the most extraordinary, often incompatible causes, in matters of race, gender, empire, and politics – the things that worried England in the last half of the nineteenth century. From that time on, "Darwin studies" often told you more about what the concerns of contemporary culture were than about Darwin's actual arguments. This volume itself fits that description. Famously, Marx immediately saw Darwin as building laissez faire into the very structure of the world. More remarkably for me, knowing how Darwin thought about the development of the female, he was enlisted in feminist causes (in Chapter 9, Carol Colatrella gives an extensive overview of the various ways Darwin's work was regarded in feminist movements). His work, at the same time, became entangled in racial discourse. On the one hand, as Moore and Desmond (1991) have shown, he was a mono-geneticist whose theory of sexual selection was partly driven by revulsion from slavery. At the same time, he was enlisted in the racist work of imperial England, taken by some as justifying racial hierarchies. His cousin enrolled Darwin's theorizing in the case for eugenics, even if, as Angelique Richardson shows in Chapter 14, Darwin disapproved of the eugenics more or less invented by his cousin, the polymath Francis Galton. Empire and free enterprise were justified in Darwinian terms. In Chapter 5, Allen MacDuffie shows that while Darwin is justly regarded as the thinker who most radically decentered the human, the "anthropo," "his ideas were ... readily and notoriously pressed into legitimating service for empire and capital." Walter Bagehot's important work on politics and human culture generally is in all its Victorian manner entitled *Physics and Politics, or Thoughts on the Application of the Principles of "Natural Selection" and "Inheritance" to Political Society* (1872, the same year as *The Descent of Man*). But as we milk Darwin for ways to make things better and study his thought with an eye to its foresight and its moral usefulness, it is critical to be aware, as MacDuffie shows, how easily his abundant ideas and his cultural situation could work to make things, in this Anthropocene moment and era, even worse. Moreover, as we list just some of the myriad ways Darwin has been enlisted to do cultural work, we recognize how easy it was to assimilate his ideas to the larger programs of social Darwinism (supported, of course, with quotations from Darwin himself). While Robert Richards is surely right that Hitler did not read Darwin and that the most fundamental Darwinian ideas are incompatible with fascism, there is no doubt that the association of fascism with a vague notion of the struggle for existence, gave faux scientific sanction of genocide. "The struggle for existence" could be invoked, as it was so brilliantly by Karl Pearson, to endorse socialism (even a kind of feminism) at home (since a strong society needed a strong social coherence) and imperialist expansion in overcoming the resistance of weaker societies, abroad. On another burning subject (still aflame here in America), Asa Gray found Darwin's thought compatible with Christianity. Richard Dawkins and Daniel Dennett find it a basis for full scale atheism. Kropotkin, appalled by the deep pessimism of Huxley's version of Darwin, read evolutionary theory as support for the anarchic ideal of "mutual aid." One might add that now, on a much smaller scale, with far less cultural significance, literary Darwinism, via evolutionary psychology, has adapted Darwinism to resist what it regards as the extravagances of literary theory, hoping to join sociobiology in turning literary criticism into a real science that works as science does by way of accumulating testable, irrefutable knowledge.

In pointing out how various and contradictory (and often more than dubious) the uses of Darwin in immediate cultural issues has been, I do not mean to suggest that they are not worth trying. Humanists have been, fairly enough, more than chary of the application of science to cultural problems, most obviously because of the appalling record of "scientific" support for racist distinctions, and for eugenic purification. I believe it is crucial in any serious consideration of large cultural issues to take the scientific fact into account. Culture is, after all, built on nature. You can't have one without the other, even if the binary can't be tossed away blithely. But, however much we have learned to distrust it, to take what it affirms as "culturally constructed," science has a way of working itself out, of imposing standards of proof that will, if carefully attended to, eventually sweep away the inevitable cultural, ideological overlay. The recent injunctions to trust the science, though they may get a little strident, are certainly right with regard to COVID-19 vaccines, although the anti-vaxxers regard the scientific facts as culturally constructed. Lives depend upon it. It is crucial to winnow through the cultural overlays and work as responsibly as possible toward the scientific ideal – rarely of course implemented with total adequacy – of objective, substantial evidence. In putting Darwin to our uses, our first responsibility is to get straight what it is that Darwin actually said.

Darwin's own career in regard to the idea of female choice in sexual selection is a strong piece of evidence for this way of reading him (see Richards, 2017). Through that great "mask of theory," as Whewell (1840) put it, by which scientific fact is put to ideological use, even by Darwin himself, Darwin emerged with world-changing theories that withstand the onslaughts of ideology even as they are variously employed to do ideological work. Moreover, not all the cultural implications have been in the interests of various unwelcome assertions of power. Despair at recognizing our animal roots was one response to Darwin's just about irrefutable demonstration of continuity and consanguinity. But another was an extension of human compassion to animals.

As we attempt to enlist Darwin in our current problems, the trick is to attend as carefully as possible both to what it is that Darwin actually said and thought, and to what it is that science has been able to substantiate, no matter where that might take us ideologically. I take Angelique Richardson's Chapter 14 as a model of such attentiveness. Making a case for the uses of Darwin in arguments against racial and sexual hierarchies, gendered stereotypes, and androcentric perspectives, she attempts to distinguish between Darwin's scientifically substantiated arguments for dimorphism and the "rigid Western gender norms and coercions that were inculcated and policed among both colonizers and colonized." That is, there is a distinction here between irrefutable scientific argument and ideological twisting of the irrefutable. Richardson enlists Darwin on the feminist side by honoring Darwin's scientific discoveries, not by discounting his own culturally inflected ideology or by imposing her own. Reading Darwin carefully, contextually, with the keenest attention to his language, continues to open possibilities for approach to the problems that "haunt us now."

More than any work I know (dare I include even *Middlemarch*?) Darwin's invests nature and matter itself with meaning and value, and Darwinian nature in all its materiality replaces with more force (and I would say more effective attraction) the world of Paleyan order and non-natural, external intelligence. At the center of Darwin's work, for example, the drive to disenchant the relation between human and animal by demonstrating the absolute continuities between them is certainly not a move to evict "meaning" from the world. As Shaw put it, "Now the general conception of Evolution provides the humanitarian with a scientific basis, because it establishes the fundamental equality of all living things" (Shaw, 1921). One cannot encounter the sheer fact of continuity between human

and animal without a fundamental change in one's moral relation to animals. Hardy (1985: 377) had it right: "the most far-reaching consequence
of the establishment of the common origin of all species is ethical ... the
application of what has been called 'The Golden Rule' beyond the area of
mere mankind to that of the whole animal kingdom." There is no help for
it: culture is based in natural fact. There is no point in shying away from
the biology; the problem is to use it right.

It is a long way from the manner in which I began my Darwin studies
to the larger, more-than-Victorian considerations that figure prominently
in my Darwin studies today. While I still feel it profitable, in the mode
of Ian Duncan's Chapter 11, to speculate about the strategies and effects
of Darwin's writing, and while I continue to take the *Origin* as a great
Victorian work, I am less reluctant to follow him, in what I take to be
a great "Darwinian tradition," into our current big issues, the questions
of race and gender and art. Less reluctant, but yet more careful to check
my ideology at the door and watch where the science allows us to go. We
know the ways in which the Victorians read him and we can be pretty
sure about the sorts of cultural impact his works have had; we want here
to be thinking about Darwin confronting the twenty-first century, where
all must be hypothetical, and where we can explore once again Darwinian
possibilities in those fields he left open for the future's exploration.

References

Aarseth, A. (2005). Ibsen and Darwin. *Modern Drama*, 48(1), 1–10.

Adhikari, R. (2020). Bringing an End to Deadly "Menstrual Huts" Is Proving Difficult in Nepal. *British Medical Journal*, 368. https://doi.org/10.1136/bmj.m536.

Agamben, G. (2004). *The Open: Man and Animal*, trans. K. Attell. Stanford, CA: Stanford University Press.

Alaimo, S. (2013). Sexual Matters: Darwinian Feminisms and the Nonhuman Turn. *J19: The Journal of Nineteenth-Century Americanists*, 1(2), 390–396.

Alcock, J. (2001). *The Triumph of Sociobiology*. Oxford: Oxford University Press.

Alleyne, B. W. (2002). *Radicals Against Race: Black Activism and Cultural Politics*. New York: Berg.

Anonymous. (1863). Darwin on the Descent of Man. *Edinburgh Review*, 134, 195–235.

Anonymous. (1870). The Act of Natural Selection on Man. *Westminster Review*, 93(April), 540–541.

Anonymous. (1889). Review of Wallace, Alfred, An Exposition of the Theory of Natural Selection. *Dublin Review*, 3(22), 476.

Appiah, K. A. (1986). The Uncomplete Argument: Du Bois and the Illusion of Race. In H. L. Gates, Jr. and K. A. Appiah, eds., *"Race," Writing and Difference*. Chicago: University of Chicago Press, pp. 21–37.

Appiah, K. A. (1996). Race, Culture, Identity: Misunderstood Connections. The Tanner Lectures on Human Values, Delivered at University of California at San Diego, October 27 and 28, 1994. https://philpapers.org/archive/APPRCI.pdf.

Appiah, K. A. (2006). *Cosmopolitanism: Ethics in a World of Strangers*. New York: W. W. Norton & Co.

Ardrey, R. (1966). *The Territorial Imperative: A Personal Inquiry into the Animal Origins of Property and Nations*. New York: Atheneum.

Aristotle. (1984). On the Generation of Animals. In J. Barnes, ed., *The Complete Works of Aristotle*, vol. 1. Princeton, NJ: Princeton University Press, pp. 1111–1218.

Austen, J. 2003 (1816). *Emma*, ed. James Kinsley. Oxford: Oxford University Press.

Baetens, J. and Trudel, É. (2014). Backward/Forward: Thalia Field's Metanarratives. *Modern Fiction Studies*, 60(3), 599–615.

Baguley, D. (2011). Zola and Darwin: A Reassessment. In N. Saul and S. J. James, eds., *The Evolution of Literature: Legacies of Darwin in European Cultures*. Amsterdam and New York: Rodopi, pp. 202–212.

Bailey, S. P. and Boorstein, M. (2020). Several Black Pastors Break with the Southern Baptist Convention over a Statement on Race. *Washington Post.* December 23. www.washingtonpost.com/religion/2020/12/23/black-pastors-break-southern-baptist-critical-race-theory/.

Bar-On, M., Phillips, R., and Milo, R. (2018). The Biomass Distribution on Earth. *PNAS*, 115(25), 6506–6511. https://doi.org/10.1073/pnas.1711842115.

Barker-Benfield, G. J. (2000). *The Horrors of the Half-Known Life: Male Attitudes toward Women and Sexuality in Nineteenth-Century America*, 2nd edn. New York: Routledge.

Barlow, N. (1945). *Charles Darwin and the Voyage of the Beagle*. London: Pilot Press.

Barlow, N. (1963). Darwin's Ornithological Notes. *Bulletin of the British Museum, Historical Series*, 2(7), 201–278.

Barrow, Jr., M. V. (2009). *Nature's Ghosts: Confronting Extinction from the Age of Jefferson to the Age of Ecology.* Chicago: University of Chicago Press.

Baskin, J. (2015). Paradigm Dressed as Epoch: The Ideology of the Anthropocene. *Environmental Values*, 24(1), 9–29.

Bataille, G. (1989). *Theory of Religion*, trans. R. Hurley. New York: Zone Books.

Beauvoir, S. de. (1974). *The Second Sex*. Trans. H. M. Parshley. New York: Random House/Vintage Books.

Beer, G. (2000). *Darwin's Plots: Evolutionary Narrative in Darwin, George Eliot and Nineteenth-Century Fiction*, 2nd edn. Cambridge: Cambridge University Press.

Beer, G. (2009a). Darwin and the Uses of Extinction. *Victorian Studies*, 51(2), 321–331.

Beer, G. (2009b). *Darwin's Plots: Evolutionary Narrative in Darwin, George Eliot and Nineteenth-Century Fiction*, 3rd edn. Cambridge: Cambridge University Press.

Behrend-Martínez, E. (ed.) (2021). *A Cultural History of Marriage in the Age of Enlightenment*. London: Bloomsbury.

Bekoff, M. (2002). *Minding Animals: Emotions, Awareness, and Heart*. New York: Oxford University Press.

Bekoff, M. (2013). Afterword: The Emotional and Moral Lives of Animals: What Darwin Would Have Said. In A. Richardson, ed., *After Darwin: Animals, Emotions, and the Mind*. Amsterdam: Rodopi, pp. 305–332.

Benjamin, R. (2019). *Race after Technology: Tools for the New Jim Code*. New York: Polity.

Bennett, J. (2020). *Being Property Once Myself: Blackness and the End of Man*. Cambridge, MA: Belknap Press.

Bertrand-Jennings, C. (1984). Zola's Women: The Case of a Victorian "Naturalist." *Atlantis*, 10(1), 26–36.

Bevis, J. (2019). A Complete History of Collecting and Imitating Birdsong. *MIT Press Reader.* December 12. https://thereader.mitpress.mit.edu/a-complete-history-of-collecting-and-imitating-birdsong.

Bewell, A. (2017). *Natures in Translation: Romanticism and Colonial Natural History*. Baltimore, MD: Johns Hopkins University Press.

Birkhead, T., Wimpenny, J., and Montgomerie, B. (2014). *Ten Thousand Birds: Ornithology Since Darwin.* Princeton: Princeton University Press.

Blackwell, A. B. (1875). *The Sexes Throughout Nature.* New York: G. P. Putnam's Sons.

Bloomfield, M., Garratt, P., Mackay, et al. (2015). Beyond the Gene Roundtable Discussion. *Textual Practice,* 29 (3), 415–432. https://doi.org/10.1080/09502 36X.2015.1020094.

Boisseron, B. (2018). *Afro-Dog: Blackness and the Animal Question.* New York: Columbia University Press.

Borello, M. (2010). *Evolutionary Restraints: The Contentious History of Group Selection.* Chicago: University of Chicago Press.

Botanical Society. (1786). *The Families of Plants, with Their Natural Characters … Translated from the Genera Plantarum … of … Linneus.* Lichfield: Botanical Society.

Boston Dynamics. (2020). Do You Love Me? Online video clip. www.youtube .com/watch?v=fn3KWMikuAw.

Bowler, P. J. (2013). *Darwin Deleted: Imagining a World Without Darwin.* Chicago: The University of Chicago Press.

Bowler, P. J. (2019). How the History of Genetics Charts the Rise and Fall of Eugenics. *British Academy Blog.* August 1. www.thebritishacademy.ac.uk/blog/ how-history-genetics-charts-rise-and-fall-eugenics/.

Boxer, M. (2012). Linking Socialism, Feminism, and Social Darwinism in Belle Epoque France: The Maternalist Politics and Journalism of Aline Valette. *Women's History Review,* 21(1), 1–19.

Boyd, R. (2017). *A Different Kind of Animal: How Culture Transformed Our Species.* Princeton, NJ: Princeton University Press.

Brain, R. M. (2015). *The Pulse of Modernism: Physiological Aesthetics in Fin-de-Siècle Europe.* Seattle: University of Washington Press.

Brand, S. (2009). *Whole Earth Discipline: An Ecopragmatist Manifesto.* New York: Viking.

Brantlinger, P. (2003). *Dark Vanishings: Discourse on the Extinction of Primitive Races, 1800–1930.* Ithaca, NY: Cornell University Press.

Bregman, R. (2020). *Humankind: A Hopeful History,* trans. E. Manton and E. Moore. New York: Little Brown.

Brilmyer, S. P. (2017). Darwinian Feminisms. In S. Alaimo, ed., *Gender: Matter. Macmillan Interdisciplinary Handbook.* New York: Palgrave Macmillan, pp. 19–34.

Brougham, H. (1839). *Dissertation on Subjects of Science Concerned with Natural Theology.* 2 vols. London: Knight.

Brower, V. (2002). Is Health Only Skin-Deep? Do Advances in Genomics Mandate Racial Profiling in Medicine?. *EMBO (European Molecular Biology Organization) Reports,* 3(8) (2002), 712–714. https://doi.org/10.1093/ embo-reports/kvf168.

Brown, B. R. (2010). *Until Darwin: Science, Human Variety and the Origin of Race.* London: Pickering & Chatto.

Browne, J. (1998). I Could Have Retched All Night: Charles Darwin and His Body. In C. Lawrence and S. Shapin, eds., *Science Incarnate: Historical Embodiments of Natural Knowledge*. Chicago: The University of Chicago Press, pp. 240–287.

Browne, J. (2002). *Charles Darwin: The Power of Place*. Princeton, NJ: Princeton University Press.

Burkhardt, F. (1999). An Appeal. In F. Burkhardt, ed., *The Correspondence of Charles Darwin*. Cambridge: Cambridge University Press, pp. 776–781.

Burkhardt, Jr., R. W. (2005). *Patterns of Behavior: Konrad Lorenz, Niko Tinbergen, and the Founding of Ethology*. Chicago: The University of Chicago Press.

Butler, J. (2007). *Gender Trouble: Feminism and the Subversion of Identity*. New York: Routledge.

Cadell, H. (1892–1893). Geological Changes Wrought by Man Within the Forth Basin. *Transactions of the Edinburgh Geological Society*, 5–6, 275–286.

Canavan, G. (2019). There's No Sheriff on This Planet: A Conversation with Kim Stanley Robinson. *Edge Effects*. Podcast. May 7. https://edgeeffects.net/kim-stanley-robinson/.

Canguilhem, G. (1988). *Ideology and Rationality in the History of the Life Sciences*. Cambridge, MA: MIT Press.

Caracciolo, M. (2020). Flocking Together: Collective Animal Minds in Contemporary Fiction. *PMLA*, 135(2), 239–253.

Carpenter, E. (1921). *The Intermediate Sex: A Study of Some Transitional Types of Men and Women*. London: Mitchell Kennerley.

Carpenter, W. B. (1875). *The Doctrine of Human Automatism: A Lecture, with Additions*. London: The Sunday Lecture Society.

Carrington, D. (2018). Humans Just 0.01% of All Life but Have Destroyed 83% of Wild Mammals. *The Guardian*, May 21, https://amp.theguardian.com/environment/2018/may/21/human-race-just-001-of-all-life-but-has-destroyed-over-80-of-wild-mammals-study.

Carroll, S. (2013). Crusades against Frost: Frankenstein, Polar Ice, and Climate Change in 1818. *European Romantic Review*, 24(2), 211–230.

Catford, J. C. (2001). *A Practical Introduction to Phonetics*, 2nd edn. Oxford: Clarendon Press.

Cavallo, G. and Chartier, R. (1999). Introduction. In L. G. Cochrane, trans., *A History of Reading in the West*. Amherst: University of Massachusetts Press, pp. 1–36.

Chakrabarty, D. (2009). The Climate of History: Four Theses. *Critical Inquiry*, 35(2), 197–222.

Churchill, F. B. (2015). *August Weismann: Development, Heredity, and Evolution*. Cambridge, MA: Harvard University Press.

Churchland, P. S. (2019). *Conscience: The Origins of Moral Intuition*. New York: W. W. Norton & Co.

Chutkan, N. (1996). The Administration of Justice As a Contributing Factor in the Morant Bay Rebellion of 1865. *Jamaican Historical Review*, 19(9). https://www.proquest.com/docview/1348048066.

Clark, L. L. (1981). Social Darwinism in France. *Journal of Modern History*, 53(1), D1025–D1044.

Clark, T. (2015). *Ecocriticism on the Edge: The Anthropocene as a Threshold Concept.* London: Bloomsbury.

Clifford, W. K. (1999). The Ethics of Religion. In T. J. Madigan, ed., *The Ethics of Belief and Other Essays.* New York: Prometheus Books, pp. 97–121.

Cohen, C. (2017). "How Nationality Influences Opinion": Darwinism and Paleontology in France (1859–1914). *Studies in History and Philosophy of Science: Part C: Studies in History and Philosophy of Biological and Biomedical Sciences,* 66, 8–17.

Colatrella, C. (2011). *Toys and Tools in Pink: Cultural Narratives of Gender, Science, and Technology.* Columbus: Ohio State University Press.

Colatrella, C. (2016). *Evolution, Sacrifice, and Narrative: Balzac, Zola, and Faulkner.* London: Routledge.

Colgan, W., Machguth, H., MacFerrin, M., et al. (2016). The Abandoned Ice Sheet Base at Camp Century, Greenland, in a Warming Climate. *Geophysical Research Letters,* 43(15), 8091–8096.

Colp, Jr., R. (2008). *Darwin's Illness.* Gainesville: University Press of Florida.

Commoner, B. (1971). *The Closing Circle: Nature, Man, and Technology.* New York: Dover.

Confino, M., and Rubinstein, D. (1992). Kropotkine savant. Vingt-cinq lettres inédites de Pierre Kropotkine à Marie Goldsmith, 27 juillet 1901–9 juillet 1915. *Cahiers du monde russe et soviétique,* 33(2/3), 243–301.

Cook, E. A. (1912). Review of Religion and the Struggle for Existence by Simon N. Patten. *American Journal of Theology,* 16(2), 312–315.

Costa, J. T., ed. (2009). *The Annotated "Origin."* Cambridge, MA: Harvard University Press.

Costa, J. T. (2020). Wallace, Darwin, and Natural Selection. In C. H. Smith, J. T. Costa, and D. Collard, eds., *An Alfred Russel Wallace Companion.* Chicago: University of Chicago Press, pp. 97–144.

Courtiol, A., Pettay, J., Jokela, M., et al. (2012). Natural and Sexual Selection in a Monogamous Historical Human Population. *PNAS,* 109 (21), 8044–8049.

Crenshaw, K., Gotanda, N., Peller, G., and Thomas K. (1995). *Critical Race Theory: The Key Writings that Formed the Movement.* New York: New Press.

Crist, E. (1999). *Images of Animals: Anthropomorphism and Animal Mind.* Philadelphia, PA: Temple University Press.

Crist, E. (2019). *Abundant Earth: Toward an Ecological Civilization.* Chicago: University of Chicago Press.

Curry, O. (2006). Who's Afraid of the Naturalistic Fallacy? *Evolutionary Psychology,* 4(1), 234–247.

Cuvier, G. (1822). *Essay on the Theory of the Earth.* Edinburgh: William Blackwood.

d'Udine, J. (1910). *L'Art et le geste.* Paris: Alcan.

Danta, C. (2018). *Animal Fables after Darwin: Literature, Speciesism, and Metaphor.* Cambridge: Cambridge University Press.

Darwin, C. (1832a). Catalogues of *Beagle* Specimens: Animals. MS DAR 29.1. pp. 1–50. Digitized by *Darwin Online Manuscripts.* http://darwin-online.org.uk/manuscripts.html.

Darwin, C. (1832b). Letter no. 176. July 5. Darwin Correspondence Project. www
.darwinproject.ac.uk/letter/DCP-LETT-176.xml.

Darwin, C. (1832–1836). Ornithological Notes. MS DAR 29.2. Digitized
by *Darwin Online Manuscripts.* http://darwin-online.org.uk/manuscripts
.html.

Darwin, C. (1837–1838). Notebook B: Transmutation of species (1837–1838).
Transcribed by Kees Rookmaaker. http://darwin-online.org.uk/content/
frameset?itemID=CUL-DAR121.-&pageseq=38&viewtype=side.

Darwin, C. (1837–1840). Old and Useless Notes about the Moral Sense and Some
Metaphysical Points. *Darwin Online Manuscripts.* http://darwin-online.org
.uk/content/frameset?itemID=F1582&viewtype=text&pageseq=1.

Darwin, C. (1838). Notebook M: Metaphysics on Morals and Speculations on
Expression. CUL-DAR125. Reproduced with permission of Wilma M. Barrett,
the Syndics of Cambridge University Library and William Huxley Darwin.

Darwin, C. (1838). Notebook C: Transmutation. *Darwin Online Manuscripts.*
http://darwin-online.org.uk/content/frameset?itemID=CUL-DAR116&viewty
pe=image&pageseq=1.

Darwin, C. (1838–1839). Notebook N: Metaphysics and Expression. CUL-
DAR126. Ed. Paul Barrett and John van Wyhe. *Darwin Online Manuscripts.*
http://darwin-online.org.uk/.

Darwin, C. (1845). Letter no. 905. August 25. Darwin Correspondence Project.
www.darwinproject.ac.uk/letter/DCP-LETT-905.xml.

Darwin, C. (1848). Letter no. 1176. May 20–21. Darwin Correspondence Project.
www.darwinproject.ac.uk/letter/DCP-LETT-1176.xml.

Darwin, C. (1854). Letter no. 1573. June 27. Darwin Correspondence Project.
www.darwinproject.ac.uk/letter/DCP-LETT-1573.xml.

Darwin, C. (1858). Letter No. 2285. June 18. Darwin Correspondence Project.
www.darwinproject.ac.uk/letter/DCP-LETT-2285.xml.

Darwin, C. (1859). *On the Origin of Species by Means of Natural Selection, or The
Preservation of Favoured Races in the Struggle for Life.* London: John Murray.

Darwin, C. (1861a). Letter no. 3176. June 5. Darwin Correspondence Project.
www.darwinproject.ac.uk/letter/DCP-LETT-3176.xml.

Darwin, C. (1861b). Letter no. 3216. July 21. Darwin Correspondence Project.
www.darwinproject.ac.uk/letter/DCP-LETT-3216.xml.

Darwin, C. (1862a). Letter no. 3404. January 22. Darwin Correspondence Project.
www.darwinproject.ac.uk/letter/DCP-LETT-3404.xml.

Darwin, C. (1862b). Letter no. 3612. June 20. Darwin Correspondence Project.
www.darwinproject.ac.uk/letter/DCP-LETT-3612.xml.

Darwin, C. (1867). Letter no. 5430. March 4. Darwin Correspondence Project.
www.darwinproject.ac.uk/letter/DCP-LETT-5430.xml.

Darwin, C. (1868a). *The Variation of Animals and Plants under Domestication,* vol. 1.
London: John Murray.

Darwin, C. (1868b). *The Variation of Animals and Plants under Domestication,* vol. 2.
London: John Murray.

Darwin, C. (1869a). Sir Charles Lyell on Geological Climates and the Origin of Species. *Quarterly Review*, 126 (April), 359–394.

Darwin, C. (1869b). *On the Origin of Species*. 5th edn. London: Murray.

Darwin, C. (1870). Letter no. 7124. February 8. Darwin Correspondence Project. www.darwinproject.ac.uk/letter/DCP-LETT-7124.xml.

Darwin, C. (1871a). *The Descent of Man and Selection in Relation to Sex*. London: John Murray.

Darwin, C. (1871b). Letter no. 7560. March 9. Darwin Correspondence Project. www.darwinproject.ac.uk/letter/DCP-LETT-7560.xml.

Darwin, C. (1871c). Letter no. 7612. Darwin Correspondence Project. www .darwinproject.ac.uk.

Darwin, C. (1871d). Letter no. 7685. April 14. Darwin Correspondence Project. www.darwinproject.ac.uk/letter/DCP-LETT-7685.xml. emphasis in original.

Darwin, C. (1873). *The Expression of the Emotions in Man and Animals*. New York: Appleton

Darwin, C. (1874). *The Variation of Animals and Plants under Domestication*. 2nd edn. 2 vols. London: John Murray.

Darwin, C. (1876–1882). Recollections of the Development of My Mind & Character. Darwin Online CUL-DAR26.1.-121. http://darwin-online.org.uk/ content/frameset?viewtype=side&itemID=CUL-DAR26.1-121&pageseq=1.

Darwin, C. (1877). Letter no. 10746. Darwin Correspondence Project. www .darwinproject.ac.uk/letter/DCP-LETT-10746.xml.

Darwin, C. 1916 (1872). The Expression of the Emotions in Man and Animals. In F. Darwin, ed., *Selected Works of Charles Darwin*. New York: Appleton.

Darwin, C. (1964). *On the Origin of Species*. Cambridge, MA: Harvard University Press.

Darwin, C. (1969). *The Autobiography of Charles Darwin*, ed. N. Barlow. New York: Norton.

Darwin, C. 1977 (1862). *The Collected Papers of Charles Darwin*, ed. P. H. Barrett. 2 vols. Chicago and London: University of Chicago Press.

Darwin, C. (1980). *The Red Notebook of Charles Darwin*, ed. S. Herbert. London: British Museum of Natural History.

Darwin, C. 1981 (1871). *The Descent of Man, and Selection in Relation to Sex*. 2 vols. Princeton, NJ: Princeton University Press.

Darwin, C. (1987). Notebook B (1837–1838). In P. H. Barrett, ed., *Charles Darwin's Notebooks, 1836–1844: Geology, Transmutation of Species, Metaphysical Enquiries*. Cambridge: Cambridge University Press, pp. 167–236.

Darwin, C. (2001). *Charles Darwin's Beagle Diary*, ed. R. Keynes. Cambridge: Cambridge University Press.

Darwin, C. 2002 (1859). On the Origin of Species by Means of Natural Selection; or the Preservation of Favoured Races in the Struggle for Life. In J. van Wyhe, ed., *The Complete Works of Charles Darwin Online*. http://darwin-online.org .uk/content/frameset?itemID=F373&viewtype=text&pageseq=1.

Darwin, C. 2002 (1862). On the Various Contrivances by Which British and Foreign Orchids are Fertilised by Insects, and on the Good Effects of Intercrossing. In J. van Wyhe, ed., *The Complete Works of Charles Darwin Online*. www.darwin-online.uk.

Darwin, C. 2002 (1868). The Variation of Animals and Plants under Domestication. In J. van Wyhe, ed., *The Complete Works of Charles Darwin Online*. http://darwin-online.org.uk/contents.html.

Darwin, C. 2002 (1871). The Descent of Man and Selection in Relation to Sex. 2 vols. In J. van Wyhe, ed., *The Complete Works of Charles Darwin Online*. http://darwin-online.org.uk/contents.html.

Darwin, C. 2002 (1881). *The Formation of Vegetable Mould through the Actions of Worms*. In J. van Wyhe, ed., *The Complete Works of Charles Darwin Online*. www.darwin-online.uk.

Darwin, C. (2003 [1969]). *On the Origin of Species*. New York: Penguin.

Darwin, C. 2004 (1871). *The Descent of Man, and Selection in Relation to Sex*, ed. A. Desmond and J. Moore. London: Penguin.

Darwin, C. 2006 (1859). On the Origin of Species. In E. O. Wilson, ed., *From So Simple a Beginning: The Four Great Books of Charles Darwin*. New York: W.W. Norton, pp. 441–760.

Darwin, C. 2006 (1871). The Descent of Man, and Selection in Relation to Sex. In E. O. Wilson, ed., *From So Simple a Beginning: The Four Great Books of Charles Darwin*. New York: W.W. Norton, pp. 767–1248.

Darwin, C. 2006 (1872). The Expression of Emotions in Man and Animals. In E. O. Wilson, ed., *From So Simple a Beginning: The Four Great Books of Charles Darwin*. New York: W.W. Norton & Company. 1253–1477.

Darwin, C. (2006). The Voyage of the Beagle. In E. O. Wilson, ed., *From So Simple a Beginning: The Four Great Books of Charles Darwin*. New York: W.W. Norton, pp. 30–432.

Darwin, C. (2008a). Recollections of the Development of My Mind and Character (1876–1881). In J. A. Secord, ed., *Evolutionary Writings*. Oxford: Oxford University Press, pp. 355–425.

Darwin, C. (2008b). *The Beagle Letters*, ed. F. Burkhardt. Cambridge: Cambridge University Press.

Darwin, C. (2009). Notebook C (1838). In P. H. Barrett, ed., *Charles Darwin's Notebooks, 1836–1844: Geology, Transmutation of Species, Metaphysical Enquiries*. Cambridge: Cambridge University Press.

Darwin, C. 2009 (1859). *On the Origin of Species by Means of Natural Selection*, ed. W. Bynum. London: Penguin.

Darwin, C., and Darwin, C. (1835). Letter no. 266. January 28. Darwin Correspondence Project. www.darwinproject.ac.uk/letter/DCP-LETT-266.xml.

Darwin, C., and Darwin, F. (1892). *Charles Darwin: His Life Told in an Autobiographical Chapter and in a Series of His Published Letters*, vol. 5. London: John Murray.

Darwin, Erasmus (1793). *The Botanic Garden; A Poem, In Two Parts*. Dublin: J. Moore.

Darwin, Emma (1863). Letter no. 4359. December 26. Darwin Correspondence Project. www.darwinproject.ac.uk/letter/DCP-LETT-4359.xml.

Darwin, F. (1887). *The Life and Letters of Charles Darwin, Including an Autobiographical Chapter*, ed. Francis Darwin, 3 vols. London: John Murray.

Darwin, H. (n.d.). Letter no. 7112F. Darwin Correspondence Project. www.darwinproject.ac.uk/letter/DCP-LETT-7112F.xml.

Daston, L. J. (1978). British Responses to Psycho-Physiology, 1860–1900. *Isis*, 69(2), 192–208.

Daston, L. and Galison, P. (2007). *Objectivity*. New York: Zone Books.

Davis, L. J. (2013). Introduction: Disability, Normality, and Power. In L. J. Davis, ed., *The Disability Studies Reader*, 4th edn. New York and London: Routledge, pp. 1–14.

Dawkins, M. S. (1980). *Animal Suffering: The Science of Animal Welfare*. London: Chapman & Hall.

Dawkins, R. (1976). *The Selfish Gene*. Oxford: Oxford University Press.

Dawson, A. (2016). *Extinction: A Radical History*. New York: OR Books.

Dayan, C. (2015). *With Dogs at the Edge of Life*. New York: Columbia University Press.

De Vos, R. (2017). Extinction in a Distant Land: The Question of Elliot's Bird of Paradise. In D. B. Rose, T. Van Dooren, and M. Chrulew, eds., *Extinction Studies: Stories of Time, Death, and Generations*. New York: Columbia University Press, pp. 89–115.

de Lamarck, J.-B. (1815–1822). *Histoire naturelle des animaux sans vertèbres*. 7 vols. Paris: Verdière.

de Lamarck, J.-B. 1994 (1809). *Philosophie zoologique*, ed. A. Pichot. Paris: Garnier-Flammarion.

de Maupassant, G. (2015). *The Necklace and Other Stories*, trans. Sandra Smith. London: Norton.

De Vos, J. M., Joppa, L. N., Gittleman, J. L., Stephens, P. R., and Pimm, S. L. (2015). Estimating the Normal Background Rate of Species Extinction. *Conservation Biology*, 29(2), 452–462.

De Waal, F. (1997). *Good Natured: The Origins of Right and Wrong in Humans and Other Animals*. Cambridge, MA: Harvard University Press.

De Waal, F. (2009). *The Age of Empathy: Nature's Lessons for a Kinder Society*. Crown.

Deen, D., Hollis, B., and Zarpentine, C. (2013). Darwin and the Levels of Selection. In Michael Ruse, ed., *The Cambridge Encyclopedia of Darwin and Evolutionary Thought*. Cambridge: Cambridge University Press, pp. 202–210.

Del Barco, M. (2014). How Kodak's Shirley Cards Set Photography's Skin-Tone Standard. *National Public Radio*. www.npr.org/2014/11/13/363517842/for-decades-kodak-s-shirley-cards-set-photography-s-skin-tone-standard.

Delgado, R. (1984). The Imperial Scholar: Reflections on a Review of Civil Rights Literature. *University of Pennsylvania Law Review*, 132(3), 561–578.

Delgado, R. (1995). *Critical Race Theory: The Cutting Edge*. Philadelphia, PA: Temple University Press.

Delgado, R., and Stefancic, J. (2001). *Critical Race Theory: An Introduction.* New York: New York University Press.

Dennett, D. C. (1987). *The Intentional Stance.* Cambridge, MA: MIT Press.

Derrida, J. (2008). *The Animal That Therefore I Am,* trans. D. Wills, ed. M.-L. Mallet. New York: Fordham University Press.

Desmond, A. (1994). *Huxley: From Devil's Disciple to Evolution's High Priest.* Reading, MA: Addison-Wesley.

Desmond, A., and Moore, J. (1991). *Darwin.* New York: Warner Books.

Desmond, A., and Moore, J. (2009). *Darwin's Sacred Cause: Race, Slavery and the Quest for Human Origins.* London: Penguin.

Diamond, J. (1997). *Guns, Germs and Steel: The Fates of Human Societies.* New York, Norton: 1997.

Dixon, T. (2003). *From Passions to Emotions: The Creation of a Secular Psychological Category.* Cambridge: Cambridge University Press.

Dixon, T. (2008). *Invention of Altruism: Making Moral Meanings in Victorian Britain.* Oxford: Oxford University Press.

Dixon, T. (2013). "Emotion": The History of a Keyword in Crisis. *Emotion Review,* 4(4), 338–344. https://doi.org/10.1177/1754073912445814.

Doyle, R. (2011). *Darwin's Pharmacy: Sex, Plants, and the Evolution of the Noosphere.* Seattle: University of Washington Press.

Driscoll, C. (2018). Sociobiology. In E. N. Zaita, ed., *Stanford Encyclopedia of Philosophy.* plato.stanford.edu/archives/spr2018/entries/sociobiology.

Dryzek, J., and Pickering, J. (2019). *The Politics of the Anthropocene.* Oxford: Oxford University Press.

Duncan, I. (2013). On Charles Darwin and the Voyage of the Beagle. *BRANCH: Britain, Representation, and Nineteenth-Century History.* www.branchcollective .org/?ps_articles=ian-duncan-on-charles-darwina-and-the-voyage-of-the-beagle-1831-36.

Duncan, I. (2019). *Human Forms: The Novel in the Age of Evolution.* Princeton, NJ: Princeton University Press.

Duncan, I. (2020). Natural Histories of Form: Charles Darwin's Aesthetic Science. *Representations,* 151(1), 51–73.

Dupré, J. (1995). *The Disorder of Things: Metaphysical Foundations of the Disunity of Science.* Cambridge, MA: Harvard University Press.

Elhacham, E., Ben-Uri, L., Grozovski, J., M. Bar-On, Y., and Milo, R. (2020). Global Human-Made Mass Exceeds all Living Biomass. *Nature,* 588: 442–444. https://doi.org/10.1038/s41586-020-3010-5.

Eliot, G. 1981 (1860). *The Mill on the Floss,* ed. G. S. Haight. Oxford: Oxford University Press.

Ellis, H. (1926). *Man and Woman: A Study of Secondary Sexual Characters.* 6th edn. London: A. & C. Black.

Elshakry, M. (2013). *Reading Darwin in Arabic, 1860–1950.* Chicago: University of Chicago Press.

Faris, R. 1968 (1956). Evolution and American Sociology. In S. Persons, ed., *Evolutionary Thought in America.* New York: George Braziller, pp. 160–180.

Fawcett, H. (1861). Letter no. 2868. July 16. Darwin Correspondence Project. www.darwinproject.ac.uk/letter/DCP-LETT-2868.xml.

Feeley-Harnik, G. (2007). "An Experiment on a Gigantic Scale": Darwin and the Domestication of Pigeons. In R. Cassidy and M. Mullin, eds., *Where the Wild Things Are Now*. Oxford: Berg, pp. 147–182.

Feld, S. (2015). Acoustemology. In D. Novak, ed., *Keywords in Sound*. Durham, NC: Duke University Press, pp. 12–21.

Feller, D. A. (2009). Dog Fight: Darwin as Animal Advocate in the Antivivisection Controversy of 1875. *Studies in History and Philosophy of Science Part C: Studies in History and Philosophy of Biomedical Sciences*, 40(4), 265–271.

Felluga, D. F., Gilbert, P. K., and Hughes, L. K., eds. (2015). *Encyclopedia of Victorian Literature*. Chichester: Blackwell-Wiley.

Ferraro, J. M. (2021). *A Cultural History of Marriage in the Renaissance and Early Modern Age*. London: Bloomsbury.

Fessenbecker, P., and Nottelmann, N. (2020). Honesty and Inquiry: W.K. Clifford's Ethics of Belief. *British Journal for The History of Philosophy*, 28(4), 797–818.

Fisher, R. A. (1930). *The Genetical Theory of Natural Selection*. Oxford: Clarendon Press.

Ford, R. T. (2001). Race and the Law. In P. Baltes and N. J. Smelser, eds., *International Encyclopedia of the Social & Behavioral Sciences*. Amsterdam: Elsevier, pp. 12684–12689.

Foucault, M. (2001). *Security, Territory, Population*. New York: Picador.

Fraiman, S. (2012). Pussy Panic Vs. Liking Animals: Tracking Gender in Animal Studies. *Critical Inquiry*, 39(1), 89–115.

Frederickson, K. (2014). *The Ploy of Instinct: Victorian Sciences of Nature and Sexuality in Liberal Governance*. New York: Fordham University Press.

Freud, S. (1961). *Civilization and Its Discontents*. New York: W. W. Norton.

Fries, K. (2007). *The History of My Shoes and the Evolution of Darwin's Theory*. New York: Carroll & Graf.

Galison, P. (1998). Judgment against Objectivity. In C. A. Jones and P. Galison, eds., *Picturing Science, Producing Art*. Abingdon and New York: Routledge, pp. 327–359.

Gamble, E. B. (1894). *The Evolution of Woman: An Inquiry into the Dogma of Her Inferiority to Man*. New York: Putnam's.

Gamble, E. B. (1916). *The Sexes in Science and History: An Inquiry into the Dogma of Woman's Inferiority to Man*. New York: G. P. Putnam's Sons.

Garcia, R. (2015). *La nature de l'entraide: Pierre Kropotkine et les fondements biologiques de l'anarchisme*. Paris: ENS Éditions.

Garland-Thomson, R. (2012). The Case for Conserving Disability. *Bioethical Inquiry*, 9(3), 339–355.

Gayon, J. (2013). Darwin and Darwinism in France before 1900. In M. Ruse, ed., *The Cambridge Encyclopedia of Darwin and Evolutionary Thought*. Cambridge: Cambridge University Press, pp. 243–249.

Gelb, S. A. (2008). Darwin's Use of Intellectual Disability in the Descent of Man. *Disability Studies Quarterly*, 28(2). https://dsq-sds.org/article/view/96/96.

Gerrard, M. B. (2015). America's Forgotten Nuclear Waste Dump in the Pacific. *SAIS Review of International Affairs*, 35(1), 87–97.

Ghesquier-Pourcin, D. (2010). L'énergie et le vivant: les colloïdes du protoplasme, acteurs de la vie et de son evolution. In D. Ghesquier-Pourcin, M. Guedj, G. Gohau and M. Paty, eds., *Énergie, science et philosophie au tournant des XIXe et XXe siècles, vol. 1: L'émergence de l'énergie dans les sciences de la nature*. Paris: Hermann, pp. 261–274.

Ghesquier-Pourcin, D., M. Guedj, G. Gohau and M. Paty, eds. (2010). *Énergie, science et philosophie au tournant des XIXe et XXe siècles, vol. 1: L'émergence de l'énergie dans les sciences de la nature*. Paris: Hermann.

Gianquitto, T., and Fisher, L., eds. (2014). *America's Darwin: Darwinian Theory and U. S. Literary Culture*. Athens: University of Georgia Press.

Goldsmith, J. A., and Laks, B. (2019). *Battle in the Mind Fields*. Chicago: University of Chicago Press.

Goodall, J. (1986). *The Chimpanzees of Gombe: Patterns of Behavior*, Cambridge, MA: Belknap Press.

Gordon, L. (2019). Philosophical Methodologies of Critical Race Theory. *APA Online*. https://blog.apaonline.org/2019/08/20/philosophical-methodologies-of-critical-race-theory/.

Gordon, R. B. (2009). *Dances with Darwin 1875–1910: Vernacular Modernity in France*. London: Routledge.

Gould, S. J. (2002). *The Structure of Evolutionary Theory*. Cambridge, MA: Harvard University Press.

Griffin, D. R. (2001). *Animal Minds: Beyond Cognition to Consciousness*. Chicago: University of Chicago Press.

Griffiths, D. (2015). Flattening the World: Natural Theology and the Ecology of Darwin's Orchids. *Nineteenth-Century Contexts*, 37(5), 431–452.

Griffiths, D. (2016). *The Age of Analogy: Science and Literature between the Darwins*. Baltimore, MD: Johns Hopkins University Press.

Griffiths, D. (2021). The Ecology of Form. *Critical Inquiry* 47(4).

Griffiths, P. (2002). Emotions. In S. P. Stich and T. A. Warfield, eds., *The Blackwell Guide to Philosophy of Mind*. Oxford: Blackwell, pp. 288–308.

Griffiths, P., and Stotz, K. (2013). *Genetics and Philosophy: An Introduction*. Cambridge: Cambridge University Press.

Grosz, E. (2004). *The Nick of Time: Politics, Evolution, and the Untimely*. Durham, NC: Duke University Press.

Grosz, E. (2005). *Time Travels: Feminism, Nature, Power*. Durham, NC: Duke University Press.

Grosz, E. (2011). Becoming *Undone: Darwinian Reflections on Life, Politics, and Art*. Durham, NC: Duke University Press.

Gruber, H. (1974). *Darwin on Man*. New York: Dutton.

Gudding, G. (1996). The Phenotype/Genotype Distinction and the Disappearance of the Body. *Journal of the History of Ideas*, 57 (3 July), 525–545.

Guibilini, A. (2016). Conscience. In E. N. Zaita, ed., *Stanford Encyclopedia of Philosophy*. plato.stanford.edu/archives/spr2021/entries/conscience.

Haac, O. A., ed. And trans. (1995). *The Correspondence of John Stuart Mill and Auguste Comte*. New Brunswick, NJ, and London: Transaction Publishers.

Hall, S. (1996). The Meaning of New Times. In D. Morley and K.-H. Chen, eds., *Stuart Hall: Critical Dialogues in Cultural Studies*. London: Routledge, pp. 222–236.

Hall, S. (2017). *The Fateful Triangle: Race, Ethnicity, Nation*. Cambridge, MA: Harvard University Press.

Halliwell, S. (1987). *The Poetics of Aristotle: Translation and Commentary*. London: Duckworth.

Hamilton, W. D. (1963). The Evolution of Altruistic Behavior. *American Naturalist*, 97 (896), 354–356.

Hamlin, K. A. (2014). Sexual Selection and the Economics of Marriage: "Female Choice" in the Writings of Edward Bellamy and Charlotte Perkins Gilman. In T. Gianquitto and L. Fisher, eds., *America's Darwin: Darwinian Theory and U.S. Literary Culture*. Athens: University of Georgia Press, pp. 151–180.

Harari, Y. H. (2015). *Sapiens: A Brief History of Humankind*. New York: HarperCollins.

Haraway, D. (2002). *The Companion Species Manifesto*. Chicago: Prickly Paradigm Press.

Haraway, D. (2003). *The Companion Species Manifesto: Dogs, People, and Significant Otherness*. Chicago: Prickly Paradigm Press.

Haraway, D. (2008). *When Species Meet*. Minneapolis: University of Minnesota Press.

Haraway, D. (2016). *Staying with the Trouble: Making Kin in the Chthulucene*. Durham, NC: Duke University Press.

Hayward, E. (2010). Spider City Sex. *Women and Performance: a Journal of Feminist Theory*, 20(3), 225–251.

Heise, U. (2016). *Imagining Extinction: The Cultural Meanings of Endangered Species*. Chicago: University of Chicago Press.

Hennessy, E. (2019). *On the Backs of Tortoises: Darwin, the Galapagos, and the Fate of an Evolutionary Eden*. New Haven, CT: Yale University Press.

Heringman, N. (2015). Deep Time at the Dawn of the Anthropocene. *Representations*, 129(1), 56–85.

Higham, T. (2021). *The World before Us: How Science is Revealing a New Story of Our Human Origins*. New York: Viking.

Hirsh, A. (2020). The Human Error Darwin Inspired: How the Demotion of Homo Sapiens Led to Environmental Destruction. *Nautilus*, 90. https://nautil.us/issue/90/something-green/the-human-error-darwin-inspired.

Hofstadter, R. (1955). *Social Darwinism in American Thought*. Boston, MA: Beacon.

Hogarth, W. (1753). *The Analysis of Beauty*. London: J. Reeves.

Hooker, J. D. (1862). Letter no. 3395. January 19. Darwin Correspondence Project. www.darwinproject.ac.uk/letter/DCP-LETT-3395.xml.

Hopkins, G. M. (1948). *The Poems of Gerard Manley Hopkins*, ed. W. H. Gardner. Oxford: Oxford University Press.

Horton, Z. (2019). The Trans-scalar Challenge of Ecology. *ISLE: Interdisciplinary Studies in Literature and Environment*, 26(1), 5–26.

House of Lords. (1832). West India Interest. *Hansard*, vol. 12. April 17. https://hansard.parliament.uk/lords/1832-04-17/debates/9fe00ad1-544b-4f4d-9741-4b20a275ce84/West-IndiaInterest.

House of Lords. (1833). Slavery—Petition and Ministerial Plan for the Abolition of Slavery. Hansard. August 12. https://hansard.parliament.uk/Lords/1833-08-12.

Hovanec, C. (2018). *Animal Subjects: Literature, Zoology, and British Modernism.* Cambridge: Cambridge University Press.

Hovanec, C. (2019). Darwin's Earthworms in the Anthropocene. *Victorian Review*, 45(1), 81–96.

Humboldt, A. (1819–1829). *Personal Narrative of Travels to the Equinoctial Regions of the New Continent, during the Years 1799–1804*, trans. H. M. Williams. London: Longman, Hurst, Rees, Orme & Brown.

Huxley, T. H. (1853). The Cell Theory. *British and Foreign Medico-Chirurgical Review*, 221–243.

Huxley, T. H. (1863). *Evidence as to Man's Place in Nature.* London: Williams and Norgate.

Huxley, T. H. 1888 (1874). *Science and Culture, and Other Essays.* London: Macmillan.

Irvine, W. (1955). *Apes, Angels, and Victorians: The Story of Darwin, Huxley, and Evolution.* New York: McGraw-Hill.

Iser, W. (1993). *The Fictive and the Imaginary: Charting Literary Anthropology.* Baltimore, MD: Johns Hopkins University Press.

Jacob, F. (1982). *The Possible and the Actual.* Seattle: University of Washington Press.

Jackson, Z. I. (2020). *Becoming Human: Matter and Meaning in an Antiblack World.* New York: New York University Press.

James, S. M. (2011). *An Introduction to Evolutionary Ethics.* Oxford: Wiley-Blackwell.

Janet, P. (1889). *L'automatisme psychologique: essai de psychologie expérimentale sur les formes inférieures de l'activité humaine.* Paris: Alcan.

Jann, R. (1994). Darwin and the Anthropologists: Sexual Selection and Its Discontents. *Victorian Studies*, 37(2), 287–306.

Jann, R. (1997). Revising the Descent of Woman. In B. T. Gates and A. B. Shteir, eds. *Natural Eloquence: Women Reinscribe Science.* Madison: University of Wisconsin Press.

Jerdon, T. C. (1864). *The Birds of India; Being a Natural History of All the Birds Known to Inhabit Continental India, With Descriptions of the Species, Genera, Families, Tribes, and Orders, and a Brief Notice of Such Families as are Not Found in India, Making it a Manual Of Ornithology Specially Adapted for India.* Calcutta: George Wyman and Co.

Johnson, M. L. and McRuer, R. (2014). Proliferating Cripistempologies: A Virtual Roundtable. *Journal of Literary & Cultural Disability Studies*, 8(2), 149–169.

Kafer, A. (2013). *Feminist, Queer, Crip.* Bloomington: Indiana University Press.

Kaufman, M. (2020). The Carbon Footprint Sham. *Mashable,* July 13. https://mashable.com/feature/carbon-footprint-pr-campaign-sham.

Keita, M. (2019). Our Discussions of Intersectionality Are Going Nowhere. Here's Why. *Arc Digital,* July 12. https://medium.com/arc-digital/our-discussions-of-intersectionality-are-going-nowhere-heres-why-4fd5a99bfcab.

Kelman, A.Y. (2010). Rethinking the Soundscape. *The Senses and Society,* 5(2), 212–234.

Kendall-Morwick, K. (2021) *Canis Modernis: Human/Dog Coevolution in Modernist Literature.* University Park: Pennsylvania State University Press.

Kim, C. J. (2015). *Dangerous Crossings: Race, Species, and Nature in a Multicultural Age.* Cambridge: Cambridge University Press.

King-Hele, D. (1981). *The Letters of Erasmus Darwin.* Cambridge: Cambridge University Press.

Kingsley, C. (1867). Letter no. 5673. November 8. Darwin Correspondence Project. www.darwinproject.ac.uk/letter/DCP-LETT-5673.xml.

Kmietowicz, Z. (2019). Ending Child Marriage: Five Minutes with ... Mabel van Oranje. *British Medical Journal,* 365. https://doi.org/10.1136/bmj.l4141.

Kolbert, E. (2014). *The Sixth Extinction: An Unnatural History.* New York: Henry Holt.

Korzybski, A. (1933). *Science and Sanity: An Introduction to Non-Aristotelian Systems and General Semantics.* Lakeville, CT: The Institute of General Semantics.

Kreilkamp, I. (2018). *Minor Creatures: Persons, Animals, and the Victorian Novel.* Chicago: University of Chicago Press.

Kropotkin, P. (1910). The Theory of Evolution and Mutual Aid. *The Nineteenth Century and After,* 86: 86–107.

Kropotkin, P. (1912). Inheritance of Acquired Characters: Theoretical Difficulties. *The Nineteenth Century and After,* 88: 511–531.

Kuhn, T. (1970). *The Structure of Scientific Revolutions.* Chicago: University of Chicago Press.

LaFleur, G. (2018). *The Natural History of Sexuality in Early America.* Baltimore, MD: Johns Hopkins University Press.

Laqueur, T. (1987). Orgasm, Generation, and the Politics of Reproductive Biology. In C. Gallagher and T. Laqueur, eds. *The Making of the Modern Body: Sexuality and Society in the Nineteenth Century,* Berkeley: University of California Press, pp. 1–41.

Larson, B. (2013). Introduction. In B. Larson and S. Flach, eds., *Darwin and Theories of Aesthetics and Cultural History.* Farnham and Burlington, VT: Ashgate, pp. 1–16.

Larson, B., and Flach, S., eds. (2013). *Darwin and Theories of Aesthetics and Cultural History.* Farnham and Burlington, VT: Ashgate.

Latour, B. (2009). Will Non-humans Be Saved? An Argument in Ecotheology. *Journal of the Royal Anthropological Institute,* 15(3), 459–475.

Le Dantec, F. (1907). *De l'Homme à la science: philosophie du XXe siècle.* Paris: Flammarion.

Le Dantec, F. (1908). *Science et conscience: philosophie du XXe siècle.* Paris: Flammarion.

Le Dantec, F. (1909). *La Crise du transformisme: leçons professées à la Faculté des sciences de Paris en novembre et décembre 1908.* Paris: Alcan.

Leclerc, G.-L. (1778). Epochs of Nature. In *Natural History, General and Particular*, trans. W. Smellie, 2nd edn. London, 9:306.

Ledger, S. (1997). *The New Woman: Fiction and Feminism at the Fin de Siècle.* Manchester: Manchester University Press.

Lennox, J. G. (2013). Darwin and Teleology. In M. Ruse, ed., *The Cambridge Encyclopaedia of Darwin and Evolutionary Thought.* Cambridge: Cambridge University Press, pp. 152–157.

Leung, C. (2014). Eugenics in Popular Culture. http://eugenicsarchive.ca/discover/tree/535eed7a7095aa000000024a.

Levine, G. (1988). *Darwin and the Novelists: Patterns of Science in Victorian Fiction.* Cambridge, MA: Harvard University Press.

Levine, G. (2006). *Darwin Loves You.* Princeton, NJ: Princeton University Press.

Levine, G. (2011). *Darwin the Writer.* Oxford: Oxford University Press.

Lewes, G. H. (1887). *Comte's Philosophy of the Sciences: Being an Exposition of the Principles of the Cours de Philosophie Positive of Auguste Comte.* London: Bell.

Lewis, S., and Maslin, M. (2018). *The Human Planet: How We Created the Anthropocene.* New Haven, CT: Yale University Press.

Linnaeus, C. (1787). *The Families of Plants.* Trans. E. Darwin. Lichfield: Botanical Society of Lichfield.

Lippit, A. M. (2000). *Electric Animal: Toward a Rhetoric of Wildlife*, Minneapolis: University of Minnesota Press.

Loison, L. (2010). Thermodynamique et historicité de l'évolution chez les Néolamarckiens français. In D. Ghesquier-Pourcin, M. Guedj, G. Gohau and M. Paty, eds., *Énergie, science et philosophie au tournant des XIXe et XXe siècles, vol. 1: L'émergence de l'énergie dans les sciences de la nature.* Paris: Hermann, pp. 307–322.

Lomolino, M. V. (2019). Wallace at the Foundations of Biogeography and the Frontiers of Conservation Biology. In C. H. Smith, J. T. Costa, and D. Collard, eds., *An Alfred Russel Wallace Companion.* Chicago: University of Chicago Press, pp. 341–355.

Lopez, I. F. H. (2000). The Social Construction of Race. In R. Delgado, and J. Stefancic, eds., *Critical Race Theory: The Cutting Edge.* Philadelphia, PA: Temple University Press, pp. 191–203.

Lowenthal, D. (2009). *George Perkins Marsh: Prophet of Conservation.* Seattle: University of Washington Press.

Lukacs, G. (1974). *The Theory of the Novel: A Historico-Philosophical Essay on the Forms of Great Epic Literature*, trans. A. Benstock. Cambridge, MA: MIT Press.

Lyell, C. (1863). *The Geological Evidence of the Antiquity of Man.* London: Murray.

Lyell, K. M. (ed) (1881). *Life, Letters and Journals of Charles Lyell*, vol. 2, Cambridge: Cambridge University Press.

Lyell, C. 2002 (1830). Principles of Geology, Being an Attempt to Explain the Former Changes of the Earth's Surface, by Reference to Causes Now in Operation. In J. van Wyhe, ed., *The Complete Works of Charles Darwin Online*: www.darwin-online.uk.

MacDuffie, A. (2014). "Childe Roland to the Dark Tower Came" and the Landscapes of the Anthropocene. *Philological Quarterly*, 93(3), 315–338.

MacDuffie, A. (2018). Charles Darwin and the Victorian Pre-History of Climate Denial. *Victorian Studies*, 60(4), 543–564.

Macfarlane, A. (1986). *Marriage and Love in England: Modes of Reproduction, 1300–1840*. Oxford: Blackwell.

McHugh, S. (2011). *Animal Stories: Narrating Across Species Lines*. Minneapolis: University of Minnesota Press.

Mackenzie, D. (2019). Sex-Selective Abortions May Have Stopped the Birth of 23 Million Girls. New Scientist, April 16. https://www.newscientist.com/article/2199874-sex-selective-abortions-may-have-stopped-the-birth-of-23-million-girls/#ixzz7TxrOJd48.

McKibben, B. (1989). *The End of Nature*. New York: Random House.

Maienschein, J., and Ruse, M. eds. (2009). *Biology and the Foundation of Ethics*. Cambridge: Cambridge University Press.

Malm, A. (2018). *The Progress of This Storm: Nature and Society in a Warming World*. New York: Verso.

Mance, H. (2019). Frans de Waal: "We Are Very Much Like Primates." *Financial Times Magazine*, March 8, www.ft.com/content/da283f36-3f9e-11e9-9bee-efab61506f44.

Marsh, G. P. (1885). The Earth as Modified by Human Action: A Last Revision of "Man and Nature." New York: C. Scribner's Sons.

Marsh, G. P. 2003 (1865). *Man and Nature, or the Earth as Modified By Human Action*, ed. David Lowenthal. Seattle: University of Washington Press.

Martineau, trans. (1853). *The Positive Philosophy of Auguste Comte*. London: J. Chapman.

Marx, K. (1904). *A Contribution to the Critique of Political Economy*, trans. N. I. Stone. Chicago: Charles H. Kerr & Company.

Marx, K. (1921). *Theorien über den Mehrwert*, vol. 2. Stuttgart: Dietz.

Marx, K. (1972 [1909]). *On History and People*, ed. Saul K. Padover. New York: McGraw-Hill, Karl Marx Library.

Maudsley, H. (1878). *The Physiology of Mind*. New York: Appleton.

Menely, T. (2004). Traveling in Place: Gilbert Cosmopolitan Parochialism. *Eighteenth-Century Life*, 28(3), 46–65.

Menely, T. (2017). Commodify. In J. J. Cohen and L. Duckert, eds., *Veer Ecology: A Companion for Environmental Thinking*. Minneapolis: University of Minnesota Press, pp. 44–59.

Merchant, C. (2016). *Autonomous Nature: Problems of Prediction and Control from Ancient Times to the Scientific Revolution*. New York and London: Routledge.

Milam, E. L. (2010). *Looking for a Few Good Males: Female Choice in Evolutionary Biology*. Baltimore, MD: Johns Hopkins University Press.

Mill, J. (1863). *Utilitarianism*. London: Parker, Son, and Bourn.

Millgate, M., ed. (1984). *The Life and Work of Thomas Hardy*. 2 vols. London: Macmillan.

Millgate, M. (1985). *Thomas Hardy: A Biography*. Oxford: Oxford University Press.

Millikan, R. G. (1984). *Language, Thought and Other Biological Categories: New Foundations for Realism*. Cambridge, MA: MIT Press.

Milton, J. (1667). *Paradise Lost*. London: Parker, Boulter, and Walker.

Miscellaneous Notes (1918). Bulletin of Miscellaneous Information, 9–9: 341–352.

Mitchell, D. (2003). Unexpected Adaptations: Disability and Evolution. *Disability & Society*, 18(5), 691–696.

Mollow, A. (2012). Is Sex Disability? In R. McRuer and A. Mollow, eds., *Sex and Disability*. Durham, NC: Duke University Press, pp. 285–312.

Monbiot, G. (2014). *Feral: Rewilding the Land, the Sea, and Human Life*. Chicago: University of Chicago Press.

Moore, G. E. (1903). *Principia Ethica*. Cambridge: Cambridge University Press.

Moore, J. W. (2016a). *Capitalism in the Web of Life*. New York: Verso.

Moore, J. W. (2016b). Introduction. In J. W. Moore, ed., *Anthropocene or Capitalocene?: Nature, History, and the Crisis of Capitalism*. Oakland, CA: PM Press, pp. 1–13.

Morris, D. (1967). *The Naked Ape: A Zoologist's Study of the Human Animal*. London: Jonathan Cape.

Morton, T. (2010). Ecology as Text, Text as Ecology. *Oxford Literary Review*, 32(1), 1–17.

Moses, C. G. (1984). *French Feminists in the Nineteenth Century*. Albany, NY: State University of New York Press.

Müller-Wille, S. and Rheinberger, H.-J. (2012). *A Cultural History of Heredity*. Chicago and London: University of Chicago Press.

Murray, R. (2020). *The Modernist Exoskeleton: Insects, War, Literary Form*. Edinburgh: Edinburgh University Press.

Nagel, T. (1974). What Is it Like to Be a Bat? *Philosophical Review*, 83, 435–450.

National Institutes of Health (n.d.). Klinefelter Syndrome (KS). www.nichd .nih.gov/health/topics/klinefelter#:~:text=KS%20describes%20a%20set%20 of,treated%20in%20a%20timely%20manner.

Newman, J. H. (1874). *An Essay in Aid of a Grammar of Assent*. London: Burns, Oates, & Co.

Norris, M. (1985). *Beasts of the Modern Imagination: Darwin, Nietzsche, Kafka, Ernst & Lawrence*. Baltimore, MD: Johns Hopkins University Press.

Nott, J. C., and Gliddon, G. R. (1857). Indigenous Races of the Earth, or New Chapters in Ethnological Inquiry. Philadelphia, PA: Lippincott & Co.

O'Hear, A. (1997). Beyond Evolution. Human Nature and the Limits of Evolutionary Explanation. Oxford: Clarendon Press.

Offen, K. (1984). Depopulation, Nationalism, and Feminism in Fin-de-Siècle France. *The American Historical Review*, 89(3), 648–676.

Otis, L. (2002). Introduction. In L. Otis, ed., *Literature and Science in the Nineteenth Century: An Anthology*. Oxford: Oxford University Press, pp. xvii–xxviii.

Pagano, T. (1999). *Experimental Fictions: From Emile Zola's Naturalism to Giovanni Verga's Verism.* Madison, WI: Fairleigh Dickinson University Press.

Palmeri, F. (2016). *State of Nature, Stages of Society: Enlightenment Conjectural History and Modern Social Discourse.* New York: Columbia University Press.

Pannell, J. (2009). Plants, Sex, and Darwin. Interview by Pete Wilton. *Oxford Science Blog.* March 12. www.ox.ac.uk/news/science-blog/plants-sex-darwin.

Paul, D. B. (1995). *Controlling Human Heredity: 1865 to the Present.* Amherst, NY: Humanity Books.

Paul, D. (2003). Darwin, Social Darwinism, and Eugenics. In J. Hodge and G. Radick, eds., *The Cambridge Companion to Darwin.* Cambridge: Cambridge University Press, pp. 214–239.

Paul, D., Stenhouse, J., and Spencer, H. G. (2013). The Two Faces of Robert Fitzroy, Captain of HMS Beagle and Governor of New Zealand. *The Quarterly Review of Biology,* 88, 219–225.

Persson, I., and Savalescu, J. (2012). *Unfit for the Future: The Need for Moral Enhancement.* Oxford: Oxford University Press.

Phillips, C. (28 July 2020). My Talk with Jane Goodall: Vegetarianism, Animal Welfare and the Power of Children's Advocacy. *The Conversation.* www.theconversation.com/my-talk-with-jane-goodall-vegetarianism-animal-welfare-and-the-power-of-childrens-advocacy-140735.

Picker, J. M. (2003). *Victorian Soundscapes.* Oxford: Oxford University Press.

Piepzna-Samarasinha, L. L. (2018). *Care Work: Dreaming Disability Justice.* Vancouver: Arsenal Pulp Press.

Potts, T. C. (1980). *Conscience in Medieval Philosophy.* Cambridge: Cambridge University Press.

Price, M. (2011). *Mad at School: Rhetorics of Mental Disability and Academic Life.* Ann Arbor: University of Michigan Press.

Prum, R. O. (2017). *The Evolution of Beauty: How Darwin's Forgotten Theory of Mate Choice Shapes the Animal World – and Us.* New York: Anchor.

Prystash, J. (2012). Zoomorphizing the Human: How to Use Darwin's Coral and Barnacles. *Rhizomes: Cultural Studies in Emerging Knowledge,* 24. www.rhizomes.net/issue24/prystash/index.html.

Purdy, J. (2015). *After Nature: A Politics for the Anthropocene,* Cambridge, MA: Harvard University Press.

Ramirez, J. J. (2020). Race and Robots. *American Quarterly,* 72(1), 291–299.

Rampino, M. R., and Shen, S.-Z. (2019). The End-Guadalupian (259.8 Ma) Biodiversity Crisis: The Sixth Major Mass Extinction? *Historical Biology,* 33(5), 716–722. https://doi.org/10.1080/08912963.2019.1658096.

Ratcliffe, R. (2019). India's Wild Tiger Population Rises 33% in Four Years. *The Guardian,* July 29. https://www.theguardian.com/world/2019/jul/29/india-wild-tiger-population-rises-conservation.

Reade, W. (1872). *The Martyrdom of Man.* London: Trübner.

Reynolds, J. (1997). *Discourses on Art,* ed. R. R. Wark. New Haven, CT and London: Yale University Press.

Rhee, J. (2018). *The Robotic Imaginary: The Human and the Price of Dehumanized Labor.* Minneapolis: University of Minnesota Press.

Richards, E. (1997). Redrawing the Boundaries: Darwinian Science and Victorian Women Intellectuals. In B. Lightman, ed., *Victorian Science in Context*. Chicago: University of Chicago Press, pp. 119–142.

Richards, E. (2017). *Darwin and the Making of Sexual Selection*. Chicago: University of Chicago Press.

Richards, R. J. (1987). *Darwin and the Emergence of Evolutionary Theories of Mind and Behavior*. Chicago: University of Chicago Press.

Richards, R. (2002). *The Romantic Conception of Life*. Chicago: University of Chicago Press.

Richardson, A. (2003). *Love and Eugenics in the Late Nineteenth Century: Rational Reproduction and the New Woman*. Oxford: Oxford University Press.

Richardson, A. (2010). Darwin and Reductionisms: Victorian, Neo-Darwinian and Postgenomic Biologies. *19: Interdisciplinary Studies in the Nineteenth Century*, 11. https://doi.org/10.16995/ntn.583.

Richardson, A. (2011a). Against Finality: Darwin, Mill and the End of Essentialism. *Critical Quarterly*, 53 (4), 21–44.

Richardson, A. (2011b). Essentialism in Science and Culture. *Critical Quarterly*, 53 (4), 1–11.

Richardson, A. (2013). George Eliot, G. H. Lewes, and Darwin: Animals, Emotions, and Morals. In A. Richardson, ed., *After Darwin: Animals, Emotions, and the Mind*. Amsterdam: Rodopi, pp. 136–171.

Richardson, A. (2014). "I differ widely from you": Darwin, Galton and the Culture of Eugenics. In E. Voigts-Virchow, B. Schaff, and M. Pietrzak-Franger, eds., *Reflecting on Darwin*. Farnham: Ashgate, pp. 17–40.

Richardson, A. (2020). No Coloureds. London Review of Books. October 20. www.lrb.co.uk/blog/2020/october/no-coloureds.

Richardson, E. (2019). Man is Not a Meat-Eating Animal: Vegetarians and Evolution in Late-Victorian Britain. *Victorian Review*, 45(1), 117–134.

Ritvo, H. (1987). *The Animal Estate: The English and Other Creatures in the Victorian Age*. Cambridge, MA: Harvard University Press.

Robson, J. M., et al. (1965–1991). System of Logic. In *The Collected Works of John Stuart Mill*, 33 vols. Toronto: University of Toronto Press.

Rohman, C. (2009). *Stalking the Subject: Modernism and the Animal*. New York: Columbia University Press.

Rollin, B. E. (2007). Animal Mind: Science, Philosophy, and Ethics. *Journal of Ethics*, 11 (3), 253–274.

Rose, S. (2003). *Lifelines: Life Beyond the Gene*. Oxford: Oxford University Press.

Rose, S. (2006). Commentary: Heritability Estimates—Long Past Their Sell-By Date. *International Journal of Epidemiology*, 35(3), 525–527.

Rosenberg, J. (2014). The Molecularization of Sexuality: On Some Primitivisms of the Present. *Theory & Event* 17(2). https://muse.jhu.edu/article/546470.

Ross, S. (1962). Scientist: The Story of a Word. *Annals of Science: A Quarterly Review of the History of Science and Technology Since the Renaissance*, 18(2), 65–85.

Roughgarden, J. 2013. *Evolution's Rainbow*. 10th anniversary edn. Berkeley: University of California Press.

Rudwick, M. J. S. (2008). *Worlds before Adam: The Reconstruction of Geohistory in the Age of Reform*. Chicago: University of Chicago Press.

Ruse, M. (1986a). Evolutionary Ethics. A Phoenix Arisen. *Journal of Religion & Science*, 21(1), 95–112.

Ruse, M. (1986b). *Taking Darwin Seriously: A Naturalistic Approach to Philosophy*. Oxford and New York: Blackwell.

Ruskin, J. (1884). *The Storm Cloud of the Nineteenth Century*. Kent: G. Allen.

Russett, C. (1989). *Sexual Science: The Victorian Construction of Womanhood*. Cambridge, MA: Harvard University Press.

Saini, A. (2020). *Superior: The Return of Race Science*. Boston, MA: Beacon Press.

Saldanha, A. (2006). Reontologising Race: The Machinic Geography of Phenotype. *Environment and Planning D: Society and Space*, 24 (1), 9–24.

Saldanha, A., and Song, H. (2015). *Sexual Difference between Psychoanalysis and Vitalism*. New York: Routledge.

Sapp, J. (1994). *Evolution by Association: A History of Symbiosis*. Oxford: Oxford University Press.

Saul, N., and James, S. J., eds. (2011). *The Evolution of Literature: Legacies of Darwin in European Cultures*. Amsterdam and New York: Rodopi.

Saussy, H. (2021). Bioinformatics. In M. Kennerly, S. Frederick, and J. E. Abel, eds., *Information Keywords*. New York: Columbia University Press, 57–71.

Sax, L. (2002). How Common Is Intersex? A Response to Anne Fausto-Sterling. *Journal of Sex Research*, 39(3), 174–178. https://doi.org/10.1080/00224490209552139. PMID: 12476264.

Sayre, G. M. (2017). The Alexandrian Library of Life: A Flawed Metaphor for Biodiversity. *Environmental Humanities*, 9(2), 280–299.

Schalk, S. (2018). Bodyminds Reimagined: (Dis)ability, Race, and Gender in Black Women's Speculative Fiction. Durham, NC: Duke University Press.

Schiebinger, L. (1987). Skeletons in the Closet: The First Illustrations of the Female Skeleton in Eighteenth-Century Anatomy. In C. Gallagher and T. Laquer, eds., *The Making of the Modern Body: Sexuality and Society in the Nineteenth Century*. Berkeley: University of California Press, pp. 42–82.

Schmitt, C. (2009). *Darwin and the Memory of the Human: Evolution, Savages, and South America*. Cambridge: Cambridge University Press.

Schroeder, G. (2020). Seminary Presidents Reaffirm BFM, Declare CRT Incompatible. *Baptist Press*, November 30. www.baptistpress.com/resource-library/news/seminary-presidents-reaffirm-bfm-declare-crt-incompatible/.

Sepkoski, D. (2020). *Catastrophic Thinking: Extinction and the Value of Diversity from Darwin to the Anthropocene*. Chicago: University of Chicago Press.

Sesardis, N. (2010). Race: A Social Destruction of a Biological Concept. *Biology and Philosophy*, 25, 143–162.

Sharpe, R. V. (2019). Disaggregating Data by Race Allows for More Accurate Research. *Nature Human Behavior*, 3, 1240.

Shaw, G. B. (1921). Preface. In *Back to Methuselah: A Metabiological Pentateuch*. Online: Gutenberg Project, p. 14.

Sheller, M. (2019). Complicating Jamaica's Morant Bay Rebellion: Jewish Radicalism, Asian Indenture, and Multi-ethnic Histories of 1865. *Cultural Dynamics*, 31(3), 200–233.

Shepherd-Barr, K. (2017). *Theatre and Evolution from Ibsen to Beckett.* New York: Columbia University Press.

Siebers, T. (2008). *Disability Theory.* Ann Arbor: University of Michigan Press.

Singer, P. (2005). Ethics and Intuitions. *Journal of Ethics,* 9(3/4), 331–352.

Sirugo, G., Tishkoff, S. A., and Williams, S. M. (2021). The Quagmire of Race, Genetic Ancestry, and Health Disparities. *The Journal of Clinical Investigation,* 131(11), e150255. https://doi.org/10.1172/JCI150255.

Smith, C. (2001). Across the Widest Gulf: Nonhuman Subjectivity in Virginia Woolf's Flush. *Twentieth Century Literature,* 48(3), 33–71.

Smith, J. (2006). *Charles Darwin and Victorian Visual Culture.* New York: Cambridge University Press.

Smith, M. M. (2015). Sound—So What? *The Public Historian,* 37(4), 132–144.

Smuts, B. (1985). *Sex and Friendship in Baboons.* London: Transaction.

Snow Leopard Trust (2017). Statement on IUCN Red List Status Change of the Snow Leopard. www.snowleopard.org/statement-iucn-red-list-status-change-snow-leopard/.

Sober, E. (1998). What is Evolutionary Altruism? In D. L. Hull and M. Ruse, eds., *The Philosophy of Biology.* Oxford: Oxford University Press, 459–478.

Spencer, H. (1866). Letter no. 5265. November 2. Darwin Correspondence Project. www.darwinproject.ac.uk/letter/DCP-LETT-5265.xml.

Spencer, H. (1871). Recent Discussions in Science, Philosophy, and Morals. New York: Appleton.

Spencer, H. (1904). *Essays Scientific, Political, and Speculative,* vol. 1. New York: Appleton.

Spencer, J. (2013). "Love and Hatred are Common to the Whole Sensitive Creation": Animal Feeling in the Century before Darwin. In A. Richardson, ed., *after Darwin: Animals, Emotions, and the Mind,* Amsterdam: Rodopi, pp. 24–50.

Springer, A.-S., and Turpin, E. (2017). The Science of Letters. In A.-S. Springer and E. Turpin, eds., *Reverse Hallucinations in the Archipelago.* Berlin: K. Verland & Haus der Kulturen der Welt, pp. 1–52.

Star, S. L., and Griesemer, J. R. (1989). Institutional Ecology, "Translations," and Boundary Objects: Amateurs and Professionals in Berkeley's Museum of Vertebrate Zoology, 1907–39. *Social Studies of Science,* 19: 387–420.

Steffen, W., Grinevald, J., Crutzen, P., and McNeill, J. (2011). The Anthropocene: Conceptual and Historical Perspectives. *Philosophical Transactions of the Royal Society A: Mathematical, Physical and Engineering Sciences,* 369(1938), 842–867.

Stepan, N. (2001). *Picturing Tropical Nature.* Ithaca, NY: Cornell University Press.

Stephens, M. (2009). What Is This Black in Black Diaspora? *Small Axe,* 13(2), 26–38.

Stowe, H. B. (1889). *Uncle Tom's Cabin; Or, Life among the Lowly.* Boston and New York: Houghton, Mifflin and Company.

Strohm, P. (2011). *Conscience. A Very Short Introduction.* Oxford: Oxford University Press.

Subramaniam, B. (2014). Ghost Stories for Darwin: The Science of Variation and the Politics of Diversity. Champaign: University of Illinois Press.

Subramaniam, B. (2019). *Holy Science: The Biopolitics of Hindu Nationalism.* Seattle: University of Washington Press.

Tattersall, I. (2009). Charles Darwin and Human Evolution. *Evolution: Education and Outreach,* 2, 28–34. https://doi.org/10.1007/s12052-008-0098-8.

Taylor, J. O. (2022). Darwin after Nature: Evolution in an Age of Extinction. In D. Griffiths & D. Kreisel, eds., *After Darwin.* Cambridge: Cambridge University Press, pp. 19–32.

Taylor, J. O. (2016). *The Sky of Our Manufacture: The London Fog in British Fiction from Dickens to Woolf.* Charlottesville: University of Virginia Press.

Taylor, S. (2020). Being Human, Being Animal: Species Membership in Extraordinary Times. Interview by S. E. S. Orning. *New Literary History,* 51(4), 663–685.

The Evolution of Honeycomb. Darwin Correspondence Project. www .darwinproject.ac.uk/commentary/life-sciences/evolution-honeycomb.

Torrens, H. (2016). William Smith (1769–1839): His Struggles as a Consultant, in Both Geology and Engineering, to Simultaneously Earn a Living and Finance His Scientific Projects, to 1820. *Earth Sciences History,* 35(1), 1–46.

Townshend, E. (2009). *Darwin's Dogs: How Darwin's Pets Helped Form a World-Changing Theory of Evolution.* London: Frances Lincoln.

Tsing, A. (2012). Unruly Edges: Mushrooms as Companion Species. *Environmental Humanities,* 1(1), 141–154.

Tsing, A. L. (2018). Nine Provocations for the Study of Domestication. In *Domestication Gone Wild: Politics and Practices of Multispecies Relations.* Durham, NC: Duke University Press, 231–251.

Vogt, C. (1864). *Lectures on Man: His Place in Creation, and in the History of the Earth.* London: Longman, Green, Longman, and Roberts.

Voss, J. (2010). *Darwin's Pictures: Views of Evolutionary Theory, 1837–1874.* New Haven, CT: Yale University Press.

Wailoo, K., Nelson, A., and Lee, C., eds. (2012). *Genetics and the Unsettled Past: The Collision of DNA, Race, and History.* New Brunswick, NJ: Rutgers University Press.

Wallace, A. R. (1855). On the Law Which Has Regulated the Introduction of New Species. *Annals and Magazine of Natural History,* 16(2), 184–196.

Wallace, A. R. (1859). On the Tendency of Varieties to Depart Indefinitely Form the Original Type. *Zoological Journal of the Linnean Society,* 3–4, 53–62.

Wallace, A. R. (1863). On the Physical Geography of the Malay Archipelago. *The Journal of the Royal Geographical Society of London,* 33, 217–234.

Wallace, A.R. (1869). Review of Principles of Geology by Charles Lyell, 10th ed., and Elements of Geology by Charles Lyell, 6th ed. *Quarterly Review* 126, 359–394.

Wallace, A. R. (1872). *The Malay Archipelago.* London: Macmillan.

Wallace, A. R. (1876). *On the Geographical Distribution of Animals, with a Study of the Relations of Living and Extinct Faunas as Elucidating Past Changes of the Earth's Surface.* London: Macmillan & Co.

Wallace, A. R. (1898). *Wonderful Century: Its Successes and Failures.* New York: Dodd, Mead.

Wallace, A. R. (1908). *The Darwin-Wallace Celebration Held on Thursday, 1st July 1908, by the Linnean Society of London.* London: Longmans, Green & Co.

Wallace, A. R. (1916). *The World of Life: A Manifestation of Creative Power, Directive Mind, and Ultimate Purpose.* New York: Moffat, Yard, & Co.

Wallace, A. R. 1962 (1890). *The Malay Archipelago: The Land of the Orang-utan and the Bird of Paradise, a Narrative of Travel with Studies of Man and Nature.* 10th ed. New York: Dover.

Wang, X. (2020). *The World is a Factory Farm. Public Books,* 26 November, www .publicbooks.org/the-world-is-a-factory-farm/.

Weber, M. (1946). Science and Politics. In H. H. Girth and C. Wright Mills, eds., *From Max Weber.* Oxford: Oxford University Press.

Weir, J. J. (1868). Letter no. 5939. After February 27. Darwin Correspondence Project. www.darwinproject.ac.uk/letter/DCP-LETT-5939.xml.

Weil, K. (2012). *Thinking Animals: Why Animal Studies Now?* New York: Columbia University Press.

Weismann, A. (1883). *Ueber die Vererbung: Ein Vortrag.* Jena, Germany: Fischer.

Wells, H.G. (1919–1920). *The Outline of History: Being a Plain History of Life and Mankind,* 2 vols. London: George Newnes.

West, C. (1995). Preface. In K. Crenshaw, N. Gotanda, G. Peller and K. Thomas, eds., *Critical Race Theory: The Key Writings that Formed the Movement.* New York: New Press, pp. xi–xii.

Whewell, W. (1840). *Philosophy of the Inductive Sciences.* London: J. W. Parker.

Wilcox, W. (1975). *The Papers of Benjamin Franklin, January 1 through December 31, 1772,* vol. 19. New Haven, CT: Yale University Press, pp. 210–212.

Williams, D. (2017). Victorian Ecocriticism for the Anthropocene. *Victorian Literature and Culture,* 45(3), 667–684.

Wilson, E. O. (1975). *Sociobiology: The New Synthesis.* Cambridge, MA: Harvard University Press.

Wilson, E. O. (2016). *Half-Earth: Our Planet's Fight for Life.* New York: Norton.

Woloch, A. (2003). *The One Vs. The Many: Minor Characters and the Space of the Protagonist in the Novel.* Princeton, NJ: Princeton University Press.

Woods, R. J. H. 2017. *The Herds Shot Round the World: Native Breeds and the British Empire, 1800–1900.* Chapel Hill: University of North Carolina Press.

Wordsworth, W. (1814). *The Excursion: Being a Portion of the Recluse.* London: Longmans.

Wulf, A. (2015). *The Invention of Nature: Alexander von Humboldt's New World.* New York: Knopf.

Wynter, S. (2003). Unsettling the Coloniality of Being/Power/Truth/Freedom: Towards the Human, after Man, Its Overrepresentation—an Argument. *CR: The New Centennial Review,* 3(3), 257–337.

Wynter, S., and McKittrick, K. (2015). Unparalleled Catastrophe for Our Species? Or, to Give Humanness a Different Future: Conversations. In K. McKittrick, ed., *Sylvia Wynter: On Being Human as Praxis.* Durham, NC: Duke University Press, pp. 9–89.

Young, R. M. (1971). Darwin's Metaphor: Does Nature Select? *The Monist*, 55 (3), 442–503.

Zalasiewicz, J., Williams, M., Haywood, A., and Ellis, M. (2011). The Anthropocene: a New Epoch of Geological Time? *Philosophical Transactions of the Royal Society A: Mathematical, Physical and Engineering Sciences*, 369(1938), 835–841.

Zeder, M. 2015. Core Questions in Domestication Research. *Proceedings of the National Academy of Sciences of the United States of America*, 112(11), 3191–3198.

Zola, E. (1871). *The Fortune of the Rougon*, trans. E. A. Vizetelly. Project Gutenberg eBook. www.gutenberg.org/files/5135/5135-h/5135-h.htm.

Zola, E. (1972). *The Debacle (1870–71)*, trans. L. Tancock. London and New York: Penguin.

Zola, E. (1984). *The Attack on the Mill and Other Stories*, trans. D. Parmee. Oxford: Oxford University Press.

Index

on evolution of imagination, 140–141
on evolution of reason, 148
on evolution of sympathy, 145–146
exceptionalist interpretations of, 60
on extinction, 20–21, 25–27, 43, 64, 121, 123, 173
family of, 180
female collaborators of, 187
feminist interpretations of, 73–75, 187
fictions of, 139
on gender difference, 190
on "grandeur of nature", 31
on habit, 202
health diary of, 81
and history of science, 2
on human evolution, 137–139
and human exceptionalism, 33
imagination of, 4–5
imaginative fictions of, 5
and imperialism, 21–23
influence on narrative fiction, 122
influence on realism of, 214
influences of, 221
intentions of, 200
interest in hemaphroditism of, 119
Lamarck's influence on, 200–204
language of, 3, 49, 167, 218
love of science, 179
and "modern conception of nature", 23
and "modern synthesis", 4
and modernity, 14
on monogenesis, 84
on moral evolution, 152–157
in museums, 19–20
narrative patterns of, 66
and novelists, 194
observations of, 169
as part of history, 1
philosophical responses to, 157–162
philosophy of, 6–9, 67, 196
on pigeon breeding, 105, 167
on plants, 60
pluralism in thinking of, 197
poetic education of, 69
and polysexuality, 80
on prehumans, 145
and process philosophy, 15
and queer theory, 95–97
and race, 10–12
on racial development, 37–38
on racial extinction, 147
racism in writings of, 79
on reform, 181–182
rejection of human exceptionalism, 27
in relation to Mill, 191–194
relational analysis of, 191–194

responses to, 66
rhetoric of, 218, 220
scalar thinking of, 57–58, 61–62, 171
on science, 179
as scientist, 1
on slavery, 180, 186, 221
and socialism, 104
and sound studies, 46–47, 55
on "Species Question", 83
on sublime vs. beautiful, 172
as theorist, 213, 223
as writer, 3, 165–168, 199, 213, 217, 218
Darwin, Charles Waring, 81
Darwin Correspondence Project, 212
Darwin, Emma, 186
Darwin, Erasmus, 47–48, 171, 190, 197, 198
Darwin, Francis, 212
Darwin, Henrietta, 187, 197
Darwin industry, 212
Darwin's Plots, 215
Darwin's 1842 sketch, 98
Darwin vs. Wallace
Darwinian feminism, 10
Darwinian narratives, 75
"Darwinian tradition", 220, 224
Darwiniana, 211
Darwinism, 194
  communist response to, 204
  and humanism, 222
  social, 114
Daston, Lorraine, 202
Davis, Lennard J., 73
Dawkins, Marian Stamp, 39
Dawkins, Richard, 66, 162, 222
de Beauvoir, Simone, 119
"deep time," 58, 60, 215
Delgado, Richard, 87
de Maupassant, Guy, 108, 117, 118
Dennett, Daniel, 222
Derrida, Jacques, 33
Descent of Man, 10–12, 153
  and aesthetic selection, 166
  aesthetics in, 12
  animal/human relations in, 200
  and animal studies, 33
  anthropomorphism of, 163
  and critical race theory (CRT), 87
  criticism of human exceptionalism in, 139–140
  disability in, 75–76
  and emergence, 138
  evolution of imagination in, 140–141
  evolution of language in, 175
  evolution of sympathy in, 145–146
  gender bias of, 188

gradualist, 147
of humanity, 151
and imperialism, 21
of man, 137
museums of, 27
and race, 85
and religion, 151
revolution of, 220
natural selection, 2, 13, 162, 203, *See also*
   selection, sexual selection
   and the Anthropocene, 23
   and artificial selection, 24
   criticism of, 29
   critiques of, 182–183
   and economics, 104
   as evolutionary "base", 104–105
   and extinction, 25–27
   French resistance to, 116
   and narratives, 167
   perception of, 169
   and psychology, 161
   reactions to, 217
   vs. sexual selection, 104
   in writing, 199
   as writing process, 166
naturalism, 115, *See also* realism
   manifesto of, 117
   and war, 117
nature
   abstract, 172
   as abstraction, 63
   abundance of, 196
   animal, 12, 33
   anthropocentric, 80
   autonomous, 21
   autonomy of, 28, 31
   commodification of, 23
   continuity of, 138
   control of, 61
   and culture, 3, 200, 208, 222
   Darwinian, 223
   Darwin's, 167
   definition of, 24
   designed, 84
   and disability, 132
   divinely governed, 152
   and domestic species, 97
   domestication and, 24, 98, 99
   economy of, 10, 96, 106
   equilibrium of, 64
   evolved vs. vulnerable, 19
   exploitation of, 28
   and feminism, 114
   fragmentation of, 30
   freedom in, 105
   of genocide, 156

human, 69, 113, 137, 141, 148, 151, 175
of human species being, 7, 23
humanity's place within, 67, 84, 186
Humboldtiam, 52
the imagination of, 4
impoverishment of, 43
inorganic and organic, 64
and instrumental reason, 7
intentionality of, 199
local, 21
mausoleum of, 19
messiness of, 7
mindful, 219
modern, 23
nonhuman, 1, 220
vs. nurture, 182, 184
orderliness of, 5
otherness of, 59
of race, 91, 93
racialized, 92
"red in tooth and claw", 219
of sexual selection, 103
vs. society, 20
of sound, 47
state of, 100, 128
sublime, 61
"supplanted" by humanity, 60
as system, 22
teleological, 79
travelling, 21
unthinking, 7
variations in, 90, 98
Neanderthals, 143
neo-Darwinism, 161
neo-Lamarckism, 204, 208, *See also* Lamarck,
   Jean Baptiste
neurodiversity, 12
neurology, 202
neurophysiology, 163
Newman, Cardinal John Henry, 152
"New Woman", 114
Nicholson, Daniel J., 6–8
Nietzsche, Friedrich, 6
Norris, Margot, 34, 60
Nott, Josiah, 94
Nottelmann, Nikolaj, 13
novels, 115, 124, 125, 143, 187
   vs. scientific treatises, 220
nurture vs. nature, 182, 184

Odyssey, 133
Offen, Karen, 116
O'Hear, Anthony, 159
orchids, 189
organicism, 7–9, *See also*
   inorganicism

CPSIA information can be obtained
at www.ICGtesting.com
Printed in the USA
LVHW101608140123
737185LV00001B/52